Crime Science

This book comprehensively examines the rapidly changing tactics and technologies used to combat crime. The authors delve into the intricacies of how scientific methodologies and technological advancements are employed to investigate and prevent various forms of crime, exploring topics such as forensic science, cybercrime, data analytics, crime mapping, predictive policing, and other technological and scientific advancements that aid law enforcement and criminologists in their work. It explores the interplay between criminology, technology, and science and arms readers with knowledge about cutting-edge techniques and technologies utilized in the fight against crime.

Through engaging narratives, case studies, and expert insights, this book sheds light on the intricate web of scientific disciplines that play a pivotal role in uncovering and solving crimes. The technologies covered represent a complex web of tools available to law enforcement and other criminal justice agencies. However, it is important to recognize that integrating these technologies requires careful consideration of legal, ethical, and social issues, including privacy rights and potential biases in predictive algorithms. As technology continues to evolve, so will the tools available for crime prevention, detection, and prosecution. It is an ongoing process of balance and adjustment as society seeks to ensure safety and justice while preserving individual rights and freedoms.

Appropriate as a textbook for crime science, criminal investigation, and crime prevention courses in criminology and criminal justice programs, *Crime Science: Modern Technologies to Combat Crime* is also useful for professionals and others intrigued by the world of crime and investigation. This book is a groundbreaking exploration into the important role science plays in comprehending, preventing, and solving crimes in the modern era.

Lisa Stolzenberg is a criminologist and professor known for her research in criminal justice, particularly in areas related to crime trends, sentencing, and the effects of social policies on crime. She has published extensively on topics such as gun control, juvenile delinquency, and racial disparities in the criminal justice system. Stolzenberg is a faculty member at Florida International University (FIU) and has contributed significantly to the field through empirical studies that analyze crime patterns and policy effectiveness.

Stewart J. D'Alessio is a criminologist and professor at Florida International University (FIU), specializing in criminal justice research. His work focuses on crime trends, sentencing disparities, juvenile delinquency, and the impact of public policies on crime and justice outcomes. D'Alessio has coauthored numerous studies examining issues such as racial and ethnic disparities in the criminal justice system, gun violence, and the effects of pretrial detention. His research employs quantitative methodologies to analyze crime patterns and inform policy decisions.

Crime Science Series

Edited by: **Richard Wortley**, *University College London*

Crime science is a new way of thinking about and responding to the problem of crime in society. The distinctive nature of crime science is captured in the name.

First, crime science is about crime. Instead of the usual focus in criminology on the characteristics of the criminal offender, crime science is concerned with the characteristics of the criminal event. The analysis shifts from the distant causes of criminality – biological makeup, upbringing, social disadvantage and the like – to the near causes of crime. Crime scientists are interested in why, where, when and how particular crimes occur. They examine trends and patterns in crime in order to devise immediate and practical strategies to disrupt these patterns.

Second, crime science is about science. Many traditional responses to crime control are unsystematic, reactive, and populist, too often based on untested assumptions about what works. In contrast crime science advocates an evidence-based, problem-solving approach to crime control. Adopting the scientific method, crime scientists collect data on crime, generate hypotheses about observed crime trends, devise interventions to respond to crime problems, and test the adequacy of those interventions.

Crime science is utilitarian in its orientation and multidisciplinary in its foundations. Crime scientists actively engage with front-line criminal justice practitioners to reduce crime by making it more difficult for individuals to offend, and making it more likely that they will be detected if they do offend. To achieve these objectives, crime science draws on disciplines from both the social and physical sciences, including criminology, sociology, psychology, geography, economics, architecture, industrial design, epidemiology, computer science, mathematics, engineering, and biology.

Agent-Based Modelling for Criminological Theory Testing and Development
Edited by Charlotte Gerritsen and Henk Elffers

Eliminating Online Child Sexual Abuse Material
Rick Brown

Psychological Criminology
An Integrative Approach
Richard Wortley

Insider Threat
A Systemic Approach
Pierre Skorich and Matthew Manning

Crime Science
Modern Technologies to Combat Crime
Lisa Stolzenberg & Stewart J. D'Alessio

For more information about this series, please visit:
www.routledge.com/criminology/series/CSCIS

Crime Science
Modern Technologies to Combat Crime

Lisa Stolzenberg and Stewart J. D'Alessio

Routledge
Taylor & Francis Group
NEW YORK AND LONDON

Designed cover image: Getty Images

First published 2026
by Routledge
605 Third Avenue, New York, NY 10158

and by Routledge
4 Park Square, Milton Park, Abingdon, Oxon OX14 4RN

Routledge is an imprint of the Taylor & Francis Group, an informa business

© 2026 Lisa Stolzenberg & Stewart J. D'Alessio

The right of Lisa Stolzenberg & Stewart J. D'Alessio to be identified as authors of this work has been asserted in accordance with sections 77 and 78 of the Copyright, Designs and Patents Act 1988.

All rights reserved. No part of this book may be reprinted or reproduced or utilised in any form or by any electronic, mechanical, or other means, now known or hereafter invented, including photocopying and recording, or in any information storage or retrieval system, without permission in writing from the publishers.

Trademark notice: Product or corporate names may be trademarks or registered trademarks, and are used only for identification and explanation without intent to infringe.

ISBN: 978-1-032-90538-9 (hbk)
ISBN: 978-1-032-90539-6 (pbk)
ISBN: 978-1-003-55849-1 (ebk)

DOI: 10.4324/9781003558491

Access the Support Material: www.routledge.com/9781003558491

Typeset in Sabon
by Taylor & Francis Books

Contents

About the Authors

The journey of Professors Lisa Stolzenberg and Stewart D'Alessio in the dynamic field of criminology resembles the chapters of a compelling crime novel. Individually, they are formidable scholars; together, they have redefined the boundaries of criminological research. Their collaborative journey highlights the confluence of their passions and demonstrates the power of synergy in academic pursuits.

Upon completing their undergraduate studies, Stolzenberg and D'Alessio met in 1986 at Florida State University while pursuing postgraduate degrees in criminology. A casual conversation over pizza evolved into a brainstorming session and a collaborative partnership that has lasted nearly four decades. After initially accepting faculty positions at Indiana-Purdue University Fort Wayne, they relocated to Florida International University (FIU) in Miami, where they spent their childhood years. Today, they are tenured professors of criminology at FIU's Steven J. Green School of International and Public Affairs.

Drs. Stolzenberg and D'Alessio's combined expertise and passion for criminology have led to significant contributions in the fields of criminology and criminal justice. Working in tandem, they have published numerous books and influential scholarly articles on topics such as race and crime, criminal sentencing, and criminal justice policy. They were also instrumental in developing two unique degree programs in the United States: the PhD in International Crime and Justice and the Bachelor of Science in Crime Science.

Today, criminologists worldwide are inspired by their dedication, innovative spirit, and ability to break down silos in the pursuit of knowledge. Their story is a testament to the power of collaboration and the profound impact that committed individuals can have when they unite to pursue knowledge and justice.

1 The Origins and Evolution of Crime Science

Crime science emerged as a distinct and rapidly growing field of study at the beginning of the 21st century, born out of the need to address the complexity and diversity of modern criminal activities. While traditional models of criminal justice and criminology focused primarily on preventing crime and explaining criminal behavior after it occurred, these methods have proven ineffective against newer forms of criminality, such as cybercrime, organized crime, and terrorism.

The arrival of crime science marked a shift from reactive approaches to crime prevention. Unlike criminology, which investigates the social and psychological causes of criminal activity, crime science emphasizes crime reduction through scientific and pragmatic approaches. This innovative discipline combines insights from psychology, sociology, law, and forensic science to develop a comprehensive strategy for combating crime. Integrating technology and data analysis has further empowered crime science to create more efficient, research-backed strategies.

Understanding the evolution of crime science is crucial for grasping its current methodologies and future developments. This chapter examines the evolution of the field, the influence of interdisciplinary approaches, and the potential advancements. It explores the historical background and key theories underpinning crime science alongside the roles of technology, data analytics, and major institutions, such as the Jill Dando Institute of Security and Crime Science. Additionally, it discusses the role of crime science within contemporary criminal justice systems and its potential for technological innovation, international collaboration, and ethical practices. The chapter highlights the contribution of crime science to fostering positive societal change and promoting a more secure society.

Theoretical Foundations of Crime Science

Several theories and early influences can be traced and identified in the development of crime science. The Chicago School of Sociology was well-established in the early 20th century, focusing on social and ecological theories of crime. Originating from the University of Chicago, it was grounded in urban sociology and featured prominent theorists such as Robert E. Park, Ernest Burgess, and Clifford Shaw.

Park and Burgess are considered the founders of the Chicago School. Their research on urban environments and social structures significantly contributed to understanding crime (Jørgensen & Smith, 2009). Park and Burgess formulated the concentric zone model, which posits that certain zones of a city exhibit characteristics that influence behaviors and crime rates.

Shaw, with the assistance of Henry D. McKay, developed these ideas, emphasizing juvenile delinquency within the urban context. Their research indicated that crime was not random but concentrated in large cities marked by poverty, overcrowding, and

DOI: 10.4324/9781003558491-1

various social problems (Shaw & McKay, 1969). Shaw and McKay introduced the social disorganization theory, suggesting that crime is associated with the breakdown of social institutions in these areas, such as families, schools, and communities.

Social disorganization theory emerged as one of the initial theories in criminology, emphasizing the influence of social and environmental factors on criminality. The theory states that crime rates are high in societies with low social organization due to the lack of structures that restrain individuals (Hardyns & Pauwels, 2018). Residential mobility, ethnic heterogeneity, and poverty weaken informal social control, increasing vulnerability to crime. The findings of the Chicago School highlighted the contextual nature of crime, marking a shift from biological explanations to social factors. This shift developed crime science, which adopts a multifaceted approach to understanding criminal behavior.

When reviewing the development of crime science in the 1970s and 1980s, situational crime prevention theories emerged as one of the main drivers. These theories propose that altering the conditions for committing crimes can prevent criminal activity. Two notable scholars associated with this movement are Ronald V. Clarke and Marcus Felson.

According to Clarke's Rational Choice Theory, offenders consider the consequences of their actions. This theory posits that crime can be prevented if perceived risks increase and the perceived benefits of crime decrease. Clarke asserts that regulating the situational aspects of the decision-making process can deter crime. He developed several crime prevention methods, collectively known as situational crime prevention strategies, which include target hardening (making crime targets less attractive or easier to protect), increased surveillance (enhancing the likelihood of offender identification), and environmental management (altering the physical environment to reduce crime opportunities). These strategies have significantly influenced crime prevention approaches and shaped the field of crime science.

Felson's Routine Activity Theory elaborates on situational crime prevention by suggesting that crime occurs when three elements converge: a motivated offender, a suitable target, and a lack of capable guardians (Felson, 2008). This theory posits that crimes arise from everyday interactions and routines. Felson argues that addressing the situational factors that enable crimes is essential, as preventing criminal behavior requires attention to all three elements. For instance, enhancing the abilities of capable guardians—such as security personnel or vigilant neighbors—can deter potential offenders while reducing the attractiveness of targets (e.g., by using anti-theft devices), making crimes less appealing.

Beyond the Chicago School and situational crime prevention, several prominent theories and sources have significantly contributed to crime science. In addition to examining sociological and environmental factors, researchers have also considered biological influences. This research explores the genetic and neurological factors that may lead to criminal behavior. For example, studies have investigated the roles of neurotransmitters, hormones, and brain anatomy in aggression and impulsive behavior (Anderson, 2019). Although crime science does not prioritize biological aspects, understanding these factors enhances the study of crime and its causes.

Environmental criminology is another key driver of crime science (Bottoms & Wiles, 2020). This study area analyzes the spatial and temporal aspects of crime, considering the physical environment and geography of criminal activity. Environmental criminologists use Geographic Information Systems (GIS) to map crimes and identify areas more prone to criminal activities, offering a more practical approach to crime fighting.

Other researchers have expanded Routine Activity Theory to account for additional factors and conditions. For instance, the framework of crime scripts has been proposed to analyze the steps involved in committing crimes (Henson, 2020). By examining these scripts, researchers can identify opportunities to disrupt criminals' actions.

Other theories incorporating elements from various criminological frameworks have also influenced crime science. These integrated theories recognize the complexity of crime, asserting that the offender, the environment, and the opportunities for committing crimes determine its frequency (Krohn & Eassey, 2014). By adopting features from different theoretical paradigms, crime science can develop more effective strategies for addressing criminal behavior.

The early development and fundamental theories of crime science can be traced to a rich and evolving background. The Chicago School of Sociology offered a sociological perspective emphasizing social and environmental disorders. In contrast, situational crime prevention theories provide helpful strategies for altering specific contexts in which crimes occur (Jørgensen & Smith, 2009). Similarly, biological factors, environmental criminology, and integrated theories have promoted more comprehensive and interdisciplinary methods for analyzing and combating crime.

The Evolution and Growth of Crime Science

Crime science has significantly revolutionized the study of crime. It emerged from the increasing complexity of criminal activities, which traditional criminology could no longer effectively address. The rise of computer crime, organized crime, terrorism, and other new threats demonstrated the necessity for a more practical approach to countering crime.

Crime science developed at the end of the twentieth century, responding to challenges that classical criminology and criminal justice were ill-equipped to tackle. Historically, criminology has focused on the sociological and psychological factors influencing criminal behavior, exploring why individuals commit crimes and how social processes affect crime (Vilks & Kipāne, 2021). However, this traditional approach often reacted to crime after it occurred, proving ineffective against new, complex, and sophisticated types of criminality.

Considering these challenges, crime science evolved into a proactive, multidisciplinary field that seeks to study and combat crime scientifically. Scholars such as Professor Ken Pease advocated for systematic approaches to learning about and preventing crime (Farrell & Sidebottom, 2018). Whereas criminology seeks to explain the causes of crime, crime science aims to prevent crime by studying and managing the contexts or environments that facilitate it.

To better understand crime science, recognizing its distinctiveness from conventional crime analysis approaches is essential. Crime science is inherently interdisciplinary, drawing from psychology, sociology, law, forensics, and technology to understand the nature of crime and its prevention (Farrell & Sidebottom, 2018). This integration allows crime science to focus on factors that may lead to criminality and apply evidence to develop improved solutions.

One key characteristic of crime science is that its concepts are primarily evidence-based. This approach distinguishes it from traditional criminology, which often emphasizes theoretical and hypothetical orientations. Crime science is an emerging field that studies crime and develops strategies for containment and prevention (Farrell & Sidebottom, 2018). For instance, GIS and predictive policing algorithms represent crime science's application of technology and analytical reasoning to identify crime hot spots and optimize resource utilization for crime prevention.

Moreover, crime science embraces the concept of situational crime prevention, seeking to alter the immediate environments in which crime is likely to occur. This approach is grounded in the understanding that changes in environmental and situational factors can reduce crime risk (Lawless, 2022). Real-life examples include installing better streetlights, implementing surveillance cameras, and establishing access control barriers in high-risk areas to deter potential offenders. This proactive approach marks a clear shift from traditional criminology, which primarily responds to crime after its occurrence.

The field of crime science distinguishes itself by focusing on translating research findings into practical applications. Some scholars argue that the theoretical emphasis of traditional criminology limits its applicability to real-world crime prevention (Lawless, 2022). In contrast, crime science seeks to implement research findings into operational strategies and policies, ensuring that the knowledge gained has a tangible positive impact on reducing crime and enhancing safety. Its development reflects a broader trend toward interdisciplinary solutions for complex social challenges. By integrating knowledge and methods from various disciplines, crime science is better equipped to address the intricate nature of contemporary criminal acts (Vilks & Kipāne, 2021). For example, crime science can create more effective crime prevention strategies by analyzing the mental states of offenders—such as intentions and emotions—alongside sociological theories, crime patterns, legal provisions, and technological trends in forensic science and data processing.

Additionally, crime science is characterized by an evidence-based framework that continually develops new approaches to crime prevention and control. These strategies are regularly updated and compared against actual data, enhancing their effectiveness and adaptability to emerging criminal activities (Farrell & Sidebottom, 2018). For instance, predictive policing has proven effective in recent years, enabling law enforcement to prevent crimes before they occur. However, the findings also highlight the need for further research and ethical considerations to balance the biases in predictive technologies.

The Role of Technology and Data Analytics in Crime Science

Technology and data analytics have significantly influenced the development and efficiency of crime science. Computer technology and the advent of the internet have equipped researchers and police departments with powerful tools for collecting, processing, and analyzing vast amounts of information about crime and its trends. In their 2021 publication, Baraka and Murimi noted that tools such as GIS and predictive policing algorithms have made forensic science, crime prevention, and investigative processes more proactive and accurate.

GIS have revolutionized crime mapping and spatial analysis. By visualizing crime data on maps, GIS help researchers and law enforcement agencies identify geographic patterns and distributions of crime, thereby guiding effective interventions (Baraka & Murimi, 2021). For example, hot-spot policing policies reliant on GIS to pinpoint high-crime areas enable law enforcement agencies to prioritize their resources and direct their efforts to essential tasks (Chainey & Ratcliffe, 2013). Kenyan police officers are optimistic about using GIS for spatiotemporal crime analysis, recognizing its benefits to their daily operations.

Another technological breakthrough in crime science is predictive policing algorithms. These algorithms employ statistical methods and artificial intelligence (AI) to predict when and where crimes are most likely. By analyzing historical crime statistics and other relevant factors, predictive policing can forecast future crime trends. This capability allows law enforcement agencies to allocate their resources better and address crimes before occurrence (Chauhan & Aluvalu, 2016). However, predictive policing has raised concerns regarding fairness and bias. Critics argue these algorithms may perpetuate existing biases and disproportionately target specific groups (Pramanik et al., 2017). Contemporary research, transparency, and ethical oversight are crucial for preventing irresponsible predictive policing.

Technology in crime science extends beyond GIS and predictive policing. Advancements in forensic science have transformed the investigation and prosecution of offenses.

For instance, DNA analysis in forensic science has significantly improved the identification of criminals because of the more precise collection of biological evidence at crime scenes. DNA can help pinpoint a suspect's presence at a crime scene, facilitating arrests and ensuring justice (Delgado et al., 2021). Additionally, DNA databases have enhanced the efficiency of solving cold cases and tracking repeat offenders, demonstrating the effectiveness of forensic science.

Furthermore, technology has shaped digital forensics. Modern technologies related to cybercrime and communication and information storage devices present new challenges for forensic investigation. Digital forensics retrieves electronic evidence from computers, mobile devices, and networks, aiding in the detection, deterrence, and prosecution of cybercrimes by analyzing the behaviors of cybercriminals (Chapman, 2016). This discipline enables investigators to trace and reconstruct digital activities, addressing the growing threat of cybercrime.

However, applying technology and data analytics in crime science has drawbacks. One primary concern is data credibility, as much information is gathered online. Discrepancies in crime data can lead to incorrect conclusions and misguided actions (Pramanik et al., 2017). Additionally, deploying predictive algorithms raises privacy and civil liberties issues. Surveilling and collecting large amounts of personal information may violate the privacy rights of individuals. Therefore, data collection and usage must be appropriate and secure to mitigate these concerns.

Bias and fairness are critical ethical issues when using technology and data analytics in crime science. Some predictive policing algorithms have been accused of replicating the biases inherent in policing practices. If the historical crime data for training these algorithms contain biases against certain groups, the predictions will reflect those biases (Chauhan & Aluvalu, 2016). To address these problems, greater transparency and accountability in algorithm development are essential, along with continuous analysis to minimize bias.

Another ethical concern is the potential overreliance on technology at the expense of rationality and professional judgment. Integrating technological tools and insights with the expertise of law enforcement practitioners is crucial (Delgado et al., 2021). Ensuring that technology enhances human decision-making is vital to maintaining the integrity and efficiency of crime prevention and investigation efforts.

The Jill Dando Institute and Its Contributions to Crime Science

The Jill Dando Institute of Security and Crime Science was established at University College London (UCL) in 2001 and has since become a significant academic institution in crime science. Founded in memory of Jill Dando, a British television presenter murdered in 1999, the institute greatly emphasizes crime and security research (University College London, n.d.). The institute was pivotal in advancing crime science as a specialized and multidisciplinary approach.

The institute was founded on the premise that existing methods for understanding and combating crime were inadequate. Its founders believed that integrating knowledge from various fields, including psychology, sociology, law, forensic science, and technology, would develop a rational and preventative model of crime (Smith & Tilley, 2013). This multidisciplinary foundation allows the institute to address complex crime issues effectively.

Since its inception, the institute has emphasized the importance of applied crime prevention and control. Its organizational research priorities are comprehensive and specialized, covering various issues pertinent to contemporary security concerns (Laycock, 2023). The creation of the Dando Institute underscores the necessity for collaboration among scholars, law enforcement officers, and officials to apply research findings and enhance societal safety effectively.

During its development, the Dando Institute has significantly contributed to several areas of crime science, including terrorism, cybercrime, and situational crime prevention.

Terrorism: Terrorism is one of the most important fields researched at the Dando Institute of Security and Crime Science. Scholars at the institute have investigated the aims, actions, and tactics of terrorists. By studying terrorist activity and the factors leading to radicalization and recruitment, the institute has developed counterterrorism and deradicalization interventions grounded in research (Laycock, 2023). This work has informed national and international policies and significantly contributed to the global fight against terrorism. The institute's efforts highlight that the social and psychological dimensions of terrorism must be considered in prevention and intervention strategies.

Cybercrime: Cybercrime has emerged as a significant issue in the digital landscape due to its increasing complexity. The Dando Institute has actively developed new techniques for addressing cybercrime. Researchers analyze the behaviors and strategies of cybercriminals, work on identifiers and methodologies in cyber forensics, and investigate the legal and ethical implications of combating cybercrime (Smith & Tilley, 2013). This research is vital for tracking the ever-evolving attack tactics and equipping law enforcement agencies to meet these challenges. The institute's contributions to the study of cybercrime underscore the need for constant enhancement and evolution of crime control measures.

Situational Crime Prevention: The Dando Institute has also pioneered research on situational crime prevention based on the theoretical framework of Clarke and Felson. Their empirical investigations into various situational interventions have informed the development of effective strategies for preventing crime in specific contexts. These strategies include changes in urban planning and design, environmental modifications, and community interventions aimed at minimizing crime opportunities (Meško et al., 2022). Situational crime prevention focuses on the specific environments in which criminal activities occur and seeks to deter crime by making it more difficult. Through its research, the institute has significantly contributed to formulating social policies and enhancing urban development practices that promote public safety.

Some of the groundbreaking findings of the Dando Institute include its advocacy for evidence-based policing, which emphasizes using statistical data and scientific research in policing practices and decision-making (Laycock, 2023). This approach has increased the efficacy of crime prevention efforts and enhanced agency performance by directing resources to areas of greatest need.

In addition to policing strategies, the research by the institute has significantly impacted national and international public policies. The institute's studies on terrorism, cybercrime, and situational crime prevention have informed policies and programs to reduce crime rates and improve security (Smith & Tilley, 2013). By providing informed, sound recommendations to policymakers, the institute has substantially advanced crime prevention and public safety.

The institute's interdisciplinary nature has fostered collaboration among scholars, law enforcement, and policymakers. This synergistic approach ensures the effective use of research outcomes and facilitates the deployment of innovative crime prevention strategies (Meško et al., 2022). The institute emphasizes applying scientific knowledge to enhance law enforcement agencies and develop effective public policies against crime.

The Dando Institute is actively involved in research, education, and training. It offers programs such as bachelor's and master's degrees in security and crime science, ensuring comprehensive knowledge for students, including theories, practices, and skills related to technology and methodologies. The institute's courses are designed to equip students with the education and skills necessary for employment with police forces, government agencies, private security firms, and other related organizations. Given the complexity of crime prevention in modern society, the institute's training prepares students to address these challenges effectively (Smith & Tilley, 2013). Furthermore, the institute contributes to advancing crime science and implementing evidence-based practices by training young and enthusiastic crime science specialists.

The Integration of Crime Science in Criminal Justice Systems

Crime science has influenced contemporary criminal justice systems by promoting predictive policing, situational crime prevention, and technological policies in crime analysis and identification. These innovations have transformed traditional policing by increasing the crime-fighting capacities of police agencies.

A significant development in this field is predictive policing in which the likelihood of a crime is estimated using statistical analysis and AI. Predictive policing algorithms generate patterns and trends based on past crime statistics and other environmental characteristics, resulting in a shift from reactive to proactive policing to prevent crimes from occurring in the first place (Gore & Bennett, 2022). For example, predictive policing has been employed in Los Angeles to identify areas with the highest probability of burglaries and to allocate police resources accordingly. However, predictive policing is not without controversy and ethical concerns, particularly regarding data bias and its impact on vulnerable populations. Critics argue that relying on historical crime rates may perpetuate biases and lead to the overpolicing of specific communities (Ho et al., 2022). Thus, further study and evaluation are necessary to ensure responsible and ethical predictive policing.

Police and similar authorities have endorsed the principles of situational crime prevention as effective strategies for minimizing the propensity for criminal activity in specific settings. This approach modifies the physical environment to reduce the likelihood of offenses (Clarke, 2016). Practical solutions include improved lighting on streets, the installation of security cameras, and the implementation of security access systems. For instance, enhancing lighting in parking lots or residential areas may make it more difficult for offenders to operate undetected (Ho et al., 2022). Similarly, placing surveillance cameras, particularly in communal areas, reduces crime rates due to the increased likelihood of apprehension. Physical security barriers, such as gates in residential compounds and offices, also eliminate avenues for criminal activities. The effectiveness of situational crime prevention underscores that the success of crime prevention depends on the specific circumstances of particular crimes, thereby enhancing safety and reducing crime levels (Ho et al., 2022).

Technology has dramatically transformed the analysis and investigation of crime within law enforcement. Innovations such as DNA matching have significantly enhanced criminal investigations and prosecution. This method accurately identifies suspects at crime scenes and can be used in court proceedings. Recent advancements in DNA database systems have also solved cold cases and identified repeat offenders, demonstrating that DNA analysis plays a critical role in contemporary criminal investigations (Oosthuizen & Howes, 2022). Digital forensics represents another area that has benefited from technological advancements. Computer crimes have necessitated retrieving and analyzing information from computers, devices, and networks. Digital forensics techniques enable tracing evidence, elucidating cybercrimes, and gathering data for legal proceedings (Delgado et al., 2021). This capability is vital in combating the rising incidence of cybercrime and equipping law enforcement to address emerging operational methods.

Behavioral and Social Sciences in Crime Science

Combining behavioral and social sciences with crime science has provided deeper insights into criminal conduct and improved crime-fighting strategies. Crime science can explore how individual, social, and environmental factors contribute to unlawful behavior, using psychological and sociological theories and information from other social sciences.

Criminal psychology theories are particularly relevant as they enhance understanding of the cognitive and decision-making aspects of the crime. The cognitive-behavioral model, a widely accepted theoretical orientation in psychology, focuses on the relationships among cognition, emotion, and behavior. Cognitive-behavioral interventions aim to alter an offender's thinking and, consequently, their behavior to reduce the likelihood of re-offending. For instance, cognitive behavior therapy has been implemented for an extended period in correctional centers to assist offenders in changing their cognitive patterns and responses to specific events (Gore & Bennett, 2022). Meta-analyses have demonstrated that cognitive behavior therapy effectively decreases the number of re-offenders, as it addresses the thought patterns and stimuli leading to criminal conduct.

Another important perspective in crime science is the social psychological strain theory of Robert Agnew. This theory attributes criminal involvement to stress from the failure to achieve culturally valued goals through legal means. Stress can stem from financial factors, social prejudice or discrimination, or individual failures and disappointments. More specifically, as confirmed by Agnew (2020), individuals experiencing significant stress are more likely to offend or commit a crime. This theory underscores the importance of considering stress-triggering social and economic factors in the fight against crime. Strain theory interventions aim to help individuals achieve objective success and alleviate structural strain factors.

Sociological concepts of crime emphasize that elements within the social environment contribute to criminal behavior. For example, social control and disorganization theories explain how the breakdown of social structures, such as the family, school, and community, leads to criminality. According to social control theory, individuals with strong bonds to society or societal structures are less likely to engage in criminal activities. Initiatives that strengthen social ties and rebuild cohesive communities have been linked to reduced crime levels (Hipp & Williams, 2020). Community-policing programs, which enhance relationships between the police and citizens, are an example of initiatives designed to reduce crime.

Spatial criminology is a discipline closely related to crime science, behavioral science, and social science. Criminology can be defined as a branch of knowledge that studies crime and its conditions (Gore & Bennett, 2022). Recent methodological developments have enabled scholars to describe and explain the spatial patterns of crime. Examining the spatial distribution of crimes allows researchers to design appropriate, effective prevention measures in specific environments in which crime is likely to occur (Hipp & Williams, 2020). For instance, environmental design principles that modify surroundings to minimize opportunities for criminal activities, such as improved lighting and natural surveillance, have been shown to reduce crime in urban areas.

Integrating behavioral and social sciences in crime science has also facilitated the development of complex strategies for crime prevention. These strategies often incorporate elements from various theoretical orientations, reflecting the complexity of criminal behavior. For example, cognitive-behavioral methods and community-based and environmental design initiatives demonstrate the potential for a holistic approach to crime reduction (Gore & Bennett, 2022). By addressing key individual, social, and environmental factors contributing to crime, such programs can significantly and durably reduce criminal activity.

Forensic science has expanded rapidly over the last few decades due to technological advancements and improved analytical methods. Indeed, genetic identification constitutes one of the most significant innovations in forensic studies. This technology has transformed criminal investigations by enabling law enforcement agencies to associate suspects with crime scenes effectively (Oosthuizen & Howes, 2022). When executed correctly, DNA collection and analysis yield irrefutable evidence indicating the suspect's presence at the crime scene, enhancing the likelihood of solving cases and securing convictions. The development of comprehensive DNA databases has further increased this potential, allowing cold cases to be reexamined and repeat offenders to be easily identified.

Digital forensics has also become crucial to crime scene science, particularly cybercrime. If cyber threats proliferate at their current pace, the ability to recover and analyze electronic evidence will become essential. Digital forensics enables investigators to observe the techniques and trends employed by cyber criminals and aids in tracking digital traces and networks of unlawful activities. This field requires ongoing research and development to counter emerging threats and enhance the technical aspects of cybercrime investigations (Weyermann et al., 2023). Therefore, advancing this evolving area of law is vital to prevent the erosion of the admissibility of such evidence within the justice system.

Significant improvements have also been observed in fingerprinting, facial recognition, and iris scans, enhancing police effectiveness in apprehending criminals. These technologies positively impact crime fighting, detection, data analytics, and AI. For example, facial recognition technology can match the footage of suspects with images in databases in real-time, thus improving response times and reducing reliance on potentially inaccurate witness testimony (Khan & Rizvi, 2021). However, the implementation of these technologies must be regulated to align with privacy policies and prevent misuse.

Data analytics and predictive modeling are now core components of contemporary crime science. These technologies assist researchers and practitioners in learning how to prevent or contain crime (Delgado et al., 2021). In predictive policing, computers forecast where and when a particular crime is most likely to occur, and police agencies worldwide have implemented this strategy. By analyzing crime rates, situational factors, and the social environment, predictive policing can ensure the appropriate allocation of available resources to prevent potential crimes.

Although predictive policing aims to reduce crime rates and optimize resource allocation, it has faced significant criticism and ethical concerns. One primary issue is that algorithms are not immune to bias and can exacerbate existing inequalities in policing practices. When the data input into these systems reflects biases against specific societal groups, the outputs may disproportionately target those groups, intensifying social injustice. Addressing these concerns and fully harnessing the potential of predictive analytics requires further research, transparency, and regulation (Ferguson, 2019).

In addition to predictive policing, data analytics is employed to study crime-related data, including social media posts and economic statistics. Crime cannot be combated with general solutions but requires targeted strategies that integrate multiple data sources. For instance, analyzing social media trends can help identify new threats or changes in criminal behavior (Lavorgna & Ugwudike, 2021). This approach enables law enforcement agencies to adopt more flexible strategies for evolving crime trends.

Data analytics in crime science and forensic intelligence connect forensic science to policing. Analytical tools extract intelligence from forensic data, thereby enhancing the investigation process. For example, forensic intelligence may identify signs of serial offenses or link various incidents based on specific characteristics (Delgado et al., 2021). Integrating forensic science with data analytics strengthens the effectiveness of crime investigation and prevention measures.

Emphasis should be on the fact that crime science is a highly interdisciplinary subject incorporating a wide range of knowledge from various fields. Institutions such as the Jill Dando Institute have fostered this cooperation and promoted multidisciplinary research. In its broadest sense, crime science can encompass knowledge from psychology, sociology, law, forensic science, and technology to enhance crime-fighting and prevention efforts. This collaborative framework integrates diverse skills to address modern, complex crime.

This process is not limited to academic circles but includes collaboration among police, government and nongovernmental organizations, private individuals, and society. Such partnerships are crucial for applying research findings, particularly in formulating sustainable and effective crime-prevention strategies. For example, collaboration between police departments and universities can implement evidence-based practices in policing, enhancing the overall effectiveness of police operations (Anderson et al., 2021). These collaborations also exchange information and resources, improving the efficacy of crime prevention measures.

Interdisciplinary research is essential, as it involves multiple disciplines that help identify the best solutions to crime-related problems. For instance, combining psychological theories of criminality with sociological perspectives on social factors can deepen the understanding of the causes of criminal behavior. This integration enables researchers to develop comprehensive interventions that address the root causes of criminal conduct rather than merely its symptoms (Laycock, 2023). Such holistic strategies are more likely to sustainably change crime rates and overall security.

Ethical and Legal Challenges in Crime Science

With the emergence of crime science, the field must address significant ethical concerns and questions of social justice. Apprehensions abound regarding privacy, surveillance, and the risk of discrimination when crime prevention and investigation involve technology and data analysis (Ferguson, 2019). For these tools to be employed appropriately, discussions, disclosures, and accountability must always exist. For example, if predictive policing algorithms use biased historical crime data, those biases will inevitably reflect in their outcomes. Measures should be taken to mitigate such biases, and regular checks should assess their presence.

Moreover, crime science needs to focus on social justice and equity questions. Understanding the social and economic determinants of crime is vital for informing prevention strategies that address these underlying causes (Tonry, 2020). Effective crime prevention cannot be designed and implemented without considering all population groups, especially those at risk of becoming victims of crime and those most vulnerable to predation. For instance, participatory interventions that engage community residents in designing and implementing crime prevention measures may enhance their effectiveness as they respond to cultural and environmental contexts (Browning & Arrigo, 2021). This approach is crucial for building safer and more equitable societies.

The ethical application of various surveillance tools, including facial recognition and data analysis, also raises important issues. Although these tools can benefit crime prevention, they pose serious concerns regarding individual privacy and civil liberties. Pervasive surveillance and the misuse of personal information necessitate stringent legal regulations and oversight to protect citizens' rights. Governments and policymakers must balance the leveraging of technology for public safety and human rights concerns (Khan & Rizvi, 2021). This equilibrium is essential for maintaining public support and the legal admissibility of actions to prevent crime.

Future Directions in Crime Science

Crime science is expected to be influenced by various key areas that will continue to impact its growth and effectiveness:

Technological Innovation: New technologies, such as AI, machine learning, and the Internet of Things, will transform the landscape of crime prevention and investigation. However, the full benefits can only be realized if these technologies are used responsibly and ethically.

Global Collaboration: Crime increasingly assumes an international dimension, requiring internationalization and integration. Combating transnational crimes such as human trafficking, drug trafficking, and cybercrime necessitates the cooperation of different countries and international organizations and the sharing of their resources.

Community Engagement: This activity involves actively engaging communities in crime-fighting processes and enhancing police-community relations. Community activities and involvement can increase the community's role in risk prevention.

Policy and Practice: Another challenge for crime science involves translating research into actionable policies and practices. Sustained interactions between researchers, policymakers, and practitioners will ensure that consistency is maintained in implementing best practices and that policies are informed by research.

Ethical and Legal Frameworks: Strong ethical and legal standards are needed when applying technology and data analytics to crime fighting. These frameworks must address privacy, surveillance, bias, and discrimination to advance the field of crime science ethically.

Education and Training: Continued development requires education and training for the next generation of crime scientists. Academic programs, professional development, and interdisciplinary training can prepare future researchers and practitioners to address emerging challenges.

Conclusion

Crime science is experiencing a shift in attitude toward crime, with a particular emphasis on prevention and the application of scientific knowledge. The integration of various scientific disciplines and the use of progressive technologies, including data science and forensics, have enhanced crime prevention and response. Through interdisciplinary research, academic institutions such as the Jill Dando Institute have significantly contributed to the development of counterterrorism, cybercrime, and situational crime-prevention strategies. The necessity for multidisciplinary research and collaboration cannot be overstated, as these efforts have improved crime prevention methods that take into account the various risk factors associated with crime. The potential for constructing safer societies is evident with advancements in crime science. Further progress in this field can enhance crime prevention and reduction strategies by addressing the root causes of crime while upholding high ethical standards. Therefore, ongoing development and cooperation will be essential to tackling emerging issues and improving the efficacy of criminal justice initiatives. In summary, maintaining an interdisciplinary focus and a commitment to social justice will be critical to the continued development of crime science and its beneficial impact on society.

References

Agnew, R. (2020). The contribution of social-psychological strain theory to the explanation of crime and delinquency. *The legacy of anomie theory*, 113–137. Routledge.

Anderson, G. (2019). *Biological influences on criminal behavior.* CRC Press.

Anderson, T. L., Donnelly, E. A., Delcher, C., & Wang, Y. (2021). Data science approaches in criminal justice and public health research: Lessons from opioid projects. *Journal of Contemporary Criminal Justice*, 37(2), 175–191.

Baraka, G. E., & Murimi, S. K. (2021). Why geographic information systems in spatiotemporal crime analysis? Attitude of Kenyan police officers. *Police Practice and Research*, 22(5), 1453–1468.

Bottoms, A. E., & Wiles, P. (2020). Environmental criminology. *Crime, inequality and the state*, 273–293. Routledge.

Browning, M., & Arrigo, B. (2021). Stop and risk: Policing, data, and the digital age of discrimination. *American Journal of Criminal Justice*, 46(2), 298–316.

Chainey, S., & Ratcliffe, J. (2013). *GIS and crime mapping.* Wiley.

Chapman, B. (2016). *Research on the impact of technology on policing strategy in the 21st century.* National Institute of Justice.

Chauhan, T., & Aluvalu, R. (2016). *Using big data analytics for developing a crime predictive model.* RK University's First International Conference on Research & Entrepreneurship, 1–6.

Clarke, R. V. (2016). Situational crime prevention. *Environmental criminology and crime analysis.* Routledge.

Delgado, Y., Price, B. S., Speaker, P. J., & Stoiloff, S. L. (2021). Forensic intelligence: Data analytics as the bridge between forensic science and investigation. *Forensic Science International: Synergy*, 3, 100162.

Farrell, G., & Sidebottom, A. (2018). *Realist evaluation for crime science.* Routledge.

Felson, M. (2008). Situational crime prevention. *International handbook of penology and criminal justice*, 295–320. Taylor Francis.

Ferguson, A. G. (2019). Predictive policing theory. *Cambridge handbook of policing in the United States*, 491–510. Cambridge University Press.

Gore, M. L., & Bennett, A. (2022). Importance of deepening the integration of crime and conservation sciences. *Conservation Biology*, 36(1), e13710.

Hardyns, W., & Pauwels, L. J. (2018). The Chicago School and criminology. *The handbook of the history and philosophy of criminology*, 123–139. Wiley-Blackwell.

Henson, B. (2020). Routine activities. *The Palgrave handbook of international cybercrime and cyberdeviance*, 469–489. Palgrave Macmillan.

Hipp, J. R., & Williams, S. A. (2020). Advances in spatial criminology: The spatial scale of crime. *Annual Review of Criminology*, 3(1), 75–95.

Ho, H., Ko, R., & Mazerolle, L. (2022). Situational crime prevention (SCP) techniques to prevent and control cybercrimes: A focused, systematic review. *Computers & Security*, 115, 1–24.

Jørgensen, A., & Smith, D. (2009). The Chicago School of Sociology: Survival in the urban jungle. *Encountering the everyday: An introduction to the sociologies of the unnoticed*, 45–68. Palgrave Macmillan.

Khan, Z. A., & Rizvi, A. (2021). AI-based facial recognition technology and criminal justice: Issues and challenges. *Turkish Journal of Computer and Mathematics Education*, 12(14), 3384–3392.

Krohn, M. D., & Eassey, J. M. (2014). Integrated theories of crime. *The encyclopedia of theoretical criminology*, 458–463. Wiley.

Lavorgna, A., & Ugwudike, P. (2021). The datafication revolution in criminal justice: An empirical exploration of frames portraying data-driven technologies for crime prevention and control. *Big Data & Society*, 8(2), 1–15.

Lawless, C. (2022). *Forensic science: A sociological introduction.* Routledge.

Laycock, G. (2023). *Crime, science, and policing.* Taylor & Francis.

Meško, G., Eman, K., & Hacin, R. (2022). Crime mapping in crime analysis: Developments in the past two decades. *Security Technologies and Social Implications*, 222–246. Wiley.

Oosthuizen, T., & Howes, L. M. (2022). The development of forensic DNA analysis: New debates on the issue of fundamental human rights. *Forensic Science International: Genetics*, 56, 102606.

Pramanik, M. I., Lau, R. Y., Yue, W. T., Ye, Y., & Li, C. (2017). Big data analytics for security and criminal investigations. *Wiley Interdisciplinary Reviews: Data Mining and Knowledge Discovery*, 7(4), e1208.

Shaw, C. R., & McKay, H. D. (1969). *Juvenile delinquency and urban Areas: A study of delinquency in relation to differential characteristics of local communities in American cities*. University of Chicago Press.

Smith, M. J., & Tilley, N. (2013). *Crime science*. Taylor & Francis.

Tonry, M. (2020). *Doing justice, preventing crime*. Oxford University Press.

University College London. (n.d.). Jill Dando Institute of Security and Crime Science. Retrieved 9–27–24, from https://www.ucl.ac.uk/jill-dando-institute/.

Vilks, A., & Kipāne, A. (2021). Criminology as trends in the development of science. *Socrates*, 39–48.

Weyermann, C., Willis, S., Margot, P., & Roux, C. (2023). Towards more relevance in forensic science research and development. *Forensic Science International*, 348, 111592.

2 Surveillance Systems

The evolving landscape of crime science has seen the crucial rise of surveillance systems. These technological tools have gained significance within contemporary law enforcement strategies against criminal activities, contributing to public safety, supporting investigations, and deterring criminal acts (Hassan & Ibrahim, 2023). As technology progresses, surveillance techniques have evolved, enabling law enforcement agencies to collect vital data and respond adeptly to emerging risks.

The realm of surveillance systems encompasses various technologies, each contributing uniquely to multifaceted crime science objectives. From closed-circuit television (CCTV) cameras monitoring urban areas to drones providing aerial surveillance, these tools have transformed crime prevention and investigation techniques. The distinct strength of surveillance systems lies in their dual capacity as deterrents and evidence-gathering tools. In urban settings, where high human activity can foster criminal inclinations, CCTV cameras act as vigilant sentinels, capturing real-time visuals that significantly discourage potential criminals. The awareness of being under scrutiny profoundly influences individual behavior due to the increased likelihood of apprehension.

Furthermore, these technologies have redefined the investigative process. By providing law enforcement agencies with visual records of incidents, surveillance systems create a valuable timeline of events that aid in reconstructing criminal events. Whether tracing suspect movements, identifying persons of interest, or corroborating witness statements, these systems enhance the precision and efficiency of investigative efforts.

In law enforcement, surveillance technologies have expanded operational capabilities, empowering authorities to monitor situations from previously inaccessible vantage points. Drones, in particular, have emerged as versatile assets capable of aerial reconnaissance, tracking mobile suspects, and contributing to search and rescue missions (Kashef et al., 2021). Utilizing drones in potentially hazardous situations enhances police officer safety while maintaining vigilant monitoring.

As we delve into the intricate universe of surveillance systems, the following chapter will explore two fundamental constituents: closed-circuit television cameras and drones. We shall unveil their integral roles in shaping contemporary crime science by examining their applications, advantages, obstacles, and ethical considerations. Through this exploration, we aim to illuminate how these technologies harmonize with conventional investigative methods to forge a safer and more secure societal milieu.

CCTV Surveillance

CCTV cameras play a vital role in modern surveillance systems. These cameras have transformed the administration of law enforcement and public safety through their advanced capabilities. These cameras are strategically positioned in multiple locations to

DOI: 10.4324/9781003558491-2

gather visual and audio data. Subsequently, this information is sent to a central monitoring station accessible only by authorized personnel, ensuring the security of the recorded data.

The primary functions of CCTV cameras are to monitor and deter criminal activity. Equipped with a complex network of lenses and sensors, these cameras provide a continuous and comprehensive view of selected areas. This functionality allows operators to observe events in real time, offering a dynamic digital window into the monitored environment. Law enforcement agencies benefit from this phenomenon, as it enhances their capacity for prompt responses to emerging incidents, including crises, disturbances, and illicit activities.

CCTV cameras operate differently from broadcast television. While broadcast television disseminates signals for public consumption, CCTV functions within a confined system (Surette, 2005). The video captured by CCTV is exclusively intended for authorized personnel responsible for upholding public safety and deterring criminal activities. This exclusivity protects private data from unauthorized access, preserving the integrity of investigations.

CCTV cameras produce real-time video feeds and recordings that provide law enforcement with valuable information. These cameras are utilized in various public and private spaces, such as managing traffic, crowds, and law enforcement activities in urban areas. Operators can monitor events as they unfold during disturbances, dispatching officers to the area immediately and enabling a quick resolution. The recorded video simultaneously serves as a crucial tool for post-incident analysis and investigations, assisting in reconstructing events, identifying suspects, and supporting legal proceedings.

In deterring unlawful acts, the mere presence of CCTV cameras serves as a strong deterrent. The awareness of being watched influences individual behavior, instilling a sense of accountability even in areas where police presence is not apparent (Fitwi & Chen, 2020). This psychological impact, known as the "watchfulness influence," prompts individuals to reconsider engaging in illegal activities, knowing their actions are being recorded.

Overall, CCTV cameras redefine how society combats crime and protects public safety. They exemplify the synergy between technology and law enforcement. By harnessing the power of real-time monitoring, these cameras enable authorities to respond swiftly to developing situations while fostering an environment less conducive to criminal activity. However, this powerful technology comes with substantial accountability. Therefore, CCTV systems must adhere to ethical standards and protect individuals' privacy, highlighting the delicate balance between technology and the preservation of civil liberties.

Applications of CCTV in Urban Areas

The widespread implementation of CCTV cameras in urban areas demonstrates their significant ability to address and mitigate the unique security challenges of dynamic urban environments. Urban settings, characterized by vibrant public spaces, extensive street networks, towering structures, and bustling transportation hubs, present a complex backdrop. These elements can create opportunities for criminal activities (Laufs & Borrion, 2022). The deployment of CCTV surveillance systems has emerged as a steadfast guardian, diligently monitoring various areas and enhancing overall security and societal harmony.

In public areas, such as parks and plazas, the inclusion of TV cameras serves as a deterrent to illegal activities. The constant surveillance created by these cameras fosters a visible monitoring atmosphere, prompting individuals to reconsider engaging in illicit activities. This preventive impact is particularly significant in mitigating occurrences of public disturbances, drug-related activities, and violent incidents, thereby transforming previously vulnerable areas into safer spaces that foster security and community engagement.

The extensive surveillance provided by CCTV systems extends its benefit to the intricate network of metropolitan streets and highways. Cameras assist law enforcement agencies in managing traffic and investigating accidents, making heavily trafficked roads and pedestrian areas easier to control (Laufs & Borrion, 2022). The captured video footage serves as impartial and factual documentation of occurrences, enabling authorities to effectively reconstruct sequences of events, assign accountability, and expedite claim filing Additionally, these surveillance cameras are essential in mitigating criminal activities, such as vandalism and theft (Badidi et al., 2023). These cameras act as a constant deterrent, reminding individuals that their actions are under continuous surveillance and will be recorded for future reference.

CCTV cameras are strategically placed within metropolitan buildings to enhance security measures and protect individuals inside. These cameras act as monitors for entrances, exits, and common areas, deterring unauthorized access and proactively mitigating potential threats. Their presence deters unauthorized access and proactively mitigates potential threats. Continuous surveillance through electronic monitoring reassures building residents, enhancing their safety and security.

CCTV monitoring significantly improves the security and efficiency of transportation hubs, which are vital to urban infrastructure. Airports, train stations, and bus terminals serve as bustling centers for both local and international passengers. These locations rely on surveillance systems to bolster their security measures and maintain order. Monitoring densely populated areas and tracking crowd dynamics provide authorities with valuable real-time data, facilitating prompt responses to emerging security threats and unforeseen emergencies. The use of real-time awareness measures ensures the protection and welfare of commuters, thereby maintaining the operational efficiency of these critical transit hubs.

In summary, the use of CCTV cameras in urban areas extends beyond mere observation. They hold the potential for enhanced safety, maintaining public peace, and more effectively preventing crimes. The utilization of these cameras encompasses a range of functions, such as transforming public spaces into secure areas, improving traffic management, reinforcing building security, and safeguarding busy transit centers. These cameras function as discreet monitors that protect the integrity of urban environments. However, it is essential to strike a balance between security and privacy. This balance entails recognizing that while surveillance technologies undeniably offer significant benefits, their deployment must be guided by ethical considerations and legal frameworks that uphold personal freedoms and civil liberties.

Crime Prevention and Behavioral Impact of CCTV

Extensive research and empirical evidence highlight the substantial influence of CCTV cameras in reducing unlawful activities. The utilization of CCTV systems in various urban settings has demonstrated noticeable correlations with reductions in criminal activities (Markovic et al., 2021). Research provides valuable insights into the quantifiable impact of CCTV cameras in deterring criminal activities. A study conducted by the Urban Institute examined public housing complexes and found that the implementation of CCTV cameras resulted in a substantial decline in drug-related offenses and violent acts (Markovic et al., 2021). The experiential evidence presented in this study highlights the capability of surveillance technology to positively alter community dynamics, leading to improved neighborhood safety and an elevated sense of well-being among residents.

Additionally, the retail sector demonstrates the preventive effectiveness of CCTV cameras. Retail establishments, frequently challenged by shoplifting and employee theft, have effectively harnessed the monitoring capabilities offered by CCTV systems (Beck &

Willis, 1999). The use of surveillance cameras not only serves as a preventive measure against potential shoplifters but also aids in retrospectively identifying perpetrators, assisting law enforcement in apprehending suspects and recovering stolen goods.

The psychological impact of CCTV surveillance on individual behavior goes beyond mere statistical analysis. The awareness of being watched fosters a heightened sense of accountability and self-discipline. The Hawthorne effect, originating from notable industrial research, links increased productivity to the simple awareness of being under surveillance (McCambridge et al., 2014). In crime prevention, as the knowledge that their actions are being recorded makes individuals reconsider engaging in illegal activities.

The impact of CCTV cameras on behavior extends beyond individuals to the wider community. Establishing a collective sense of safety nurtures an environment where residents and visitors experience heightened feelings of security. Consequently, individuals are more likely to engage in activities that strengthen their community, contributing to neighborhood improvement (Hall, 2020). However, it is essential to recognize that the effectiveness of CCTV systems is multifaceted. While they can help reduce certain crimes, they may not be a comprehensive solution for all types of criminal activity. A holistic crime prevention strategy requires integrating technological solutions with community involvement, effective policing, and targeted interventions.

Integrating CCTV cameras into urban landscapes has demonstrated their significance as pivotal tools in crime prevention and deterrence. The influence of surveillance systems in diminishing criminal actions has been validated by empirical research across various settings, including public spaces and retail environments. In addition to quantitative evidence, psychological mechanisms such as the Hawthorne effect highlight the profound impact of surveillance technologies on shaping human behavior. By promoting accountability and community safety, these surveillance cameras go beyond their practical use, helping to create safer, more connected urban environments.

Ethical and Legal Challenges of CCTV

The widespread use of CCTV cameras has significantly altered how people perceive modern crime science and public safety. However, this transformation raises challenges and ethical concerns. With increasing reliance on surveillance to protect communities, it becomes essential to closely evaluate its impact on privacy, civil rights, and data misuse risk.

A key concern arising from the extensive deployment of CCTV is balancing crime prevention with the potential invasion of privacy rights. Critics argue that the constant presence of surveillance systems creates an environment where citizens feel that their every move is continually monitored (Ding et al., 2022). This raises concerns about the emergence of a surveillance-driven society, where security is prioritized at the expense of personal freedoms. The debate revolves around balancing crime prevention with an individual's right to live free from constant surveillance.

Furthermore, the accumulation, preservation, and management of extensive quantities of sensitive data via CCTV systems presents significant cybersecurity risks. Unauthorized access to these data exposes individuals to threats such as identity theft and more severe forms of malicious exploitation, including extortion or harassment (Ding et al., 2022). Safeguarding the integrity of these sensitive data is paramount, particularly considering the potentially severe consequences of breaches. Thus, robust cybersecurity measures are imperative to ensure that these data remain inaccessible to malicious actors. Ethical concerns regarding CCTV cameras also include the potential for misuse by those responsible for operating them. Individuals with access to surveillance feeds wield significant power, and any misuse can result in privacy violations and false accusations (American Civil

Liberties Union, 2002). Establishing clear protocols, effective oversight, and accountability mechanisms is essential to prevent unauthorized access, tampering, or misuse.

Addressing these complexities requires a comprehensive approach that goes beyond the technical aspects of surveillance. Moral, legal, and community perspectives must be considered equally alongside technical aspects. The responsibility for balancing society's security and individual liberty rests with legislators and policymakers. The development, implementation, and maintenance of CCTV networks should be governed by well-defined regulations and guidelines. Proposed regulations should establish clear parameters regarding the acceptable scope of surveillance, data storage protocols, and procedures for retrieving and disseminating information. Equally important are public education efforts that inform citizens and allow them to engage in meaningful discussions about surveillance technology. Determining suitable surveillance parameters necessitates open dialogues, a clear understanding of the technology, issue resolution, and the formulation of universally agreeable solutions.

The role of CCTV cameras in deterring unlawful activities and facilitating investigations is undeniable. However, these cameras have concurrently raised numerous ethical and privacy concerns. It is essential to carefully consider the trade-offs between security, individual liberty, data security, and potential misuse. Our collective responsibility is to strike a balance that ensures public safety while protecting fundamental rights in an increasingly digital world.

The evolution of CCTV systems has surpassed their conventional role, driven by technological advancements that have expanded their capabilities and potential. These advancements have introduced a new era in crime science, fundamentally altering how law enforcement agencies oversee, prevent, and respond to criminal activity. The fusion of cutting-edge technologies with CCTV systems has elevated their efficiency, precision, and adaptability to evolving challenges.

High-resolution cameras present a monumental advancement in surveillance. These sophisticated optical devices capture clearer images and finer details, allowing law enforcement authorities to identify suspects with greater accuracy. By enhancing image clarity, high-resolution cameras provide valuable data that were previously inaccessible. This advancement plays a pivotal role in the investigative process, where clear visual evidence becomes a cornerstone in identifying suspects, substantiating witness statements, and constructing a robust justification for legal action.

Facial recognition software, seamlessly integrated into CCTV systems, introduces a novel dimension of real-time identification. This innovation has improved the speed and accuracy of law enforcement in capturing wanted criminals. As individuals traverse areas monitored by CCTV cameras, facial recognition algorithms promptly compare their features with watch lists of known offenders. This allows field officers to intercept suspects swiftly, ensuring rapid responses to emerging threats and enhancing law enforcement effectiveness.

One of the most remarkable advancements, real-time analytics, signifies a paradigm shift in the capabilities of CCTV cameras. This transformation stems from the integration of algorithms that detect anomalous patterns and behaviors in monitored environments. In densely populated public spaces, for instance, real-time analytics can identify sudden movements, abandoned packages, or erratic behavior that may indicate a threat (Liu et al., 2023). Automated notifications are sent to law enforcement personnel upon detecting triggers, facilitating quick intervention and preempting potentially dangerous situations. This predictive capability transforms CCTV systems from passive recorders into proactive tools, merging technology with human judgment for a more synergistic approach to public safety.

The implementation of these technological advancements underscores the evolving role of CCTV cameras within modern crime science. These cameras have evolved from mere observers into essential components of a dynamic crime prevention ecosystem (Liu et al., 2023). However, as these innovations expand the possibilities, they also raise new ethical considerations and potential pitfalls. Privacy concerns, already a significant aspect of CCTV deployment, are intensified by the precision and capabilities of high-resolution cameras and facial recognition software. Striking a balance between preventing crime and preserving individual privacy rights remains a pressing challenge. Additionally, reliance on algorithms and real-time analytics can lead to false positives (Snow, 2018), resulting in unwarranted interventions or the perpetuation of biases inherent in the foundational data.

In summary, technological advancements permeating the realm of CCTV systems have triggered a profound transformation in crime science. The integration of high-resolution cameras, facial recognition software, and real-time analytics has endowed these cameras with unparalleled capabilities, making them pivotal in investigations and essential for crime prevention. As these technologies evolve, ethical dilemmas and potential drawbacks must be addressed through comprehensive frameworks prioritizing responsible deployment, privacy protection, and impartial outcomes. The trajectory of CCTV cameras within crime science reflects the ongoing intersection of technological advancements and ethical considerations, shaping the future of surveillance and public safety.

Drone Surveillance in Law Enforcement

The emergence of drone surveillance represents a significant transformation in the field of crime science, fundamentally reshaping approaches to law enforcement, investigation, and public safety. Originally designed for recreational use, drones have undergone a transformative process, evolving into revolutionary tools that are now reshaping law enforcement approaches (Horowitz, 2020). Unmanned aerial vehicles (UAVs), commonly known as drones, have evolved from simple recreational devices to essential tools in various law enforcement contexts. The remarkable ability of these aerial devices to conduct airborne surveillance and demonstrate excellent adaptability has positioned them as prominent subjects in contemporary criminal science research.

Drones have evolved beyond their original characterization as recreational devices, assuming a multifaceted role that enables law enforcement organizations to surpass conventional constraints. Drones provide an exceptional capacity to explore areas that may otherwise be inaccessible, ranging from urban sprawl to remote landscapes. This mobility provides law enforcement with unparalleled situational awareness, enabling them to address complex and challenging circumstances with heightened efficacy.

The potential uses of UAVs in criminal science are both extensive and diverse. These aerial scouts can enhance existing techniques, offering innovative solutions to long-standing challenges (Peters, 2019). Acquiring real-time visual data from elevated viewpoints offers a heightened perspective that radically alters how law enforcement surveils suspects, monitors activities, and responds to emergencies (Kreps et al., 2023). Drone monitoring provides law enforcement agents with a comprehensive understanding of evolving circumstances, facilitating prompt and informed decision-making.

Moreover, autonomous aerial vehicles demonstrate exceptional performance in situations where human involvement may pose unnecessary risks. These flying devices are invaluable in critical circumstances, such as hostage situations or encounters with armed individuals, as they help minimize potential harm to law enforcement personnel and the public (Kreps et al., 2023). By serving as remote scouting instruments, drones offer crucial information that guides strategic choices, ensuring a careful and informed approach to law enforcement activities.

The increasing advancements in drone technology have significantly enhanced their potential to transform the field of criminal science. Law enforcement agencies have made significant contributions beyond technology, playing a crucial role in redefining community safeguarding (Peters, 2019). However, the integration of these technologies raises numerous ethical concerns, legal frameworks, and challenges that necessitate meticulous deliberation and strategic maneuvering. Exploring drone surveillance encompasses not only technological advancements but also a commitment to upholding justice, accountability, and responsible innovation.

Drones play a vital role in monitoring criminal activities. They serve as vigilant observers for the police, providing a valuable aerial perspective. This aerial perspective significantly enhances law enforcement's understanding of ongoing events, allowing for quicker responses.

In the ever-evolving realm of policing, highly precise drones are deployed to track suspects in motion. Real-time tracking provides law enforcement entities with a valuable flow of visual data, aiding them in formulating tactical responses based on the most current information (Thakur et al., 2021). For instance, in cases involving fleeing suspects, drones can effortlessly track these individuals from an aerial viewpoint. The immediate transmission of this crucial data equips field officers with precise information, enabling the swift development of strategies to intercept and block escape routes (Li & Savkin, 2021). This seamless integration of aerial pursuit surveillance enhances the effectiveness of law enforcement operations, thereby providing them with a strategic advantage.

The application of drone-enabled aerial tracking extends beyond monitoring individuals to include the tracking of vehicle movements. When vehicles are used in criminal activities, UAVs act as virtual guardians, providing continuous visual information to law enforcement personnel (Thakur et al., 2021). The aerial perspective ensures precise monitoring of vehicles and offers a comprehensive understanding of the operational area, facilitating effective interventions.

The diverse benefits of using drones for aerial surveillance in law enforcement have extensive implications. Elevated viewpoints provide a clear and comprehensive vantage point for surveying large areas that may be difficult to examine thoroughly. The agility and observational capabilities of drones dramatically enhance the efficiency of locating and monitoring suspects, even in densely populated locations. This capability is particularly significant during large-scale public events, where crowd surveillance is paramount for safety.

Furthermore, in areas with challenging topography or densely built urban environments, drones offer significant benefits through aerial perspectives. These perspectives enhance the efficiency of search and rescue operations by quickly identifying individuals in need of assistance. Drones play a crucial role in bolstering the situational awareness of law enforcement agencies during natural disasters and emergencies (Giordan et al., 2017), facilitating the coordination of effective responses that result in lifesaving outcomes.

Overall, the use of drones for aerial tracking and monitoring signifies a significant breakthrough in crime science. The critical importance of these technologies in improving the efficiency and efficacy of law enforcement is evident in their versatile applications for tracking suspects, monitoring criminal activities, and assessing various environments. The ongoing advancement of technology continues to enhance the potential for drones to significantly transform the fields of crime prevention and investigation. This emphasizes the critical importance of employing these devices responsibly while adhering to legal and ethical standards.

Non-Lethal Intervention Methods Using Drones

Drones have evolved beyond traditional surveillance roles to explore new domains that redefine law enforcement capabilities. This evolution has potential applications in several contexts, such as the provision of non-lethal force and invaluable assistance in situations requiring precision, safety, and de-escalation.

Within the domain of crowd management, drones have emerged as distinctive resources equipped with non-lethal tactics specifically designed to restore order without resorting to excessive force. Law enforcement organizations can effectively manage large gatherings or control unruly crowds by employing various technologies, such as tear gas distribution mechanisms, noise generators, or flashbangs, allowing for a controlled and strategic approach. This strategic deployment enables governing bodies to effectively address potential harm, minimize casualties, and promote de-escalation in situations that may escalate into disorder.

Incorporating autonomous aerial vehicles to monitor large gatherings exemplifies a commitment to leveraging technology to achieve desired outcomes while addressing ethical concerns. Rather than engaging in direct interactions that could exacerbate existing tensions, these aerial devices provide a means of intervention to restore harmony while prioritizing the safety and welfare of law enforcement officers and the general public. Drones offer a crucial strategic advantage in hazardous situations, prioritizing officer safety and effectiveness in crowd control. In scenarios involving hostage standoffs or encounters with armed criminals, drones are critical in gathering up-to-date intelligence. By employing aerial drones for scene assessment, law enforcement can obtain vital information to inform their actions. This proactive approach allows them to evaluate potential risks, explore exit strategies, and assess the overall dynamics of a situation before deploying personnel on-site.

Implementing UAVs in these situations helps protect officer safety by reducing uncertainty and lowering the chances of conflicts. By gathering vital information from a distant perspective, law enforcement can make well-informed decisions characterized by rationality and data-driven analysis. An organized and systematic strategy enhances the overall results while prioritizing the safety of law enforcement agents, suspects, and the public.

In summary, incorporating UAVs into the domain of non-lethal force and support demonstrates their transformative potential in contemporary criminal science. These aerial devices bridge technological advancements and ethical considerations, offering interventions that emphasize conflict reduction, accuracy, and individual safety. The ethical deployment of drones will be crucial in assessing their impact on public safety and protecting civil liberties as law enforcement organizations continue to explore their vast potential.

Ethical and Legal Considerations of Drone Surveillance

The integration of drones into law enforcement necessitates a comprehensive examination of the intricate web of legal and ethical factors. The increasing incorporation of drones into the field of crime science requires careful consideration of their deployment within frameworks that prioritize both public safety and individual rights.

Integrating UAVs necessitates rigorous compliance with established regulatory frameworks governing their use. It is crucial to institute comprehensive standards that clearly articulate the acceptable circumstances for employing drones, the required warrants, and safeguards to protect privacy to uphold constitutional values (Farber, 2014). By ensuring that drone activities are conducted within established legal frameworks, authorities can foster an atmosphere characterized by accountability, transparency, and public trust. These recommendations exhibit high clarity and specificity, mitigating the risk of excessive and arbitrary utilization of drones. Consequently, these guidelines serve as protective measures against potential encroachments on individual rights.

The ethical issues frequently associated with drone surveillance revolve around the delicate balance between public safety imperatives and personal privacy rights. Drones offer an intrinsic aerial perspective that enables the acquisition of photographs and data, which may potentially invade a person's privacy without their consent (Fleres et al., 2023). Balancing community safety and individual liberties requires a systematic and careful approach.

Transparency plays a fundamental role in effectively addressing ethical concerns. Law enforcement authorities must clearly communicate with the public regarding the use of UAVs, the objectives of surveillance operations, and the measures implemented to protect privacy. Public engagement and awareness initiatives are crucial in cultivating an informed populace, enabling their active involvement in discussions about the use of these technologies. Transparency in this context fosters trust and emphasizes the commitment to responsible drone implementation that upholds individuals' rights and freedoms.

Implementing accountability procedures is pivotal in reducing the risk of potential misuse of collected data. Data collected through drone surveillance should be limited to legitimate law enforcement purposes, supported by meticulous rules on retention, access, and oversight (Watney, 2022). These precautions mitigate unauthorized access and discourage any potential misuse of authority.

A continued commitment to addressing ethical concerns requires regular examination of practices and regulations. The rapid evolution of the technology landscape necessitates a corresponding adaptation of legal and ethical frameworks to ensure the appropriate integration of drones in accordance with society's changing values and expectations. A harmonized strategy can be achieved by fostering a cooperative atmosphere that encompasses law enforcement entities, lawmakers, civil liberties advocates, and the general populace, which duly recognizes the significance of safeguarding public welfare while upholding fundamental rights.

Future Trends and Challenges in Surveillance Systems

The trajectory of drones in crime science indicates a future marked by significant advancements and innovations. The continuous progression of technology is poised to significantly alter the role of drones, profoundly impacting law enforcement, investigation, and public safety.

Looking ahead, drones are expected to become increasingly specialized and efficient. Technological advancements are likely to usher in a new era of drones equipped with sophisticated sensors, enhanced maneuverability, and integrated artificial intelligence. The application of aerial artificial intelligence capabilities has the potential to enable the autonomous identification and tracking of individuals by drones (Anderson et al., 2021). These capabilities can significantly reduce response times and enhance the precision of interventions.

However, these advancements also raise several issues that necessitate attention to ensure the responsible and effective use of drones. The increasing capabilities of drones have brought cybersecurity concerns to the forefront. It is imperative to establish robust procedures to prevent hacking, data breaches, and unauthorized access to sensitive information obtained through drone monitoring (Majeed et al., 2021). Strengthening the cybersecurity measures of drone systems is crucial to maintaining their integrity and preventing them from being exploited for unauthorized access or misuse.

Moreover, a persistent challenge exists in achieving a balance between technological advancement and ethical considerations. The moral issues surrounding drone surveillance, particularly regarding individual privacy and civil liberties, necessitate ongoing assessment given their benefits for crime prevention and public safety. Achieving a balanced approach requires fostering a transparent and inclusive dialogue among law enforcement agencies, policymakers, privacy advocates, and the broader public. Establishing comprehensive criteria for the deployment, scope, and management of drone surveillance is crucial for preserving public trust and safeguarding individual rights.

In summary, drones have evolved from mere elements of science fiction to practical tools that are revolutionizing crime science. The aerial capabilities, adaptability, and potential for autonomous assistance offered by these technologies indicate a significant shift in law enforcement tactics. Integrating these evolving aerial sentinels necessitates prioritizing legal, ethical, and technological considerations. Law enforcement agencies can effectively incorporate drones into their operations by proactively addressing associated challenges and adequately utilizing their potential. By doing so, these agencies can harness the advancements offered by drones while upholding the fundamental principles of justice, accountability, and public trust (Yanakiev et al., 2020). The potential of drones shapes the future of crime science as they facilitate the creation of safer communities and a more equitable society.

Conclusion

In conclusion, surveillance systems have become essential tools within the field of crime science, fundamentally reshaping law enforcement and enhancing public safety. The advent of surveillance technologies such as CCTV cameras and aerial drones has engendered significant transformations in crime prevention, investigation, and response. The efficacy of surveillance extends beyond its capacity to observe and deter unlawful behaviors, encompassing its potential to reshape societal approaches to addressing criminality.

However, this power necessitates responsible execution with due regard for ethical implications. As monitoring technology continues to develop, it becomes increasingly important to establish a careful balance between ensuring public safety and upholding individual rights. The ethical utilization of these tools and the preservation of public trust rely on three fundamental pillars: transparency, accountability, and adherence to regulatory frameworks.

Thus, surveillance systems symbolize advancement in crime science, highlighting their potential to create a safer and more secure future. By embracing these technologies while adhering to ethical standards and safeguarding human rights, law enforcement agencies can effectively employ surveillance systems to address crime with accuracy, fairness, and a commitment to justice.

References

American Civil Liberties Union. (2002). What's wrong with public video surveillance?https://www.aclu.org/documents/whats-wrong-public-video-surveillance.

Anderson, T. L., Donnelly, E. A., Delcher, C., & Wang, Y. (2021). Data science approaches in criminal justice and public health research: Lessons from opioid projects. *Journal of Contemporary Criminal Justice*, 37(2), 175–191.

Badidi, E., Moumane, K., & El Ghazi, F. (2023). Opportunities, applications, and challenges of edge-AI enabled video analytics in smart cities: A systematic review. *IEEE Access*, 11, 80543–80572.

Beck, A., & Willis, A. (1999). Context-specific measures of CCTV effectiveness in the retail sector. *Surveillance of public space: CCTV, street lighting and crime prevention*, 251–269. Criminal Justice Press.

Ding, J., Qammar, A., Zhang, Z., Karim, A., & Ning, H. (2022). Cyber threats to intelligent grids: Review, taxonomy, potential solutions, and future directions. *Energies*, 15(18), 6799.

Farber, H. B. (2014). Eyes in the sky: Constitutional and regulatory approaches to domestic drone deployment. *Syracuse Law Review*, 64(1), 1–47.

Fitwi, A., & Chen, Y. (2020, August). Privacy-preserving selective video surveillance. *2020 29th International Conference on Computer Communications and Networks (ICCCN)*, 1–10. IEEE.

Fleres, A., Veling, L., Broz, F., & Damiano, L. (2023). Integrative robo-ethics: Uncovering roboticists' attitudes to ethics and moving forward. *International Journal of Social Robotics*, 1–19.

Giordan, D., Manconi, A., Remondino, F., & Nex, F. (2017). Use of unmanned aerial vehicles in monitoring application and management of natural hazards. *Geomatics, Natural Hazards and Risk*, 8(1), 1–4.

Hall, R. B., Jr. (2020). *Specialized police units: NYPD anti-crime and the effect of body-worn cameras* [Doctoral dissertation, St. John Fisher University]. https://fisherpub.sjf.edu/education_etd/478.

Hassan, S. K., & Ibrahim, A. (2023). The role of artificial intelligence in cyber security and incident response. *International Journal for Electronic Crime Investigation*, 7(2), 49–72.

Horowitz, M. C. (2020). Do emerging military technologies matter for international politics? *Annual Review of Political Science*, 23(1), 385–400.

Kashef, M., Visvizi, A., & Troisi, O. (2021). Smart city as an intelligent service system: Human-computer interaction and smart city surveillance systems. *Computers in Human Behavior*, 124, 106923.

Kreps, S., George, J., Lushenko, P., & Rao, A. (2023). Exploring the artificial intelligence "trust paradox": Evidence from a survey experiment in the United States. *PLOS ONE*, 18(7), e0288109.

Laufs, J., & Borrion, H. (2022). Technological innovation in policing and crime prevention: Practitioner perspectives from London. *International Journal of Police Science & Management*, 24(2), 190–209.

Li, X., & Savkin, A. V. (2021). Networked unmanned aerial vehicles for surveillance and monitoring: A survey. *Future Internet*, 13(7), 174.

Liu, Y., Yang, D., Wang, Y., Liu, J., & Song, L. (2023). Generalized video anomaly event detection: Systematic taxonomy and comparison of deep models. *arXiv preprint*. arXiv:2302.05087.

Majeed, R., Abdullah, N., Mushtaq, M., & Kazmi, R. (2021). Drone security: Issues and challenges. *International Journal of Advanced Computer Science and Applications*, 12(5), 720–729.

Markovic, B., Ilic, D., Milosevic, D., & Ilic, I. (2021). Academics' perception of public areas video surveillance in smart cities. *Economics, Management and Sustainability*, 6(2), 21–33.

McCambridge, J., Witton, J., & Elbourne, D. R. (2014). Systematic review of the Hawthorne effect: New concepts are needed to study research participation effects. *Journal of Clinical Epidemiology*, 67(3), 267–277.

Peters, K. M. (2019). 21st century crime: How malicious artificial intelligence will impact homeland security [Doctoral dissertation, Naval Postgraduate School].

Snow, J. (2018). Amazon's face recognition falsely matched 28 members of Congress with mugshots. American Civil Liberties Union. https://www.aclu.org/news/privacy-technology/amazons-face-recognition-falsely-matched-28.

Surette, R. (2005). The thinking eye: Pros and cons of second generation CCTV surveillance systems. *Policing: An International Journal of Police Strategies & Management*, 28(1), 152–173.

Thakur, N., Nagrath, P., Jain, R., Saini, D., Sharma, N., & Hemanth, D. J. (2021). Artificial intelligence techniques in smart cities surveillance using UAVs: A survey. *Machine intelligence and data analytics for sustainable future smart cities*, 329–353. Springer.

Watney, M. (2022, March). Ethical and legal aspects pertaining to law enforcement use of drones. *International Conference on Cyber Warfare and Security*, 17(1), 358–365.

Yanakiev, Y., Stoianov, N., Kirkov, D., & Velev, G. (2020). Defence strategy and new disruptive technologies nexus: Implications for the military organisations. *Journal of Defence and Security Technologies*, 3, 10.

3 Predictive Policing

Predictive policing refers to transforming law enforcement by anticipating, thwarting, and combating criminal behaviors through cutting-edge methodologies and technologies, representing a paradigm shift in crime science (Piotrowicz, 2019). This chapter explores the core principles of predictive policing, focusing on its two key pillars: big data analytics and machine learning. By integrating these components, law enforcement agencies can unlock data-driven insights, enhance investigative capabilities, and improve their capacity to combat crime.

The revolutionary nature of predictive policing becomes evident over the course of the chapter, demonstrating how innovation merges with traditional policing methods to create a synergy that extends beyond conventional criminal investigations. By leveraging machine learning algorithms and analyzing large datasets, this multidimensional approach enables law enforcement to forecast crime trends, predict incidents, and dynamically allocate resources to areas of greatest need (Piotrowicz, 2019). Thus, this proactive strategy addresses current crime patterns and anticipates future developments by linking past trends with present conditions.

Moreover, this chapter considers the intricate interplay between big data analytics and machine learning, revealing the vast potential of predictive policing. Big data analytics dissects spatial and temporal crime trends, uncovering connections between environmental factors and criminal behavior, while machine learning enhances human capabilities by detecting patterns often unnoticed by human observers (Fitzpatrick et al., 2019). Through this symbiotic relationship, law enforcement can engage in data-driven interventions and implement tailored strategies that prevent crime while fostering community trust.

Overall, the chapter demystifies predictive policing by outlining its essential elements and demonstrating its profound impact on modern law enforcement. The transformative power of predictive policing becomes evident as we explore data-driven insights and algorithmic expertise, ushering in a new era of crime prevention that seamlessly integrates technology with tradition.

Big Data Analytics in Predictive Policing

Within the ever-evolving field of predictive policing, big data analytics stands as a revolutionary force, enabling law enforcement agencies to extract meaningful insights from vast and complex datasets. This section explores the potential of big data analytics to enhance law enforcement's ability to predict and prevent criminal incidents. By harnessing data-driven insights, agencies can shift from reactive responses to proactive prevention—a paradigm shift with far-reaching implications for modern policing.

The advent of big data analytics has significantly transformed how law enforcement prevents and intervenes in criminal activities by dismantling traditional barriers between

DOI: 10.4324/9781003558491-3

information sources to allow agencies to integrate diverse data and surpass the limitations of conventional crime reports. This integrated approach enables law enforcement to develop a comprehensive and nuanced understanding of the complex crime landscape.

In predictive policing, data serves as the foundation for producing insights. Today, law enforcement agencies can access various data sources, including official crime records, emergency calls, weather conditions, and open-source social media data. By combining these diverse datasets, agencies enhance the depth and breadth of information available for analysis. For instance, law enforcement can detect early warning signs of criminal activity that might go unnoticed by comparing real-time social media chatter with historical crime statistics.

The strength of big data analytics lies in its ability to offer a holistic understanding of crime dynamics. This multidimensional perspective reveals the interconnections between various factors, allowing law enforcement to unravel the intricate web of causes behind criminal behavior. In addition to traditional measures, agencies can examine socioeconomic variables, population density, and urban planning features that may influence crime patterns. This broad perspective highlights the complex relationships among the environment, social dynamics, and criminal activity.

Rather than focusing on isolated incidents, big data analytics prioritizes contextual understanding. Law enforcement agencies can analyze the broader context of criminal activity by identifying root causes, triggers, and potential catalysts, which helps law enforcement design interventions that address the underlying drivers of crime rather than merely responding to its visible manifestations. For example, recognizing the correlation between rising crime rates and specific social events can prompt law enforcement to collaborate with event organizers to implement preventive security measures.

Furthermore, the integration of various datasets also enhances predictive capabilities. Analyzing real-time and historical data uncovers patterns and trends that help forecast future criminal activity. This ability to predict when and where crimes are likely to occur marks a significant advancement in policing strategies, allowing law enforcement to mitigate risks and prevent crimes before they happen by focusing on areas with a higher likelihood of criminal events. Big data analytics, thus, shifts law enforcement from a reactive approach to a proactive, preventive model. This comprehensive method not only aids in crime prevention but also deepens our understanding of the complex factors underlying criminal behavior.

Identifying Spatial and Temporal Crime Patterns

The effectiveness of big data analytics in predictive policing lies in its ability to process vast volumes of data and identify intricate spatial and temporal patterns within crime data (Ferguson, 2019). This analytical approach uncovers valuable insights that enhance law enforcement strategies.

At the core of predictive policing is the identification of crime hot spots—that is, specific geographic areas with a high concentration of criminal activity. Law enforcement agencies can analyze historical crime data through big data analytics to effectively pinpoint and map these high-crime areas. Hot spots often emerge in regions with specific characteristics such as poor street lighting, high population density, or socioeconomic challenges. By identifying and delineating these locations, law enforcement can divert resources toward these precise areas, increasing patrol frequency and visibility to deter potential criminal behavior.

Identifying crime hot spots extends beyond crime prevention; through community policing initiatives, law enforcement agencies can actively engage with local communities to foster collaboration and group problem-solving. This engagement reduces crime and strengthens trust between the police and the community, laying the groundwork for long-term crime-prevention efforts.

Further, temporal patterns also play a crucial role in predictive policing. Big data analytics allows law enforcement to analyze crime trends across various periods, revealing patterns linked to specific days, times, or seasons. Understanding these temporal factors enhances deployment strategies. For example, data analysis may reveal spikes in burglaries on particular weekdays or weekends (D'Alessio et al., 2012).

Armed with this knowledge, law enforcement can optimize resource allocation by increasing visibility when criminal activity is more likely. This temporal awareness transcends mere crime prevention by enabling agencies to synchronize their operations with projected crime surges, resulting in faster response times and improved apprehension rates. By proactively anticipating crime patterns, law enforcement can mitigate risks and create safer, more secure environments for the public.

The integration of geographic and temporal data offers even more significant benefits. By combining knowledge of crime hot spots with temporal trends, law enforcement can craft comprehensive strategies that account for the complex dynamics of crime (Sarker, 2021). For example, targeted interventions, specialized task force deployments, and public awareness campaigns can be timed to coincide with expected increases in criminal activity within specific hot spots.

Notably, these insights extend beyond law enforcement, fostering collaboration across sectors. Partnerships with social services, community organizations, and city planners can amplify the impact of these strategies. For instance, a crime hot spot with poor street lighting could prompt community-driven efforts to improve infrastructure, reduce crime, and promote safer neighborhoods.

The Role of Predictive Models in Crime Forecasting

The art of building predictive models is at the core of big data analytics' transformative potential in predictive policing. These models, powered by machine learning algorithms, unlock vast volumes of historical crime data and contextual factors, allowing law enforcement agencies to anticipate criminal activity and implement proactive interventions.

Machine learning algorithms orchestrate a sophisticated pattern recognition process involving statistical analysis and data synthesis to fuel predictive models. As they analyze crime data, these algorithms uncover trends that may otherwise go unnoticed by human researchers. Thus, machine learning provides a comprehensive view of the crime landscape by identifying correlations between crime incidents and various contextual factors, ranging from demographic data to weather conditions.

A key advantage of predictive models is their ability to incorporate diverse contextual variables, which extend beyond traditional crime analysis, enhancing the predictive power of the models. For example, whereas historical data may reveal a link between certain weather conditions and increased property crime, machine learning algorithms can detect correlations between crime rates and environmental factors such as temperature, precipitation, and visibility. This knowledge and holistic understanding equip law enforcement to anticipate and react to potential crime surges during specific weather patterns.

Predictive models perform more than the analysis of past trends, as they can forecast future criminal activity. By examining historical data and contextual elements, these algorithms predict when and where crimes are likely to occur. For example, if past evidence shows an uptick in car thefts during the holidays, this information can be used to allocate more resources in advance. Accordingly, police patrols can be increased, surveillance can be more focused, and community outreach can be expanded to deter auto theft. This proactive approach represents a significant shift away from traditional policing, where law enforcement often only responds after a crime.

Moreover, predictive models also improve resource allocation, making it more efficient. Since law enforcement agencies operate with limited resources, effective distribution is critical. Rather than spreading resources thinly across an entire city, predictive models guide agencies to concentrate their efforts in areas where criminal activity is more likely. This targeted allocation enhances law enforcement's effectiveness and maximizes the impact of their interventions.

Additionally, by harnessing machine learning, predictive models advance crime-prevention strategies in an ever-evolving criminal landscape, moving beyond the limitations of reactive policing to offer law enforcement the foresight to craft preventative strategies, anticipate crime dynamics, and create safer communities.

Machine Learning and Artificial Intelligence in Predictive Policing

Machine learning is the foundation of predictive policing and a critical component of artificial intelligence, transforming law enforcement operations by enabling algorithms to process massive datasets and uncover intricate patterns and trends. These algorithms systematically analyze data to reveal complex connections that might elude human analysts, thereby driving the data-driven revolution in predictive policing. This section examines the pivotal role machine learning plays in predictive policing, demonstrating how it equips law enforcement agencies with new insights to enhance decision-making.

The collaboration between human analysts and machine learning algorithms plays a crucial role in predictive policing (Youvan, 2023). Although human insight is invaluable, the sheer volume of data can often be overwhelming, making it difficult to detect subtle associations between different datasets. Machine learning algorithms, by applying advanced mathematical models, delve deep into complex datasets to reveal patterns and relationships that might otherwise remain hidden from human observation (Završnik, 2021). Consequently, this collaboration dramatically enhances our understanding of crime dynamics, primarily through machine learning's ability to identify intricate patterns within predictive policing.

Machine learning algorithms act as digital detectives in predictive policing, examining various factors with remarkable accuracy. These algorithms analyze multiple data points, from socioeconomic factors and environmental conditions to crime locations and the timing of incidents. Through this deep analysis, machine learning can uncover patterns that suggest criminal activity by mapping the interactions of diverse variables.

For instance, while standard statistical analysis may not detect the relationship between violent crime rates and environmental factors such as temperature and humidity, machine learning algorithms can identify these connections, supporting research that demonstrates weather can influence violent crime (Cruz et al., 2020). Moreover, machine learning augments human capabilities by rapidly analyzing and synthesizing data and identifying correlations for more accurate behavior predictions. For example, in case a particular neighborhood experiences a rise in criminal incidents during specific times of the day, machine learning can predict future occurrences, enabling law enforcement to allocate resources and implement crime-prevention initiatives strategically.

To summarize, the collaboration between human analysts and machine learning algorithms in predictive policing breaks conventional barriers. By leveraging both strengths, this partnership improves the capacity to detect complex patterns, providing law enforcement agencies with unprecedented insights into potential criminal activities. Additionally, machine learning's ability to process vast datasets and uncover hidden correlations marks a new era of informed decision-making in law enforcement.

Machine learning algorithms have emerged as the architects behind revolutionary data-driven predictive models, reshaping the landscape of law enforcement within the complex framework of predictive policing. These models navigate historical crime data and contextual information like time travelers (Ahmed, 2022). By leveraging machine learning techniques such as decision trees, neural networks, and support vector machines, these models propel law enforcement into a new era of proactive crime prevention.

At their core, data-driven predictive models function through assimilation and learning. These models are trained using historical crime data combined with various contextual variables. A suite of machine learning techniques supports these models' predictive power. For instance, decision trees methodically sift through data points, making decisions based on factors influencing criminal dynamics (Khan et al., 2019); neural networks analyze multiple layers of data to uncover intricate correlations, mimicking the complexity of the human brain; and support vector machines act as sophisticated classifiers, delineating the boundaries between different crime scenarios. Together, these methods capture past knowledge and propel it forward. The algorithms, akin to skilled detectives, analyze previous events to extract the contributing factors behind criminal behavior (Ahmed, 2022). By dissecting the interconnected elements that shape criminal activity, they learn from the past, which remains one of the best predictors of future behavior.

The development of predictive insights represents the culmination of this learning process. These insights, informed by historical data and machine learning techniques, predict the likelihood of crimes occurring in specific locations and times. With this predictive capability, law enforcement agencies can allocate resources more intelligently, implement targeted patrols, and engage in proactive interventions, creating a powerful toolkit for crime prevention.

Furthermore, these predictive models drive a fundamental paradigm shift in policing beyond statistical extrapolation. Law enforcement transitions from reactive responders to proactive defenders by predicting and preventing criminal activity. Accordingly, predictive models, empowered by data-driven insights, peer into the future, significantly reducing the incidence and impact of crime.

Integrating data-driven predictive models with machine learning algorithms transcends traditional policing methods. This collaboration fuses the precision of algorithms with the historical wisdom embedded in data. As a result, law enforcement gains unparalleled access to foresight, enabling them to predict, prevent, and intervene in crimes in ways previously unimaginable.

Real-Time Analysis and Crime Adaptation

Within predictive policing, the integration of machine learning heralds a new era characterized by the capacity for real-time analysis and adaptive decision-making. This hallmark feature harnesses algorithms' computational efficiency to rapidly analyze incoming data streams, thereby enhancing law enforcement agencies' ability to respond to the continuously evolving dynamics of criminal activities.

The ever-changing nature of criminal activity necessitates an adaptable and responsive response, a context that highlights the significance of real-time analysis. Fueled by continuous data streams flowing through digital channels, machine learning algorithms can efficiently process, interpret, and comprehend incoming information. Upon receiving new criminal reports, emergency calls, and environmental data, these algorithms promptly initiate operations, sorting through the data with remarkable speed and accuracy.

Real-time analysis exhibits superior agility than traditional crime analysis methods, which predominantly rely on historical data. Although historical insights provide significant value, they often lack the immediacy required to address evolving criminal activity swiftly. Real-time analysis bridges this gap, granting law enforcement agencies immediate access to up-to-date information on emerging crime trends, potential hot spots for criminal activity, and dynamic shifts in criminal behavior.

Adaptation and real-time analysis exist in a mutually dependent, symbiotic relationship. As algorithms process large volumes of data, they undergo concurrent evolution, continually enhancing their predictive capabilities. The adaptability of predictive models enables them to stay current by constantly learning from the latest occurrences and integrating these insights into their predictions, a process that involves data and algorithms working simultaneously to produce a cohesive and synchronized outcome. Such intricate orchestration allows for the ongoing refinement of machine learning's predictive capabilities, adjusting to the dynamic nature of criminal activities.

The significant ramifications of real-time analysis and adaptability are evident. Law enforcement agencies with real-time information can adapt swiftly, allocate resources to high-priority areas effectively, and respond to evolving crime patterns promptly. In the event of a sudden increase in criminal occurrences within a particular locality, the algorithms quickly recalibrate, alerting law enforcement to enhance patrol efforts, initiate investigations, and actively collaborate with the community to mitigate further incidents. The seamless integration of real-time data analysis and adaptive algorithms provides a predictive advantage for law enforcement, empowering them to outmaneuver criminals preemptively. By leveraging real-time insights, law enforcement agencies continuously evolve their strategies to counter the shifting techniques employed by criminals and exploit their vulnerabilities.

In predictive policing, the pivotal factor for success is the use of real-time data and adaptability. This singular attribute embodies the essence of agility, enabling law enforcement agencies to navigate the intricate dynamics of crime proactively. By employing data as a guiding tool and harnessing machine learning techniques, authorities can strategically advance toward a more secure society equipped to address the fluctuating patterns of criminal activities.

Resource Optimization through Predictive Policing

The impact of machine learning on predictive policing extends beyond merely forecasting crime trends, encompassing resource optimization. Although strategically allocating law enforcement resources remains a persistent challenge, the emergence of machine learning algorithms offers a potential solution for navigating this complex environment. These algorithms can effectively guide agencies in prudently deploying their limited assets to achieve the most significant impact possible.

In a society characterized by constrained resources and a dynamic criminal landscape, the strategic deployment of law enforcement officers is critical. Machine learning algorithms excel at identifying areas with high crime rates and efficiently allocating resources, thus functioning as analytical tools that guide the exploration of complex data networks to find patterns indicating regions and periods with elevated probabilities of criminal activity.

Using machine learning for resource optimization enhances the efficacy of law enforcement patrols. Historically, patrols often adhered to predetermined routes or reacted to events as they unfolded; however, this reactive strategy can lead to less-than-optimal resource allocation. Machine learning revolutionizes this paradigm by providing predictive insights that assist authorities in anticipating probable surges in criminal activity.

For instance, consider a hypothetical scenario where historical data reveal an uptick in street-level criminal activities during specific nocturnal hours in a particular locality. Machine learning algorithms can predict the likelihood of future incidents based on these historical patterns. Accordingly, law enforcement agencies can strategically allocate patrols to specific locations and times based on detected patterns, effectively mitigating illegal actions before they escalate. This shift from a reactive approach to a proactive strategy is a defining characteristic of resource optimization within the context of predictive policing.

Moreover, implementing machine learning algorithms to optimize resources yields significant advantages for public safety. Law enforcement enhances its presence in the most critical locations by strategically allocating resources to areas and times characterized by an elevated probability of criminal activity. This strategic deployment serves the dual purpose of deterring potential offenders and cultivating a heightened sense of security among community members (Vestby & Vestby, 2021). Reduced response times during critical situations can also drastically influence outcomes, potentially preventing the escalation of ongoing crimes.

The significance of machine learning in resource optimization has far-reaching implications for law enforcement agencies of all sizes, as allocating finite resources necessitates a meticulous approach to their use, and employing machine learning algorithms empowers organizations with the insights required to make well-informed decisions. A data-driven strategy does not seek to supplant human judgment but to enhance it by incorporating empirical insights that may otherwise be overlooked.

Resource optimization is a fundamental aspect of effective governance within a broader framework. Enforcement organizations must optimize all available resources, especially given the increasing demand for efficient crime prevention and response in communities.

Overall, integrating machine learning and resource optimization signifies the advancement of predictive policing, moving beyond reactive techniques and progressing toward a dynamic and anticipatory stance that leverages technological integration and human intuition. This collaboration redefines the role of law enforcement, transforming it from a reactive entity into a proactive guardian capable of effectively navigating the complex landscape of criminal dynamics and optimizing resource allocation.

Community Engagement and Public Trust in Predictive Policing

The human element is crucial in the complex predictive policing ecosystem, where algorithms and data often dominate. While the technological capabilities of big data analytics are evident, community engagement and trust-building also have a transformative effect on law enforcement (Tulumello & Iapaolo, 2022). This section explores how these components are vital to the predictive policing framework.

Big data analytics helps law enforcement identify trends and anticipate criminal activities, fostering stronger connections between agencies and the communities they serve. The insights from data analysis provide a comprehensive understanding of crime dynamics and the underlying causes driving criminal behavior, thus becoming a powerful tool for engaging with community members, leaders, and stakeholders.

Law enforcement agencies demonstrate transparency and a collaborative approach by sharing data-driven insights. For example, if data reveal increased property crimes in a specific area, agencies can work with community leaders to create strategies that target vulnerabilities and deter potential offenders. This collaborative decision-making process fosters a sense of shared ownership and accountability, aligning law enforcement and community efforts toward neighborhood safety enhancement.

Predictive policing, with its data-driven foundation, enables law enforcement to address the root causes of crime, the knowledge of which serves as a basis for meaningful community engagement. Rather than merely responding to criminal incidents, law enforcement can collaborate with communities to address the social, economic, and environmental factors contributing to criminal behavior. For instance, if data suggest a relationship between burglary rates and unemployment in a particular area (D'Alessio et al., 2012), law enforcement might collaborate with local organizations to offer job training programs, addressing a key contributor to crime. This proactive approach reduces crime and improves the community's quality of life.

Restoring trust between law enforcement and the community is one of the most significant outcomes of data-driven engagement. When the public perceives police as allies rather than adversaries, it often leads to a downturn in violent crime (Ammons-Blanfort et al., 2021). This is because transparency in sharing data insights and involving the community in the decision-making process fosters shared responsibility for public safety. Trust is critical to long-term crime-reduction efforts (Tyler, 2006), as communities with strong confidence in law enforcement are more likely to cooperate, report crimes, and participate in crime-prevention programs. Predictive policing, focusing on community-centered strategies, fosters this trust, laying the foundation for lasting relationships that continually enhance public safety.

Notably, predictive policing is not confined to law enforcement alone, being a holistic strategy that thrives on partnerships, collaboration, and mutual respect. By merging data analysis insights with community engagement tactics, law enforcement agencies nurture a robust ecosystem for crime prevention. This symbiotic relationship ensures that crime-prevention efforts are effective and sustainable, and the community safeguards its well-being as trust is rebuilt and collaborative strategies take root. Thus, integrating human elements into data-driven predictive policing highlights this approach's ability to reshape society and build safer, more inclusive communities.

Big data analytics constitutes a transformative thread in predictive policing, weaving together proactive crime prevention and investigative capabilities. Law enforcement agencies can prevent criminal activity and mitigate its societal impact by mastering complex patterns, identifying crime hot spots, and applying predictive models. However, this technological advancement requires a strong ethical compass to navigate the challenges of privacy and civil liberties (Feng et al., 2019). As predictive policing evolves, the need to balance enhanced security and the protection of fundamental rights becomes paramount to uphold public safety and civil liberties.

Ethical and Legal Challenges in Predictive Policing

Despite the emergence of machine learning introducing a novel phase in predictive policing, its potential is accompanied by numerous ethical considerations that loom large in the foreseeable future. The profound capacity for change inherent in machine learning necessitates a high level of technical competence and an unwavering dedication to maintaining ideals of fairness, transparency, and confidentiality. This section explores the complex terrain of ethical questions and the necessity of transparency within predictive policing.

The prominence of machine learning algorithms in developing predictive policing techniques brings the ethical dilemma of bias to the forefront. These algorithms acquire knowledge from past crime data, which may include inherent biases within the criminal justice system; consequently, the outcome may foster the continuation of inequalities in crime prediction and law enforcement practices, disproportionately impacting marginalized communities (Vestby & Vestby, 2021). The ethical obligation comprises addressing algorithmic bias to prevent these technologies from exacerbating or perpetuating existing injustices.

Privacy, a fundamental ethical concern, is intricately connected to the extensive scope of predictive policing. As law enforcement agencies collect and analyze data from diverse sources, the increasing prevalence of citizen surveillance and the potential for its misuse are becoming increasingly apparent. Therefore, a delicate balance must be struck to achieve a consonant equilibrium between the efficacy of crime-prevention measures and the protection of individual privacy (Fitzpatrick et al., 2019). This situation underscores the importance of establishing explicit norms and regulations defining acceptable data collection, utilization, and storage boundaries.

Moreover, concerns regarding over-policing overshadow the promise of transformation in predictive policing. An unintended consequence of the accuracy of machine learning algorithms in detecting crime hot spots may be the disproportionate allocation of policing resources to specific neighborhoods or populations. If this phenomenon is not adequately addressed, it can further erode trust and perpetuate the cycle of distrust between law enforcement agencies and marginalized communities. Therefore, to effectively implement predictive policing, agencies must adhere to ethical principles that prioritize preventing the exacerbation of pre-existing conflicts. This goal can be achieved through vigilant oversight and heightened sensitivity.

Transparency plays a pivotal role in effectively addressing the ethical complexities associated with predictive policing. Accordingly, law enforcement agencies must elucidate the underlying decision-making processes of machine learning algorithms as they generate predictions. Promoting openness facilitates the establishment of accountability and grants the public the capacity to comprehend how these algorithms function, how data are used, and how forecasts are generated (RAND Corporation, 2020). Regularly examining algorithms to detect and address biases is essential to promoting transparency and maintaining the integrity of machine learning as a means of promoting justice rather than perpetuating injustice.

Furthermore, the integration of an ethical framework within the realm of predictive policing requires comprehensive decision-making procedures. Therefore, law enforcement organizations must engage stakeholders, including community members, civil rights advocates, and technological specialists, to effectively create and execute predictive policing programs. The practice of "pluralistic engagement" serves as a protective measure against unforeseen repercussions and facilitates the development of strategies that align with the overall welfare of society.

The rise of machine learning in the context of predictive policing also necessitates a moral obligation to guide this influential capability toward principles of justice and equity. Ethical considerations and transparency are fundamental principles that ensure the positive impact of predictive policing on society. By adopting these principles, law enforcement organizations can effectively utilize machine learning technology while safeguarding civil rights, cultivating public trust, and promoting a safer and more equitable society.

To summarize, machine learning is a vital component within the predictive policing framework, enabling law enforcement organizations to analyze extensive datasets, unveil latent patterns, and produce precise forecasts concerning prospective criminal behaviors. Through machine learning, law enforcement agencies can bolster their crime-prevention tactics and advance data-driven decision-making, resulting in policing that is more impactful, streamlined, and centered on the community's needs. The responsible incorporation of machine learning will play a central role in creating a balanced coexistence between technological progress and protecting human liberties as predictive policing undergoes ongoing transformation.

Conclusion

Predictive policing represents a significant turning point at which the integration of data-driven insights intersects with the boundaries of modern technology. The collaboration among diverse law enforcement agencies affords them a plethora of cutting-edge resources, facilitating a substantial overhaul of crime prevention and investigation. The amalgamation of big data analytics with machine learning marks a significant departure from traditional policing approaches, requiring a profound re-evaluation of established methodologies. In this new framework, proactive anticipation supplants reactive measures, and deliberate strategic accuracy supersedes arbitrary approaches.

The potential of predictive policing is substantial, but it must effectively address ethical concerns, ensure transparency, and establish mechanisms for accountability. As law enforcement organizations use these technologies to achieve significant changes, it is crucial to balance using data for the public's benefit and protecting individuals' rights and dignity. Additionally, moving forward necessitates a steadfast commitment to ongoing self-reflection, a readiness to adapt, and an unyielding dedication to fostering safer societies.

In this dynamic environment, implementing predictive policing transcends its technological nature and assumes the status of a moral obligation. Adhering unwaveringly to ideals safeguarding justice, equity, and respect is imperative in pursuing a more secure society. Law enforcement organizations can create a future in which advanced technologies and ethical considerations coexist, leading to a better and more secure environment for everyone by fully embracing the potential and responsibilities associated with predictive policing.

References

Ahmed, Y. (2022). Data-driven framework and experimental validation for security monitoring networked systems [Doctoral dissertation, Birmingham City University].

Ammons-Blanfort, C., D'Alessio, S. J., & Stolzenberg, L. (2021). Self-help and black firearm crime. *Crime & Delinquency*, 69(1), 178–207.

Cruz, E., D'Alessio, S. J., & Stolzenberg, L. (2020). The effect of maximum daily temperature on outdoor violence. *Crime & Delinquency*, 69(6–7), 1161–1182.

D'Alessio, S. J., Eitle, D., & Stolzenberg, L. (2012). Unemployment, guardianship, and weekday residential burglary. *Justice Quarterly*, 29(6), 919–932.

Feng, M., Zheng, J., Ren, J., Hussain, A., Li, X., Xi, Y., & Liu, Q. (2019). Big data analytics and mining for adequate visualization and trends forecasting of crime data. *IEEE Access*, 7, 106111–106123.

Ferguson, A. G. (2019). Predictive policing theory. *Chapter* 24, American University, WCL Research Paper No. 2020–2010.

Fitzpatrick, D. J., Gorr, W. L., & Neill, D. B. (2019). Keeping score: Predictive analytics in policing. *Annual Review of Criminology*, 2, 473–491.

Khan, J. R., Saeed, M., Siddiqui, F. A., Mahmood, N., & Arifeen, Q. U. (2019). Predictive policing: A machine learning approach to predict and control crimes in metropolitan cities. *University of Sindh Journal of Information and Communication Technology*, 3(1), 17–26.

Piotrowicz, C. (2019). Predictive policing. *European Law Enforcement Research Bulletin* (4 SCE), 107–111.

RAND Corporation. (2020). *Predictive policing: Forecasting crime for law enforcement*. https://www.rand.org/pubs/research_reports/RR233.html.

Sarker, I. H. (2021). Data science and analytics: An overview from data-driven smart computing, decision-making and applications perspective. *SN Computer Science*, 2(5), 377.

Tulumello, S., & Iapaolo, F. (2022). Policing the future, disrupting urban policy today. Predictive policing, smart city, and urban policy in Memphis (TN). *Urban Geography*, 43(3), 448–469.

Tyler, T. R. (2006). *Why people obey the law*. Princeton University Press.
Vestby, A., & Vestby, J. (2021). Machine learning and the police: Asking the right questions. *Policing: A Journal of Policy and Practice*, 15(1), 44–58.
Youvan, D. C. (2023). Artificial intelligence: Unveiling hidden patterns in human behaviour. https://doi.org/10.13140/RG.2.2.16892.10883.
Završnik, A. (2021). Algorithmic justice: Algorithms and big data in criminal justice settings. *European Journal of Criminology*, 18(5), 623–642.

4 Biometrics

Biometric technologies play a crucial role in criminal science by leveraging unique physical and behavioral characteristics for identification and verification. Biometrics involves the systematic measurement and statistical analysis of traits intrinsic to individuals, providing a highly reliable method for distinguishing one person from another (Caldwell et al., 2020). This chapter explores the key biometric methods: fingerprint analysis, facial recognition, and DNA profiling.

Each method has proven effective in identity verification and forensic investigations. Fingerprint analysis, a well-established technique, remains a dependable means of identifying individuals. Meanwhile, facial recognition technology has emerged as a powerful tool for identifying suspects and locating missing persons. DNA profiling, a groundbreaking advancement in modern forensic science, has revolutionized criminal investigations by providing unparalleled accuracy in linking individuals to crime scenes through unique genetic markers.

Beyond identity verification and forensic investigation, biometric techniques play a crucial role in preventing and resolving criminal activities. By using these technologies, authorities can quickly identify potential threats, apprehend suspects, and dismantle complex criminal networks. However, the ethical and legal concerns surrounding the use of biometric data require careful consideration to ensure that privacy rights are respected and that the application of these technologies remains fair and unbiased.

The following sections will explore the technical aspects of fingerprint analysis, facial recognition, and DNA profiling, emphasizing their significance within the broader context of criminal science. This examination highlights the critical role biometrics play in crime prevention, investigation, and resolution.

Fingerprint Analysis: The Cornerstone of Biometric Identification

Fingerprint analysis is a fundamental component of biometrics, relying on the unique patterns found on an individual's fingertips. The intricate arrangement of ridges, valleys, and minutiae creates a distinctive configuration, providing a reliable method of identification and authentication that has stood the test of time (Daluz, 2018). This section explores the history, technological advancements, and contemporary applications of fingerprint analysis in forensic research, highlighting its enduring significance in the field.

The science of fingerprint analysis is based on the remarkable observation that the arrangement of ridge patterns on an individual's fingertips is unique. Even identical twins, despite sharing the same genetic code, exhibit distinct variations in their fingerprint patterns (Tao et al., 2012). This phenomenon arises from a complex interplay of genetic factors, environmental influences during prenatal development, and random events that shape the formation of ridges and furrows on the fingertips.

DOI: 10.4324/9781003558491-4

Genetic mutations, variations in blood flow, and mechanical forces significantly contribute to the development of intricate ridge patterns during embryonic skin formation. Once established in early fetal development, these patterns remain unchanged throughout a person's life, unless altered by injury or disease (Daluz, 2018). The enduring nature of these patterns underscores the reliability of fingerprints as a lifelong identifier.

The vast variation in fingerprint patterns is a cornerstone of forensic research. Fingerprints enable law enforcement and forensic professionals to link unique patterns to specific individuals. This principle of individuality is crucial for utilizing fingerprints as a reliable biometric tool for identity verification and criminal investigation.

The evolution of fingerprint analysis from a manual and labor-intensive process to a computerized and sophisticated system can primarily be attributed to the development of the Automated Fingerprint Identification System (AFIS). AFIS introduced advanced algorithms and computer-based pattern recognition, revolutionizing the field by accelerating identification processes and minimizing the risk of human error in manual comparisons (Yilmaz & Abouyoussef, 2022).

AFIS converts and stores fingerprint images in extensive databases. When a new fingerprint is submitted, the system rapidly compares its minutiae and ridge patterns with archived data, generating potential matches within seconds. This accelerated matching process enables law enforcement agencies to identify suspects quickly and, when necessary, retrieve their criminal histories (Gibb & Riemen, 2023). Additionally, AFIS efficiently manages large volumes of fingerprints collected from crime scenes, allowing investigators to search vast databases and find relevant matches with greater speed.

Law Enforcement Applications of Fingerprint Databases

Fingerprint databases form the foundation of accurate and efficient identification in modern criminal science. Law enforcement agencies have compiled extensive databases containing fingerprints from various sources, including individuals with criminal records, those undergoing background checks, and prints collected from crime scenes. These repositories are essential for quickly cross-referencing information and identifying potential suspects. By integrating fingerprint databases with other law enforcement resources, agencies can more easily establish connections between individuals and criminal activities. Fingerprints collected from crime scenes can swiftly match existing records, providing critical insights into illegal activities (Zahra & Lohani, 2021). Moreover, fingerprint analysis plays a salient role in various scenarios, including border crossings, employment background checks, and security clearances.

The practical application of fingerprint analysis extends beyond its primary role of confirming identity; it plays a crucial part in background checks and criminal investigations. In criminal investigations, latent fingerprints collected from crime scenes are compared with pre-existing prints stored in databases. This process helps establish connections between suspects and crime scenes, providing valuable insights for forensic analysis and assisting in apprehending those involved in criminal activities.

Beyond criminal investigations, fingerprint analysis is essential in various security processes. It is commonly used in employment background checks, security clearance evaluations, and granting access to secure facilities. This procedure helps identify individuals with criminal histories, thereby reducing risks and enhancing the security of businesses and institutions.

Despite the proven efficacy of fingerprint analysis, persistent challenges remain. The quality of latent fingerprints collected from crime scenes can vary significantly due to factors such as environmental conditions, surface characteristics, and the expertise of the personnel involved in the collection process. To address these challenges, advances in imaging technologies, image enhancement techniques, and algorithms are essential for compensating for partial or distorted prints (Ross et al., 2019). Furthermore, integrating fingerprint analysis with other biometric methods, such as DNA profiling and facial recognition, can significantly enhance the accuracy and scope of criminal investigations. Collaborative efforts across multiple biometric disciplines provide a more comprehensive understanding of individuals involved in criminal activities, thereby increasing the likelihood of solving complex cases.

In summary, fingerprint analysis remains vital in biometric identification and criminal science. Its historical significance and advancements in automated technologies underscore its continued relevance. As technological innovations reshape the field, fingerprint analysis continues to evolve, becoming increasingly pivotal in crime prevention and investigation. As unique and enduring identifiers, fingerprints will remain fundamental in addressing criminal behavior and ensuring public safety.

Facial Recognition: The Rise of Artificial Intelligence–Powered Identification

Facial recognition technology has emerged as a powerful tool in biometrics, showcasing transformative capabilities in security and criminal investigations. This section examines the expanding role of facial recognition, focusing on its development and operational procedures, as well as its growing importance in identifying suspects and locating missing persons. Additionally, it addresses the ethical and technical challenges associated with its use.

Facial recognition relies on the analysis of distinct facial features and variations that differentiate individuals. This technique focuses on key characteristics of the human face, such as the positioning of the eyes, mouth, nose, and other prominent landmarks. These features create a unique facial signature that remains consistent across different expressions and lighting conditions.

Sophisticated algorithms play a significant role in processing facial images by breaking them down into detailed data points. These points are converted into a mathematical representation known as a facial template, which is then cross-referenced with a database of existing templates to identify matches (Zulfiqar et al., 2019). The integration of machine learning has enhanced the accuracy of these comparisons, enabling real-time facial identification with greater precision.

Machine learning algorithms have been instrumental in enhancing the accuracy of facial recognition systems. By continuously learning from large datasets, these algorithms adapt to a wide range of facial features influenced by factors such as age, gender, race, and changes in facial hair or accessories (Fontes & Perrone, 2021). The adoption of deep learning, particularly through convolutional neural networks, has revolutionized facial feature detection and analysis, significantly improving identification accuracy.

Facial recognition systems enable fast and precise face matching, resulting in widespread adoption across various sectors. Law enforcement, security organizations, and commercial entities utilize these systems to enhance security, streamline access control, and expedite identification processes.

Facial recognition applications extend beyond the commercial and security sectors, demonstrating significant advancements in criminal science. Law enforcement agencies utilize facial recognition technology to identify individuals suspected of criminal activity and assist in locating missing persons (Lynch, 2020). By analyzing closed-circuit television footage, photographs from social media, and other visual sources, investigators can efficiently match facial images with established databases of known individuals. This practice significantly accelerates the process of narrowing down potential suspects and linking them to criminal activities.

Facial recognition technology is essential for identifying missing persons. Law enforcement agencies can compare facial features against databases containing photographs of missing individuals. This process has the potential to reunite families and, in some cases, identify victims of criminal activities.

Ethical and Technical Challenges of Facial Recognition

The rapid growth of facial recognition technology has raised significant ethical and technical concerns, drawing considerable attention. Privacy is a major ethical issue that requires careful consideration. The widespread and often covert collection of facial images in public spaces has led to fears of extensive surveillance and violations of individuals' rights to anonymity (Nabbosa & Kaar, 2020). Additionally, using facial recognition technology in law enforcement raises concerns about excessive surveillance and the potential for wrongful identifications, which can result in unjust detentions.

A primary technical challenge in this context is accuracy and bias. Facial recognition algorithms often exhibit reduced precision when analyzing the facial features of individuals from diverse ethnic backgrounds, genders, or age groups. This inherent bias can result in misidentifications and disproportionately affect certain demographic groups (Benedict, 2022). To effectively tackle these concerns, ongoing research, rigorous testing, and the incorporation of inclusive and comprehensive datasets during algorithm training are essential.

The increasing use of facial recognition technology underscores the need for a balanced approach that weighs its benefits against the legitimate concerns it raises. Government regulations, public discourse, and industry standards serve as frameworks for the responsible application of this technology (Smith & Miller, 2022). It is essential to implement critical measures to maintain public trust and ensure positive outcomes, such as ensuring transparency in data collection, mitigating bias, and obtaining informed consent for data usage.

Facial recognition technology, powered by advanced algorithms and machine learning techniques, is significantly transforming criminal science. This biometric technology analyzes distinct facial features and patterns, making it crucial for identifying potential offenders and locating missing persons. Its possible applications span various domains, including security, law enforcement, individual authentication, and access management. However, it is vital to address the ethical and technical challenges associated with this technology to protect personal privacy, tackle biases, and uphold principles of fairness. This assessment is essential for the responsible implementation of facial recognition technology. The rapid advancement of this technology, coupled with ongoing discussions about regulation, positions it as a potentially valuable tool for enhancing crime prevention and investigative efforts while safeguarding individual rights and liberties.

DNA Profiling: The Gold Standard in Forensic Science

DNA profiling is a technique employed in forensic investigations to establish connections between biological samples found at crime scenes. This innovative approach to biometrics has revolutionized forensic investigations (Cheng, 2004). This section provides a comprehensive examination of DNA profiling, emphasizing its significance, methodology, applications in criminal science, and its transformative impact on the accuracy and reliability of criminal justice systems worldwide.

DNA profiling relies on the unique characteristics of an individual's genetic material. The human genome contains specific regions known as genetic markers or short tandem repeats (STRs), which vary in the number of repeated nucleotide sequences (Murphy & Tong, 2020). DNA is extracted from biological samples, and certain sections are amplified using techniques such as polymerase chain reaction to analyze these markers. The resulting fragments are then separated by size using gel or capillary electrophoresis. This arrangement of bands produces a distinct DNA profile, akin to a genetic fingerprint, that illustrates an individual's uniqueness.

The fundamental significance of DNA profiling in criminal science lies in its ability to correlate biological samples obtained from crime scenes. These samples may include various trace components, such as blood, hair, saliva, semen, and skin cells left by suspects, victims, or witnesses. By employing meticulous techniques to extract and analyze the genetic material in these samples, forensic specialists can uncover vital information about the individuals connected to the crime scene.

Producing a DNA profile from a biological specimen is a rigorous and precise process. The genetic material within the cellular nucleus serves as a comprehensive blueprint for an individual's biological makeup (Kaur & Sharma, 2022). Forensic scientists generate a unique genetic profile by selectively amplifying specific sections of DNA, typically known as STRs. This genetic fingerprint acts as a distinctive identifier, akin to a genetic barcode, allowing for accurate identification even when only small or degraded samples are available.

Once a DNA profile is established, the next step involves comparing it with databases containing known DNA profiles. These databases store information about suspects, victims, individuals with criminal records, and those involved in previous investigations (Doleac, 2017). By conducting these comparisons, law enforcement agencies can identify potential connections between the DNA profile obtained from the crime scene and individuals listed in the database.

DNA profiling has profoundly transformed the criminal justice system by providing increased precision and reliability. DNA evidence in forensic science is widely acknowledged for its exceptional accuracy and unwavering dependability. The probability that two genetically unrelated individuals share an identical DNA profile is exceedingly low, underscoring DNA's unique nature as a genetic marker (Weir, 2007). This inherent distinctiveness makes DNA profiling an immensely powerful tool for establishing clear connections between individuals and crime scenes, identifying potential perpetrators, and validating or challenging their alibis.

The impact of DNA profiling on convictions and exonerations within the criminal justice system underscores its significance. Post-conviction DNA analysis has corrected wrongful convictions, revealing instances where individuals were falsely accused (LaPorte, 2018). In such cases, DNA profiling not only rectifies wrongful prosecutions and convictions but also restores confidence in the ability of forensic science to uphold the principles of equity and accuracy.

Although DNA profiling is often associated with individual identification, its applications extend far beyond this primary function. Genetic material contains extensive information that offers valuable insights into an individual's physical characteristics and ancestry. This potential has sparked scholarly investigations into predicting traits such as eye color, hair color, and craniofacial structure based on genetic profiles (Kaur & Sharma, 2022). While these predictions may be unreliable, they can provide additional investigative leads in cases where conventional methods fail to yield significant information about unidentified individuals.

DNA profiling is also beneficial in familial searching. When direct matches to a DNA database are unavailable, identifying partial matches between DNA profiles can suggest familial connections (Debus-Sherrill & Field, 2019). This technique is crucial for identifying individuals without direct profiles in databases, assisting law enforcement in investigations, and generating leads in challenging circumstances.

The rise of genetic fingerprinting has prompted noteworthy ethical considerations, particularly concerning the protection of personal privacy and the integrity of genetic information. Disclosing genetic details carries significant implications, as it can reveal distinct personal attributes and sensitive health-related information (Clayton et al., 2019). Therefore, it is essential to establish standards that ensure the secure collection, retention, and use of DNA data. Balancing the application of DNA profiling for crime-solving purposes with the protection of individuals' rights to genetic privacy is crucial for maintaining public trust and ethical integrity.

DNA profiling is poised for significant advancements with the rapid evolution of technology. Rapid DNA analysis tools are transforming the field by enabling prompt on-site testing, reducing analysis time, and accelerating investigations (Foley, 2023). Furthermore, integrating DNA profiling with other biometric methods, such as fingerprint analysis and facial recognition, can create a comprehensive profile of individuals involved in criminal activities.

However, ongoing challenges persist. Research and development must prioritize the integrity of DNA samples, address issues related to mixed samples, and improve methods for handling small or degraded specimens. Collaboration among experts in forensics, genetics, and technology is essential to tackle these challenges and enhance the accuracy and practicality of DNA profiling.

In the dynamic field of criminal science, DNA profiling undeniably demonstrates the influential role of genetics in forensic investigations. An individual's unique genetic makeup significantly enhances the precision, reliability, and ethical standards of criminal justice systems worldwide. By meticulously analyzing genetic markers, DNA profiling acts as an unparalleled method for establishing connections between biological materials and specific individuals. This process is crucial not only for identifying suspects and victims but also for exonerating the wrongfully accused. As technology advances and ethical considerations increasingly shape its application, DNA profiling emerges as a promising tool for illuminating the path toward justice and truth in the fight against criminal activities.

The Impact of Biometrics on Crime Prevention and Investigation

The field of biometrics extends beyond identification, encompassing various aspects of criminal science and significantly influencing crime prevention, investigation, and resolution. Integrating biometric technology into law enforcement activities has enhanced both efficiency and accuracy, thereby advancing the pursuit of justice and the protection of society.

In the ever-changing realm of crime prevention and investigation, the element of time often assumes paramount importance. Biometric techniques, such as fingerprint analysis and facial recognition, enable the swift identification of individuals under investigation, thereby accelerating the investigation process. Fingerprint analysis, a well-established method, allows for the efficient comparison of latent prints obtained from crime scenes with databases containing records of identified individuals. This process expedites the identification of potential suspects and establishes vital connections between individuals and criminal activity.

The use of facial recognition technology further enhances this expedited process. Law enforcement agencies can quickly determine the identities of individuals captured in public by analyzing the facial features and patterns present in images or recordings (Li et al., 2020). This ability to promptly recognize individuals has played a pivotal role in locating and apprehending offenders, thereby hindering their capacity to evade arrest or engage in further illicit activities. The effectiveness of biometrics stems from its accurate identification of individuals and its timely application within the context of ongoing investigations.

The influence of biometrics is far-reaching, even at the microscopic level, as demonstrated by the critical role of DNA profiling in establishing connections within the realm of illegal activities. DNA samples collected from crime scenes are essential for identifying individuals and creating intricate linkages among seemingly unrelated incidents. Forensic investigations have undergone a significant transformation due to technological advancements, which enable the connection of a suspect to multiple crime locations, the verification or questioning of alibis, and the identification of concealed patterns of criminal activity.

DNA fingerprinting is a unifying element that links diverse criminal acts, often transcending geographical and temporal limitations. The interconnectivity among various sources of information has been vital in resolving unsolved criminal cases, exposing patterns of serial criminal behavior, and providing essential evidence necessary for the successful prosecution of offenders (Rathnam, 2022). The impact of DNA profiling extends throughout the history of forensic research, uncovering the underlying facts of mysterious cases that might have otherwise remained unsolved.

The efficacy of biometric technologies is significantly enhanced when integrated with existing databases and surveillance systems. Law enforcement agencies utilize biometric databases that store fingerprints, facial photographs, and DNA profiles, creating a powerful resource for identifying individuals of interest. The integration of multiple systems facilitates a seamless and efficient cross-referencing process, thereby increasing the likelihood of successfully identifying suspects and uncovering their prior criminal records.

Incorporating biometric techniques into surveillance systems, such as closed-circuit television networks, expands the scope of law enforcement's vigilant monitoring. Real-time facial recognition algorithms can effectively identify individuals of interest as they navigate various public spaces, including venues, transportation hubs, and airports (Win et al., 2020). This proactive approach mitigates the risk of suspects evading detection, ensuring prompt identification and apprehension.

The application of biometrics in border security and crime prevention is both significant and compelling. Biometric identifiers, such as fingerprints and facial photographs, are highly effective in identifying individuals attempting to cross borders or gain access to secure facilities (Amelung et al., 2021). Integrating biometric verification into immigration procedures enables law enforcement agencies to swiftly detect individuals with prior criminal records or those on terrorist watch lists, thereby preventing their entry into a country.

Moreover, biometric technologies serve as a powerful deterrent against illicit activities. The mere presence of biometric systems can dissuade potential wrongdoers from attempting to evade identification or engage in illegal acts. Due to their inherent accuracy, biometric identification represents a proactive strategy that aligns with crime reduction and enhances public safety.

Overall, the implementation and implications of biometric approaches in criminal science are undeniably groundbreaking. Beyond their core identification functions, biometrics are crucial in preventing, investigating, and resolving criminal activities. Techniques such as fingerprint analysis and facial recognition enable the swift identification of suspects, facilitating investigations and obstructing the progression of illegal acts. DNA profiling, in particular, uncovers complex associations between criminal behaviors, revealing hidden patterns that elude human observation. By incorporating biometric technologies into databases and surveillance systems, law enforcement agencies significantly enhance their operational effectiveness, while improved verification methods strengthen border security. Biometrics have become a cornerstone of modern criminal science, providing law enforcement with the precision and efficiency needed to protect society and uphold the ideals of justice.

Ethical and Legal Considerations in Biometrics

The complex relationship between biometrics and criminal science raises numerous ethical and legal implications. This dynamic necessitates a thorough assessment of these powerful technologies' potential repercussions and responsibilities. While biometrics enhance crime prevention, investigation, and resolution, they also introduce challenges that must be addressed to preserve justice, privacy, and fairness.

The question of privacy is paramount in the discourse surrounding biometrics. The fundamental nature of biometric data—capturing individuals' distinct physiological and behavioral characteristics—deeply reflects their identities. The acquisition and retention of such sensitive data raise valid concerns regarding unauthorized access, data security breaches, and potential misuse.

Efforts to mitigate these risks must take priority. Protecting biometric databases from illegal breaches requires careful design and implementation of robust security protocols. Stringent access controls, encryption techniques, and continuous monitoring are essential for strengthening these repositories against potential threats (Khan & Rizvi, 2021). As the scope and significance of biometric databases expand, the ethical and legal obligation to uphold and safeguard citizens' privacy becomes increasingly critical.

The potential of biometric technology, particularly facial recognition, is contrasted by a consequential obstacle: the inherent biases in the algorithms that underpin these systems. When trained on datasets with limited diversity, facial recognition algorithms may inadvertently reinforce prejudices related to individuals' demographic characteristics (Cavazos et al., 2021). Such misidentifications carry profound implications, including the risk of unjust arrests, the exacerbation of societal inequalities, and the erosion of the fundamental principles of fairness that criminal justice systems strive to uphold.

Mitigating these biases necessitates a comprehensive and multifaceted approach. It is essential to prioritize the augmentation of datasets with diverse representations to ensure that algorithms learn from a wide range of human appearances and traits. Additionally, establishing rigorous laws and standards to hold developers and implementers of biometric technology accountable for maintaining fairness and accuracy is imperative. Continuous audits and transparent reporting mechanisms can provide valuable insights into the inherent biases within biometric systems, facilitating prompt interventions and necessary corrections.

Integrating biometrics and criminal science necessitates a critical examination of the ethical and legal dimensions at their intersection. Comprehensive laws and standards are essential for navigating the uncharted territory of biometric technologies. The collaborative involvement of policymakers, technologists, ethicists, and civil society is crucial for developing norms regarding the collection, storage, and utilization of biometric data.

Implementing more stringent laws can help protect against potential abuse or unauthorized use of biometric data. It is crucial to clearly define acceptable reasons for collecting and using biometric data to safeguard individuals' privacy rights. Additionally, these regulations can establish transparency mandates, ensuring that individuals are adequately informed about how their biometric data will be utilized. This awareness empowers individuals to exercise their autonomy by granting informed consent.

Future of Biometrics in Criminal Science

As biometric technologies advance, a complex challenge arises: effectively harnessing their potential while upholding essential rights and norms. The appropriate integration of biometrics into criminal science requires ongoing discussions that encompass technological advancements, legal frameworks, and ethical considerations. The moral and legal implications of biometrics have far-reaching effects on society, necessitating the retention of equity, confidentiality, and impartiality as foundational pillars for any biometric deployment. Collaboration among various stakeholders—including law enforcement agencies, technology developers, regulatory bodies, and advocacy groups—is crucial for shaping the future of biometrics in criminal science.

The intersection of biometrics and criminal science underscores the complex relationship between ethical responsibilities and technological advancements. The potential of biometric technology to transform crime prevention and investigation necessitates a conscientious approach that prioritizes privacy preservation, bias mitigation, and the promotion of fairness. This initiative's foundation lies in implementing stringent laws and standards designed to create an environment that maximizes the benefits of biometrics while addressing their potential drawbacks (Caldwell et al., 2020). As society moves toward integrating biometric technologies as essential tools in pursuing justice, the demand for responsible innovation increases. Establishing an ethical and legal framework that incorporates principles of fairness, privacy, and accountability can enhance the application of biometrics in criminal science (Ross et al., 2019). This approach promotes societal welfare while upholding the fundamental principles that underpin our collective understanding of justice and integrity.

Conclusion

Biometric technology has significantly advanced the ever-evolving field of criminal science. These methods encompass various approaches, including fingerprint analysis, facial recognition, and detailed DNA examination. Their contributions are undeniable, initiating noteworthy transformations in crime prevention, investigative procedures, and the resolution of legal matters. The integration of biometric methodologies has notably enhanced the operational capabilities of law enforcement agencies by expediting and accurately establishing the identities of potential offenders. Consequently, the identification of suspects has accelerated, correlations among previously unconnected incidents have been established, and concealed patterns of criminal behavior have been revealed.

However, the influence of biometrics extends beyond technical capabilities. Integrating biometric technologies into criminal science raises important ethical considerations and legal frameworks. The ethical use of biometrics requires a careful balance between the effectiveness of these technologies and the protection of personal privacy, the reduction of biases, and upholding principles of fairness and justice. In a world characterized by rapid technological advancement, the emerging field of criminal science is poised to reach significant milestones. Combining biometric elements with alternative tools and strategies holds great promise for enhancing law enforcement agencies' capabilities in maintaining legal order and improving efforts to prevent and investigate illegal activities. As society navigates this dynamic landscape, collaboration among experts in technology, ethics, legislation, and stakeholders becomes crucial to shaping a future where advancements in biometrics contribute to a secure and equitable society for all.

References

Amelung, N., Granja, R., Machado, H., Amelung, N., Granja, R., & Machado, H. (2021). A brief history of the evolution of biometrics and biometric database systems crossing borders in EU law enforcement. *Modes of bio-bordering: The hidden (dis)integration of Europe*, 15–34. Springer.

Benedict, T. J. (2022). The computer got it wrong: Facial recognition technology and establishing probable cause to arrest. *Washington Lee Law Review*, 79(2), 849–898.

Caldwell, M., Andrews, J. T., Tanay, T., & Griffin, L. D. (2020). AI-enabled future crime. *Crime Science*, 9(1), 1–13.

Cavazos, J. G., Phillips, P. J., Castillo, C. D., & O'Toole, A. J. (2021). Accuracy comparison across face recognition algorithms: Where are we on measuring race bias? *IEEE Transactions on Biometrics, Behavior, and Identity Science*, 3(1), 101–111.

Cheng, E. K. (2004). Reenvisioning law through the DNA lens. *New York University Annual Survey of American Law*, 60, 649–654.

Clayton, E. W., Evans, B. J., Hazel, J. W., & Rothstein, M. A. (2019). The law of genetic privacy: Applications, implications, and limitations. *Journal of Law and the Biosciences*, 6(1), 1–36.

Daluz, H. M. (2018). *Fundamentals of fingerprint analysis* (2nd ed.). CRC Press.

Debus-Sherrill, S., & Field, M. B. (2019). *Familial DNA searching—an emerging forensic investigative tool. Science & Justice*, 59(1), 20–28.

Doleac, J. L. (2017). The effects of DNA databases on crime. *American Economic Journal: Applied Economics*, 9(1), 165–201.

Foley, M. M. (2023). Rapid DNA profile development with applied biosystems RapidHIT™ ID system. *Forensic DNA analysis: Methods and protocols*, 367–396. Springer.

Fontes, C., & Perrone, C. (2021). *Ethics of surveillance: Harnessing the use of live facial recognition technologies in public spaces for law enforcement*. The Technical University of Munich.

Gibb, C., & Riemen, J. (2023). Toward better AFIS practice and process in the forensic fingerprint environment. *Forensic Science International: Synergy*, 7, 100336.

Kaur, L., & Sharma, S. G. (2022). Forensic DNA analysis: A powerful investigative tool. *Crime scene management within forensic science: Forensic techniques for criminal investigations*, 1–40. Springer.

Khan, Z. A., & Rizvi, A. (2021). AI-based facial recognition technology and criminal justice: Issues and challenges. *Turkish Journal of Computer and Mathematics Education (TURCOMAT)*, 12(14), 3384–3392.

LaPorte, G. (2018). Wrongful convictions and DNA exonerations: Understanding the role of forensic science. *NIJ Journal*, 279, 1–16.

Li, L., Mu, X., Li, S., & Peng, H. (2020). A review of face recognition technology. *IEEE Access*, 8, 139110–139120.

Lynch, J. (2020). Face off: Law enforcement use of face recognition technology. *SSRN*, 3909038.

Murphy, E., & Tong, J. H. (2020). The racial composition of forensic DNA databases. *California Law Review*, 108(6), 1847–1911.

Nabbosa, V., & Kaar, C. (2020, May). Societal and ethical issues of digitalization. *Proceedings of the 2020 International Conference on Big Data in Management*, 118–124. ACM.

Rathnam, M. R. (2022). An analysis of science in the investigation of crime: The criminology of the future. *Indian Journal of Law and Legal Research*, 4(2), 1–13.

Ross, A., Banerjee, S., Chen, C., Chowdhury, A., Mirjalili, V., Sharma, R., ... & Yadav, S. (2019, June). Some research problems in biometrics: The future beckons. *2019 International Conference on Biometrics (ICB)*, 1–8. IEEE.

Smith, M., & Miller, S. (2022). The ethical application of biometric facial recognition technology. *AI & Society*, 37(1), 167–175.

Tao, X., Chen, X., Yang, X., & Tian, J. (2012). Fingerprint recognition with identical twin fingerprints. *PLOS ONE*, 7(4), 1–7.

Weir, B. S. (2007). The rarity of DNA profiles. *Annals of Applied Statistics*, 1(2), 358–370.

Win, K. N., Li, K., Chen, J., Viger, P. F., & Li, K. (2020). Fingerprint classification and identification algorithms for criminal investigation: A survey. *Future Generation Computer Systems*, 110, 758–771.

Yilmaz, I., & Abouyoussef, M. (2022). FIGO: Enhanced fingerprint identification approach using GAN and one shot learning techniques. *arXiv preprint arXiv:2208.05615*.

Zahra, S., & Lohani, A. (2021). Intersection of justice, crime scene investigation and forensic evidence in Pakistani court. *Journal of Law & Social Studies*, 3(2), 202–213.

Zulfiqar, M., Syed, F., Khan, M. J., & Khurshid, K. (2019, July). Deep face recognition for biometric authentication. *2019 International Conference on Electrical, Communication, and Computer Engineering*, 1–6. IEEE.

5 Cybersecurity Tools

Criminal behavior has evolved to exploit the digital environment, permeating every aspect of life. This adaptability underscores the urgent need for constant vigilance and innovation in cybersecurity. Modern cybersecurity tools are essential to crime science, as criminals continually devise new ways to exploit vulnerabilities in digital systems (Djenna et al., 2021). The global digitization of information and communication has opened new avenues for criminal exploitation. Crime science has integrated advanced technologies to better understand threats, anticipate risks, and address emerging challenges. The following discussion explores the mechanics of firewalls and encryption, elucidating their roles in preventing unauthorized access, data breaches, and cyberattacks. It also highlights the critical function of dark web monitoring in exposing illicit activities within the hidden layers of the internet.

Protecting confidential data is critical in today's digital landscape. Firewalls and encryption serve as primary defenses against cyberattacks, ensuring data integrity and confidentiality. Firewalls, whether software- or hardware-based, monitor and regulate network traffic, blocking unauthorized access and preventing security breaches (Burke, 2021). They act as a boundary between trusted internal networks and untrusted external networks, controlling data flow.

Encryption, on the other hand, converts data into a coded format, making it unreadable without the corresponding decryption key. This ensures that even if unauthorized access occurs, the data remain inaccessible without the correct key. Encryption is essential for protecting information stored on devices and during transmission. Integrating firewalls and encryption strengthens defenses against cybercriminals exploiting vulnerabilities in networks, systems, and applications. The following sections examine the critical roles of firewalls and encryption in safeguarding sensitive information.

Firewalls: The First Line of Defense

In the dynamic and constantly evolving domain of cyber threats, firewalls have emerged as prominent guardians, establishing a crucial stronghold against the overwhelming influx of potential security breaches. These essential security measures are strategically positioned where trusted internal networks intersect with the complex web of untrusted external networks (Okumu et al., 2024). Beyond their technical nature, firewalls serve as fundamental pillars of defense that support the core objectives of crime science in the digital era.

In the complex relationship between technology and criminal behavior, firewalls assume a significance that surpasses their utilitarian function, as they encapsulate the fundamental principles of safeguarding against cyber threats. By securing digital boundaries, they strengthen the foundation of contemporary crime science. Their role extends beyond mere tactical operations; they provide robust defenses against various threats,

DOI: 10.4324/9781003558491-5

encompassing both ordinary and advanced forms. In this intricate environment, firewalls serve as the initial segment in the narrative of resilience and vigilance that crime science advocates. Their presence is not merely functional but crucial, as they foster a setting where digital vulnerabilities are mitigated and the confidentiality of sensitive data is maintained.

Firewalls are available in various configurations, each designed to address the complexities of digital vulnerabilities. One notable example is the packet-filtering firewall—a steadfast protector that rigorously examines inbound and outbound data packets based on predetermined criteria, such as source and destination IP addresses (Gillam, 2019). While this approach has proven effective in specific scenarios, it is limited in its focus on the network layer, often overlooking the intricacies and specific characteristics of the data being transmitted.

The stateful inspection firewall emerged as a more advanced iteration in response to these limitations. This type of firewall can store information about ongoing connections and assess the state of data transmissions, surpassing the basic functionality of packet filtering (Gillam, 2019). This enhancement enables the firewall to make informed decisions based on context, allowing for the detection of anomalies that may signal potential threats.

The evolving landscape of digital vulnerabilities has led to the development of increasingly sophisticated firewalls, known as application layer firewalls. These firewalls offer a deeper level of analysis by examining the fundamental structure of data and deciphering the complexities inherent in application protocols. This granular inspection allows for precise traffic control, effectively preventing vulnerabilities from emerging within specific applications.

As we have seen, firewalls transcend their technical functions to become essential guardians of confidential data. They function as protectors of virtual fortresses, establishing an impenetrable boundary that separates the secure domains of trusted networks from the hazardous landscape of online threats (Anwar et al., 2021). Within this fortified enclave, firewalls counter the persistent threat of unauthorized access, serving as steadfast bulwarks of digital security.

Firewalls in Law Enforcement and Cybercrime Prevention

Entrusted with the responsibility of safeguarding valuable digital assets, firewalls initially adopt a proactive stance to thwart potential intrusions, skillfully blocking malicious network traffic that seeks unauthorized access (Sukri et al., 2023). This unwavering defense is the primary barrier, ensuring the stronghold remains secure and impenetrable.

Moreover, these digital custodians meticulously manage systematic data transfer, adhering strictly to established security protocols. In addition to their capacity to repel external threats, firewalls ensure that internal data remains confined within predefined parameters, permitting release only after thorough scrutiny (Hermansson et al., 2022). Thus, firewalls enhance security against unauthorized external access while diligently regulating the internal flow of information.

The simultaneous execution of these roles underscores the critical significance of firewalls within the broader context of crime science. They do not merely function as passive observers but actively engage as agents committed to ensuring digital security. Their ability to hinder unauthorized entry and control data transmission protects the integrity of investigations, ensuring the preservation of untainted and incorruptible evidence. In the ongoing battle against cyber threats, firewalls stand as vigilant guardians, dedicated to safeguarding the integrity of confidential information within the ever-expanding realm of crime prevention.

While firewalls are widely recognized for their effectiveness in safeguarding cybersecurity, their success depends on adaptability. The cyber landscape is characterized by continuous shifts and evolving threats, necessitating constant vigilance and prompt, flexible responses (Anwar et al., 2021). This reality underscores the critical importance of routine updates and careful configurations within the dynamic realm of digital security.

Thus, firewalls play a pivotal role in the tactical and ever-changing cyber environment, acting as sentinels against many emerging security challenges. However, even the most robust defenses must adapt to withstand the evolving strategies employed by cybercriminals. The significance of timely updates incorporating current threat intelligence and innovative approaches cannot be overstated. By integrating additional layers of security, firewalls enhance their defensive capabilities and improve their capacity to proactively detect and mitigate unforeseen threats.

Flexibility, however, encompasses more than just updates. Configuration, like a finely tuned instrument, demands tailored modifications. A one-size-fits-all configuration strategy is inadequate in diverse organizational settings and risk profiles (Sukri et al., 2023). Striking a balance between robust security protocols and a network's practical demands is fundamental for successful implementation.

At their core, firewalls are not impenetrable fortresses; they are dynamic entities that thrive on adaptation and evolution. Their ability to counter advanced evasion techniques relies heavily on agility and responsiveness. Firewalls undergo a continuous process of receiving informed updates and adjusting their configurations based on contextual factors. This ongoing refinement enables them to serve as vigilant guardians, ready to protect digital environments from the ever-shifting landscape of cyber threats.

In the field of crime research, firewalls extend beyond their technological function to become potent agents of empowerment. They create secure digital boundaries, equipping crime science experts to protect critical data and thwart potential cyberattacks (Hermansson et al., 2022). Beyond their physical attributes, firewalls play a vital role in safeguarding digital evidence, ensuring its integrity and admissibility in legal proceedings.

As proactive prevention tools, firewalls provide invaluable support in enhancing cyber resilience. Their capability to prevent unauthorized access and block unlawful extraction of sensitive data forms the foundation for developing comprehensive strategies to systematically deter and neutralize cybercriminals (Anwar et al., 2021). By regulating the entry and exit of harmful network traffic, firewalls mitigate vulnerabilities that adversaries might exploit.

In addition to their preventive capabilities, firewalls serve as guardians of evidence integrity during investigations. In today's landscape, where digital forensics is crucial, their role in preserving information integrity is immeasurable. The robustness of digital evidence enhances its reliability, affirming its status when presented in legal contexts. This convergence of technology and jurisprudence positions firewalls as allies of justice within criminal science.

In summary, firewalls are critical components at the intersection of technological advancement and the landscape of cyber risks. Within the domain of crime science, they act as vigilant sentinels, connecting vigilance, resilience, and empowerment. Firewalls uphold trust in the digital sphere, serving as the primary custodians of digital assets. In the ever-evolving world of cyber threats, they remain essential tools in the battle against cybercrime and in protecting digital integrity. Their adaptability and flexibility are vital for maintaining a balance between these objectives.

Encryption: Securing Data Integrity

Cryptographic techniques are crucial in safeguarding sensitive data, whether in transit or at rest. The coding methodologies embedded within encryption practices create a formidable defense against unauthorized access and potential data integrity violations. Here, we explore the significance of cryptographic practices in data protection, particularly their role in preserving confidentiality and integrity.

Within the expansive realm of modern cyber defenses, encryption stands out as an essential principle, acting as a dependable guardian that transforms the data into an unintelligible cipher. This transformation, facilitated by sophisticated algorithms, establishes a robust structure that ensures exclusive access to the data is reserved solely for entities possessing the correct cryptographic key (Dizon & Upson, 2021). As a complex security apparatus, encryption shields data throughout its transfer and storage, providing a reliable means to maintain its confidentiality, integrity, and authenticity.

The encryption process significantly alters data, converting original information into an unreadable code (Morina et al., 2023). This transformation is achieved through elaborate algorithms and cryptographic keys, ensuring that if an unauthorized individual gains access to the encrypted information, its true meaning remains obscured unless the correct decryption key is obtained.

Encryption is fundamentally rooted in confidentiality, which protects sensitive information by keeping it hidden from unauthorized individuals lacking the necessary decryption key. This approach extends its protective capabilities to secure data during its vulnerable transmission through complex networks and provides vigilant protection for data stored within devices and servers. Consequently, encryption plays a vital role in a comprehensive cybersecurity strategy.

In today's digital landscape, characterized by the interconnectedness of global communication networks, data in transit is paramount. Encryption acts as a digital protector, reinforcing the channels through which information is transmitted. It serves as a protective barrier as data travels from origin to destination, employing precise cryptographic algorithms to encode the information and safeguard it against threats posed by cyberattackers and unauthorized individuals attempting to intercept, manipulate, or extract data during transmission.

In this context, encryption techniques serve a defensive role aimed at preserving the integrity of information. Digital communication relies on rapid data diffusion, made possible through the processes that underlie encryption, thereby assuring the soundness and authenticity of the data. By employing cryptographic codes, encryption deters illicit tampering, distortions, or corruption (van Daalen, 2023). This technology ensures data integrity by maintaining the accuracy and reliability of information during transmission, allowing decision-making and operational functions to benefit from unaltered data.

Encryption also plays a crucial role in protecting stored data, where information seeks refuge within devices, servers, and databases. While the risks associated with data at rest may vary, encryption remains vigilant. Inactive data are secured through sophisticated cryptographic methods, akin to safeguarding a precious historical artifact within a heavily fortified vault (van Daalen, 2023). These cryptographic techniques provide multiple layers of security, rendering the data inaccessible to unauthorized individuals who lack the necessary cryptographic keys for decryption.

Moreover, encryption assumes a broader role beyond its traditional function of protecting personal data, encompassing compliance with regulations and facilitating traceability. In a landscape characterized by strict regulations, such as the General Data Protection Regulation and the Health Insurance Portability and Accountability Act, encryption emerges as an indispensable ally (Morina et al., 2023). By employing encryption for data at rest, organizations demonstrate their commitment to protecting sensitive personal, financial, or medical information, thereby enhancing security measures and fostering trust between businesses and clients. This practice not only mitigates the severe consequences that may arise from security breaches but also bolsters compliance with legal frameworks.

The orchestration of encryption resonates through the seamless collaboration of algorithms and cryptographic keys. Algorithms function as proficient composers, skillfully coordinating data conversion into an intricate melody that may be difficult to decipher. In cryptography, cryptographic keys serve as head conductors, adept at deciphering encoded information and translating it into an intelligible format (Dizon & Upson, 2021). This complex interplay exemplifies the fundamental nature of encryption, where the harmonious integration of technology and mathematics converges to protect sensitive data.

The foundation of encryption is rooted in complex mathematical processes that convert plaintext into ciphertext, making it unreadable to anyone without the correct decryption key. An encryption algorithm's effectiveness depends on the complexity of its design and the size of the encryption key (Srihith et al., 2023). Modern cryptographic practices employ two primary types of encryption: symmetric and asymmetric keys, both of which provide robust safeguards for sensitive information.

Symmetric-key encryption, also known as private-key encryption, uses a single secret key for both encryption and decryption. Protecting the confidentiality of this key is crucial, as its exposure could compromise the security of the encrypted data. In this system, the render and recipient share the same key, making its safeguarding essential to maintain the integrity and confidentiality of the information.

In contrast, asymmetric-key encryption, or public-key encryption, employs a dual-key system. One key is used publicly for encryption, while a separate, private key is retained for decryption (Srihith et al., 2023). The public dissemination of the encryption key enables broad data encryption, while only the private key holder can decrypt the data, ensuring secure communication and data protection. This system reduces the risks associated with key sharing in symmetric encryption and provides enhanced security by limiting decryption access to the intended recipient.

The Role of Encryption in Crime Science and Law Enforcement

The need for encryption within the field of crime science is evident, as it plays a critical role in safeguarding sensitive information against unauthorized access. By employing robust encryption methods, law enforcement, and investigative agencies can create a formidable defense that protects vital data necessary for conducting thorough investigations. This cryptographic strategy is indispensable in thwarting malicious actors, providing a protective barrier for a wide range of sensitive information, including confidential details regarding criminal activities and the identities of victims and witnesses.

Furthermore, employing encryption is crucial for protecting data and maintaining the integrity of sensitive information. Effective encryption deters tampering and unauthorized manipulation, ensuring the integrity of stored data remains intact. It serves as a reliable safeguard in situations where the accuracy and authenticity of information are paramount—such as in legal proceedings or criminal investigations. Encryption guarantees that evidence remains unaltered and true to its original form, thereby preserving its credibility in the eyes of the law.

Encryption is vital for enhancing trust between the public and law enforcement agencies. When individuals know their personal information is securely encrypted, they are more likely to cooperate with investigations and report crimes. This trust is crucial when dealing with sensitive data, such as information related to witnesses or victims of crime. By protecting this information through encryption, agencies can ensure the safety of those involved while fostering a collaborative relationship with the community.

Encryption's capabilities span various temporal contexts, efficiently protecting both transmitted and stored data. In the dynamic and ever-evolving digital landscape, data are transmitted across multiple networks and pathways, making them susceptible to interception and manipulation. Encryption transforms this process into a complex expedition, wherein intercepted information resembles a puzzle, decodable only by individuals who possess the cryptographic key.

Furthermore, encryption is crucial for ensuring the security of data at rest across various storage mediums. As data repositories become increasingly vulnerable to attacks, encryption has emerged as a robust safeguard, ensuring that the information remains an insurmountable enigma in the event of a breach (van Daalen, 2023). This layer of defense, combined with other cybersecurity measures, forms an integrated shield that protects data from unauthorized access.

Within the complex vocabulary of encryption, two prevalent approaches exist: symmetric and asymmetric encryption. Symmetric encryption, similar to a mutually agreed-on secret, employs a solitary key for encryption and decryption operations. Although this system's effectiveness is beyond doubt, it requires a secure mechanism for distributing cryptographic keys (Kulkarni & Rosemeen Mansuri, 2022). In contrast, asymmetric encryption serves as a more sophisticated counterpart, using a pair of public and private keys. This configuration provides a reliable means of communication without requiring a preestablished shared key.

In the expanding field of crime science, encryption emerges as a versatile tool, transcending conventional technical applications to become a crucial defense against cyber threats. As data breaches and digital theft become more pervasive, encryption functions as a core defense mechanism, protecting sensitive information from unauthorized access by malicious entities (Stoyanova et al., 2020). Beyond its role as a shield, encryption promotes data sovereignty, ensuring that confidential data remains concealed and inaccessible to unauthorized individuals.

At its core, encryption ensures confidentiality, integrity, and authenticity. It safeguards sensitive information by allowing access only to authorized individuals with the necessary decryption permissions. Encryption fortifies information, protecting it from illegal access while preserving its integrity. As a custodian of data integrity, encryption plays a critical role in enhancing the reliability of investigative efforts (Stoyanova et al., 2020). Its ability to maintain the integrity of digital evidence strengthens its value in judicial procedures, adding legitimacy and reliability to investigations.

In the modern digital world, where individuals' online activities create detailed records of criminal behavior, encryption has become a prominent tool in crime science. It acts as a guardian, converting accessible data into cryptic forms that only authorized entities can unlock. This dual function of protection and verification empowers criminal justice professionals as they work toward fairness and accuracy. Encryption ensures that sensitive materials remain secure and accessible only to those with the appropriate credentials. This not only safeguards investigations but also enhances their credibility and precision. Employing encryption techniques builds a stronghold in the ongoing battle against cybercriminals.

Dark Web Monitoring: Detecting Hidden Threats

Within the complex network of interconnected computer systems exists a concealed domain distinct from the well-known pathways of search engines and conventional browsing. This domain, known as the dark web, remains veiled from the view of ordinary internet users (Kaur & Randhawa, 2020). This hidden digital domain has transformed into a covert realm, fostering a wide range of unlawful acts that flourish within its shadows. The dark web has become a sanctuary for those seeking to engage in activities beyond the reach of traditional law enforcement, encompassing a broad spectrum, including the trade of prohibited goods and the covert exchange of sensitive information. It is, therefore, vital to devise innovative strategies to tackle the unique challenges and threats it poses.

The dark web, a cryptic domain sometimes likened to a poorly illuminated alleyway, exists as a hidden area within the internet. It is exclusively accessible via specialized software and configurations—such as Tor (The Onion Router), which safeguards the user's identity and location by routing their connections through an intricate network of servers. While the original purpose of this anonymity cloak was to protect privacy, it has created a sanctuary where cybercriminals can operate without fear of detection.

An active ecology of unlawful marketplaces has appeared in the dark web's covert recesses. These provide a variety of illicit commodities and services, including narcotics, counterfeit documents, stolen data, and advanced hacking instruments. The dark web is a shadowy refuge for diverse forms of cybercriminal collaboration, facilitating discourse and information exchange on activities such as identity theft, financial fraud, and the coordination of cyberattacks.

Law enforcement organizations and institutions employ a multifaceted and advanced approach known as dark web surveillance to address the growing incidence of criminality within the concealed domains of the dark web (AlKhatib & Basheer, 2019). This strategic initiative employs specialized software tools and advanced strategies to infiltrate the cloak of anonymity within the dark web, thereby revealing the actions of cybercriminals and the interconnected web of their activities. Monitoring the dark web is vital for pursuing justice within the digital domain. One of the main objectives is to identify and consistently monitor individuals engaging in criminal activities and seeking anonymity to evade the law (Omar & Ibrahim, 2020). By infiltrating these covert platforms, law enforcement authorities can acquire crucial intelligence, empowering them to respond to and dismantle unlawful marketplaces. Dark web monitoring also provides law enforcement authorities with valuable insights that help them stay ahead in the ever-changing realm of cybercrime.

The combined use of firewalls and encryption creates a strong defense against cybercriminals' persistent efforts to exploit vulnerabilities in networks, systems, and applications. Acting as vigilant digital sentinels, firewalls establish barriers that prevent unauthorized access, while encryption protects sensitive data by transforming it into an indecipherable puzzle accessible only with the proper cryptographic key. The collaboration between firewalls and encryption is vital for securing investigations, maintaining the integrity of evidence, and protecting sensitive information (Singla et al., 2023). Law enforcement agencies use these technologies to shield their communications and operations from potential threats, ensuring the integrity of their cybercrime-fighting efforts.

Firewalls and encryption are essential pillars of cybersecurity. Their role in the digital landscape underscores the continuous advancement of technology in response to ever-evolving cyber threats. Crime scientists and cybersecurity professionals remain committed to protecting the digital realm from such risks.

Ethical and Legal Considerations in Cybersecurity

Engaging with dark web surveillance entails navigating a multifaceted landscape with intricate technical obstacles and significant ethical quandaries. The tools and procedures employed in this endeavor must be highly complex, enabling them to navigate the multiple levels of encryption and anonymity that act as formidable barriers within the dark web (Omar & Ibrahim, 2020). These technologies often involve crawling, indexing, and conducting in-depth research on hidden websites, all while diligently maintaining a high level of confidentiality to avoid alerting hackers to monitoring activities.

The effectiveness of dark web surveillance technologies can be better understood by examining real-life case studies demonstrating their ability to yield concrete outcomes. One example is the dismantling of the notorious Silk Road—a clandestine online bazaar on the dark web that gained notoriety for facilitating illegal transactions involving illicit commodities and services (Koch, 2019). By employing rigorous surveillance measures, law enforcement agencies exposed the orchestrator of the operation and dismantled the platform.

While dark web surveillance is often lauded for its role in pursuing justice in the realm of digital technology, significant ethical deliberations accompany it. Achieving a careful balance between the need for monitoring (to address the growing threat of cybercrime) and preserving privacy and civil liberties is a multifaceted challenge. Thorough reflection is required when considering the ethical implications of exposing individuals involved in criminal activities, collecting fragments of evidence, and intercepting conversations. Achieving a harmonious equilibrium between these factors requires implementing transparent governance, continuous discussion, and a sophisticated comprehension of the digital environment. The dynamic nature of technology and the continuing evolution of cybercrime consistently redefine the parameters of this ethical discussion (AlKhatib & Basheer, 2019). As contemporary society grapples with balancing digital security and individual rights, the domain of dark web monitoring exemplifies the broader discourse surrounding privacy, technology, and the limits of lawful surveillance.

Future of Cybersecurity in Crime Science

The future of cybersecurity in crime science will necessitate a reliance on advanced technologies, enhanced threat intelligence, and adaptive security strategies to counter the ever-evolving cyber threat. A proactive approach that integrates artificial intelligence (AI), blockchain technology, and advanced encryption methods is needed to safeguard digital environments. AI and machine learning, real-time threat detection, and response capabilities can revolutionize cybersecurity by analyzing vast amounts of data, identifying anomalies, detecting unauthorized access, and forecasting cyberattacks before they transpire with minimal human intervention. The automated incident response mechanisms within these technologies have the ability to take immediate action to isolate infected devices, block malicious traffic, and alert cybersecurity teams. These technologies can also become more resilient over time based on their interaction with improve over time based on their interaction with emerging cyber threats.

Although best known for its salient role in cryptocurrencies, blockchain technology has broader applications in cybersecurity by helping to ensure data integrity, safeguarding transactions, and assisting with identity verification. The decentralized nature of blockchain is a valuable tool for securing digital evidence and protecting sensitive data by reducing the reliance on centralized databases that are vulnerable to breaches. Undoubtedly, blockchain-based systems can facilitate and protect financial transactions by combating fraud and monitoring illicit activities on the dark web.

Cybercriminals are constantly developing new techniques to bypass security measures, requiring law enforcement and cybersecurity professionals to stay ahead of these threats. It is essential that cybersecurity strategies make the transition from traditional perimeter-based security models to zero-trust architectures, where every request for access to the system is verified and authenticated. Quantum-resistant encryption is becoming increasingly crucial as quantum computing emerges because it has the potential to break conventional encryption methods. Additionally, widespread cyber threat intelligence sharing among government agencies, private corporations, and cybersecurity firms can improve real-time responses to cyber threats by improving collective security.

Integrating cybersecurity tools into crime science is critical for preventing cybercrimes, securing digital evidence, and protecting critical infrastructure. Law enforcement agencies are leveraging sophisticated tracking techniques and other cybersecurity advancements to dismantle cybercriminal networks on the dark web. While digital forensics will continue to strengthen as more potent encryption methods ensure the authenticity of digital evidence in criminal investigations, it is salient to recognize that cybersecurity legislation will be needed to address emerging threats while balancing privacy rights and security needs.

The future of cybersecurity in crime science is dependent on technological innovation, adaptive security measures, and global collaboration. AI-driven cybersecurity, blockchain applications, and advanced encryption techniques will play a pivotal role in safeguarding digital environments. Law enforcement agencies and cybersecurity professionals must remain proactive, continuously updating security protocols to counter emerging cyber threats. There is little debate that with these advancements, cybersecurity will continue to be a cornerstone of modern crime science, ensuring digital safety in an increasingly interconnected world.

Conclusion

The significance of cybersecurity technologies in criminal science is paramount in today's interconnected global landscape. Together, they function as steadfast collaborators, fulfilling an essential role in investigating, mitigating, and preventing cybercrimes. Firewalls and encryption collaborate synergistically to provide a robust foundation for digital security by constructing resilient barriers that safeguard networks and data from persistent cyberattacks.

Within this complex environment, methods for monitoring the dark web have emerged as sources of empowerment for law enforcement authorities. These tools allow authorities to browse the less accessible areas of the internet and discover and expose various cybercriminal activities. The integration of these technologies enhances the repertoire of crime science, enabling practitioners to address the dynamic realm of cybercrime.

Appropriately exploiting these technologies is crucial in the battle between criminals and defenders. Crime science specialists can effectively use firewalls, encryption, and dark web monitoring tools to proactively predict and respond to cybercrime, thereby maintaining a strategic advantage in this ongoing struggle. The continuing expansion and evolution of the digital domain have led to the steadfast collaboration of cybersecurity tools, serving as a constant source of vigilance and empowerment. This collaboration is crucial for fostering a safe and lawful digital domain for all internet users.

References

AlKhatib, B., & Basheer, R. (2019). Crawling the dark web: A conceptual perspective, challenges and implementation. *Journal of Digital Information Management*, 17(2), 51–60.

Anwar, R. W., Abdullah, T., & Pastore, F. (2021). Firewall best practices for securing smart healthcare environment: A review. *Applied Sciences*, 11(19), 9183.

Burke, B. F. (2021). *Information domain: An argument for organization*. School of Advanced Military Studies, U.S. Army Command and General Staff College.

Djenna, A., Harous, S., & Saidouni, D. E. (2021). Internet of Things meets internet threats: New concern cyber security issues of critical cyber infrastructure. *Applied Sciences*, 11(10), 1–30.

Dizon, M. A. C., & Upson, P. J. (2021). Laws of encryption: An emerging legal framework. *Computer Law & Security Review*, 43, 105635.

Gillam, A. R. (2019). Technology threat avoidance factors are predictors of risky cybersecurity behavior within the enterprise [Doctoral dissertation, Indiana State University].

Hermansson, L., Lundberg, A., Gruber, S., Jolly, A., Lind, J., Righard, E., & Scott, H. (2022). Firewalls: A necessary tool to enable social rights for undocumented migrants in social work. *International Social Work*, 65(4), 678–692.

Kaur, S., & Randhawa, S. (2020). Dark web: A web of crimes. *Wireless Personal Communications*, 112, 2131–2158.

Koch, R. (2019). Hidden in the shadow: The dark web—a growing risk for military operations? *2019 11th International Conference on Cyber Conflict (CyCon)*. IEEE.

Kulkarni, U., & Rosemeen Mansuri, R. A. (2022). File storage on the cloud using cryptography. *International Journal for Research in Applied Science & Engineering Technology*, 10(5), 1949–1953.

Morina, M., Azemi, F., Eren, M., Zejneli, I., & Papajorgji, E. (2023). Crime scene in cybercrime criminal offenses: Evidence management and processing. *Academic Journal of Interdisciplinary Studies*, 12(2), 45–56.

Okumu, D. O., Omollo, R. O., & Raburu, G. (2024). Human firewall simulator for enhancing security awareness against business email compromise. *Journal of Global Humanities and Social Science*, 5(7), 276–299.

Omar, Z. M., & Ibrahim, J. (2020). An overview of darknet, its rise and challenges, and its assumptions. *International Journal of Computer Science and Information Technology*, 8, 110–116.

Singla, S., Subhash, S., & Mishra, A. (2023). Network and data analysis tools for forensic science. *Modern forensic tools and devices: Trends in criminal investigation*, 23–39. Wiley-Scrivener.

Srihith, I. D., Donald, A. D., Srinivas, T. A. S., Thippanna, G., & Anjali, D. (2023). Locking down big data: A comprehensive survey of data encryption methods. *International Journal of Advanced Research in Science, Communication, and Technology*, 3(2), 84–93.

Stoyanova, M., Nikoloudakis, Y., Panagiotakis, S., Pallis, E., & Markakis, E. K. (2020). A survey on the Internet of Things (IoT) forensics: Challenges, approaches, and open issues. *IEEE Communications Surveys & Tutorials*, 22(2), 1191–1221.

Sukri, M. M. N. M., Padli, N. A. F. M., & Syalwanie, S. (Eds.). (2023). Cyber-attacks and cyber security: Emerging trends and recent developments. *Proceedings of the 1st Global Symposium on Information and Social Sciences*, 118–127. Academica Press Solution.

van Daalen, O. L. (2023). The right to encryption: Privacy as preventing unlawful access. *Computer Law & Security Review*, 49, 105804.

6 Geographic Information Systems (GISs)

The rise of Geographic Information Systems (GIS) has significantly transformed crime science, offering a multidimensional perspective that surpasses traditional methods of understanding and addressing criminal behavior. By integrating geographic data with crime-related information, GIS technology provides researchers and law enforcement agencies with advanced tools to analyze crime patterns within a spatial context, overcoming the limitations often associated with raw statistical data.

Crime Mapping with GIS: Understanding Spatial Crime Patterns

GIS applications are vast, with crime mapping, in particular, gaining significant attention for its ability to visually represent crime incidents and trends geographically. This visualization enhances the understanding of criminal dynamics by integrating crime data into geographic landscapes, helping to identify high-crime areas and revealing trends and patterns that might otherwise remain concealed.

Law enforcement agencies can optimize resource allocation through data-driven approaches using GIS technology. By enabling the analysis of crime patterns and spatial distribution, GIS provide valuable insights that lead to more efficient resource management. This proactive approach enhances the effectiveness of crime-prevention efforts, aligning with community priorities by directing limited resources to areas most affected by crime. Overall, the proficiency of GIS technology, particularly in crime mapping, underscores the significant influence of spatial analysis on collective efforts to understand, mitigate, and ultimately eliminate criminal activities.

Crime mapping is an essential element within crime science as it enables a thorough understanding of criminal patterns and behaviors through the use of GISs. The proficiency of GIS technology lies in its ability to transform raw crime data into visually informative representations, thus influencing the approaches employed by law enforcement agencies, researchers, and policymakers in crime prevention and investigation (Bani-Taha & Shafiq, 2020). Research indicates that GIS play a crucial role in analyzing criminal incidents by facilitating the visualization of geographic patterns, trends, and occurrences. This technology enables the identification of areas with high crime rates, hot-spot locations, and temporal patterns (Cardone & Di Martino, 2022).

By employing various methods, such as kernel density estimation, hot-spot analysis, and spatial clustering, GIS allow researchers to uncover hidden relationships between criminal activities and environmental factors. Consequently, they support the formulation of informed decisions to advance crime-prevention strategies.

The integration of GIS significantly enhances the efficacy of crime mapping to an unprecedented level. This innovation transforms raw data into visually compelling and informative representations surpassing the limitations of mere numerical statistics. Within

DOI: 10.4324/9781003558491-6

this symbiotic relationship, GIS offer a valuable perspective for analyzing criminal incidents, patterns, and trends through spatial visualization. This methodology deepens our understanding of the complex interplay between criminal behaviors and geographic environments.

Current research methodologies effectively uncover temporal variations in crime incidents, revealing patterns that might otherwise remain unnoticed. Various GIS techniques, including hot-spot analysis, kernel density estimation, and spatial clustering, have proven to be robust tools for researchers (Cardone & Di Martino, 2022). These methods illuminate hidden correlations between criminal behavior and environmental factors, providing valuable insights into the complex factors contributing to illicit activities.

As GISs continue to reveal these concealed intricacies, the scope for informed decision-making in crime prevention expands. Incorporating GIS into crime mapping allows law enforcement agencies to move beyond traditional frameworks by gaining deeper insights into spatial dynamics. These insights enable practitioners to tailor their actions based on geographic patterns. This integration also significantly enhances crime analysis, improving the understanding of criminal activities and promoting the development of more sophisticated and effective strategies for deterrence and prevention.

Identifying High-Crime Areas and Hot Spots

GIS have become an indispensable tool in crime mapping, widely employed to identify regions with elevated crime rates and pinpoint areas of concentrated criminal activity. These technologies are crucial for the strategic allocation of police resources. GISs allow law enforcement agencies to aggregate criminal incidents within defined geographic boundaries, extracting valuable insights that inform resource allocation and intervention strategies. A key method used in this process is kernel density estimation, a mathematical procedure that generates continuous density surfaces to visually represent the spatial distribution of criminal incidents. These surfaces highlight areas of high crime rates, identifying locations that require focused and timely interventions (Milic et al., 2019). With this knowledge, law enforcement agencies can allocate resources and initiatives more effectively, thereby improving the overall efficiency of crime-prevention efforts.

Kernel density estimation plays a crucial role in crime mapping, providing a powerful analytical dimension to the identification of high-crime areas and hot spots. This method employs mathematical functions, or kernels, placed at each crime location to produce smoothed density surfaces (Cardone & Di Martino, 2022). The combined effect of these kernels generates surfaces that reveal varying degrees of crime density across a geographic region. Consequently, areas with higher concentrations of criminal activity emerge as prominent peaks on these density surfaces, indicating hot spots where crimes are clustered.

The value of hot-spot detection goes beyond visual clarity, providing significant strategic benefits for deploying police resources. By identifying areas with high crime concentrations, law enforcement can allocate resources more precisely to these locations. Strategies for reducing crime in these areas may include increasing patrols, enhancing surveillance, or implementing community engagement programs. The goal is to optimize resource distribution, concentrating law enforcement efforts in areas where their presence will have the most substantial impact.

This targeted allocation of law enforcement resources exemplifies a proactive approach to crime prevention. GIS technology enables law enforcement to anticipate and address emerging crime patterns more effectively, thereby creating safer community environments. Furthermore, this careful distribution of resources helps build public trust in the effectiveness of law enforcement strategies, encouraging greater community involvement in crime-prevention efforts.

GIS-driven hotspot detection represents a departure from traditional policing methods, offering a data-driven, spatially informed approach to resource allocation. By adopting targeted strategies based on insights from kernel density estimates and hot-spot analysis, law enforcement agencies can significantly enhance safety and security in urban areas. Integrating GIS technology into criminal science marks a new paradigm in law enforcement, enabling the deliberate and efficient use of resources to optimize crime-prevention strategies informed by spatial insights.

GIS for Law Enforcement Resource Allocation

The use of GIS in crime science represents a significant and pragmatic application for strategically allocating police resources. Law enforcement agencies leverage GISs to identify areas with elevated crime rates, analyze the spatial distribution of criminal behavior, and assign personnel and resources more effectively to address high-risk regions. By adopting a data-driven strategy, agencies can enhance the effectiveness of crime-prevention initiatives. This approach also lays the groundwork for strong community involvement by directly addressing residents' safety concerns in crime-affected areas.

Crime mapping using GIS integrates crime incidents within a spatial context, surpassing traditional data display methods. By merging crime data with geographic maps, GIS technologies enable stakeholders to generate visual representations that reveal complex patterns and trends often hidden in raw data. This visual component provides an intuitive understanding of the spatial distribution of criminal activity, offering insights that go beyond the limitations of conventional analysis using tabular data. Integrating crime occurrences with geographic characteristics provides law enforcement agencies and researchers with a comprehensive view, forming the basis for developing precise and targeted approaches to crime control and resource allocation.

Overlaying criminal incidents onto geographic maps transforms unprocessed data into a visual narrative. This narrative highlights the concentration of criminal activities, offering immediate insights into areas with higher crime frequencies. By visually analyzing crime across urban areas, law enforcement professionals can identify geographic trends that may not be evident through numerical analysis alone. Incorporating spatial context enhances the understanding of crime dynamics, allowing for better interpretation of the connections between criminal incidents and their environments.

Moreover, combining crime data with geographic characteristics provides a broader perspective on crime trends beyond basic statistics. This comprehensive view enables the identification of specific crime patterns in distinct neighborhoods, commercial zones, or residential areas (Yang, 2019). These insights assist law enforcement in tailoring their resource allocation strategies to effectively address the particular issues faced by different geographic regions.

For instance, a downtown area may experience a spike in theft during evening hours due to increased pedestrian traffic. GIS-enabled crime mapping can visually capture these patterns, allowing law enforcement to deploy additional patrols and enhance crime-prevention efforts in high-risk areas. Similarly, residential neighborhoods may exhibit trends in domestic burglaries that peak when residents are away at work. With this information, law enforcement can strategically allocate resources and focus on preventive measures during vulnerable times.

Using spatial visualization to analyze criminal incidents, patterns, and trends fosters a strong connection between evidence-based insights and practical decision-making. This approach enables law enforcement agencies to allocate resources more effectively, deploying personnel and technology to areas most susceptible to criminal activity (Hashim et al., 2019). Incorporating spatial data into crime-prevention strategies not only enhances effectiveness but also promotes community involvement by directly addressing localized crime issues.

GIS-enabled spatial visualization creates a detailed narrative that aligns with the geographic distribution of crime, transforming raw data into dynamic, actionable insights. The fusion of technology and crime science supports the development of safer urban environments by fostering collaboration among law enforcement, researchers, and communities (Bani-Taha & Shafiq, 2020). As GIS technology advances, it holds significant potential to reshape crime management by providing invaluable geographical insights and enabling the optimal allocation of resources. This innovation has the power to transform the current landscape of crime management, paving the way for more effective strategies in the future.

GIS and Crime-Environment Relationships

The extensive capabilities of GIS in crime mapping are evident in their ability to identify intricate correlations between criminal activity and environmental factors. By integrating crime data with socioeconomic, demographic, and ecological information, GISs provide a powerful tool for detecting relationships that are often difficult to uncover using traditional analytical methods (Flexon et al., 2024). This integration enables researchers and law enforcement officials to analyze the prevalence of specific crimes within particular demographic contexts. These insights form the foundation for developing targeted crime-prevention strategies that address underlying causes and risk factors, ultimately guiding decisions regarding resource allocation.

Integrating criminal incidents with diverse environmental factors deepens the understanding of crime dynamics. Beyond basic visualization, this approach explores causality, providing insights into how socioeconomic and environmental conditions influence criminal behavior. For instance, GIS analysis may reveal that certain types of property crimes occur more frequently in areas with high unemployment rates or low levels of social cohesion (Ogneva-Himmelberger et al., 2019). Such findings can lead to a re-evaluation of resource distribution, suggesting that interventions aimed at improving employment opportunities or fostering community engagement could significantly reduce crime.

GIS enables social scientists and law enforcement professionals to establish connections between crime patterns and environmental characteristics. This capability allows them to identify areas at higher risk of criminal activity and determine locations where targeted interventions would have the most significant impact. Such insights are especially critical for allocating resources for crime-prevention strategies. By understanding the contributing factors to criminal behavior, resource allocation becomes more effective and strategically focused.

In summary, GIS in crime mapping have evolved beyond mere visual representation; they have become a crucial analytical tool for exploring the complex relationship between crime and its surrounding environment. Incorporating demographic, socioeconomic, and environmental factors enhances our understanding of criminal behavior and strengthens resource allocation strategies. As GIS technology advances, it will play an increasingly valuable role in guiding law enforcement agencies and supporting informed decision-making based on comprehensive data analysis. In turn, these data-driven strategies improve crime-management efforts and contribute to building safer communities.

Temporal Crime Analysis Using GIS

The implications of GIS-enabled crime mapping extend beyond spatial analysis, incorporating the complex dimension of time. Integrating temporal data with GIS reveals patterns that unfold over specific time intervals (Hossain et al., 2020). This ability to interpret temporal patterns—such as daily fluctuations, weekly variations, and seasonal spikes in criminal activity—is critical. By analyzing these trends, law enforcement agencies can deploy resources more effectively during periods of heightened risk and adjust crime-prevention strategies with agility, ensuring a responsive and adaptable approach to managing crime.

Integrating temporal data into GIS-based crime mapping uncovers patterns often overlooked in traditional analyses. The interaction between time and geography plays a crucial role in shaping criminal behavior and influencing when and where crimes occur. GIS provide a comprehensive view of how crime fluctuates across different time frames, including hours, days, and seasons, thereby enhancing the overall understanding of crime dynamics.

Diurnal patterns, for example, provide insights into the times of day when criminal activity peaks or declines. This information enables law enforcement to strategically allocate resources by increasing patrols during high-risk periods when crimes are more likely to occur. Similarly, analyzing crime patterns by the day of the week can reveal disparities, helping agencies allocate resources effectively to address elevated risks on specific days.

GIS also uncover seasonal crime patterns, such as the tendency for property crimes to increase during holiday seasons when many homes are unoccupied (McDowall et al., 2000). With this knowledge, law enforcement agencies can implement proactive strategies to protect vulnerable areas during these peak times.

The value of temporal analysis lies in its ability to enhance the accuracy of resource allocation. Law enforcement agencies can improve performance by aligning resource deployment with observed temporal trends. This dynamic approach not only increases the effectiveness of crime-prevention measures but also highlights the adaptability of law enforcement in addressing the ever-changing nature of criminal activity.

Case Studies: GIS Applications in Law Enforcement

The tangible effects of GIS on criminal research are well-illustrated through various compelling case studies and practical examples. These instances demonstrate the substantial impact of GIS-powered crime mapping on law enforcement operations and the advancement of safer communities through evidence-based resource allocation strategies. This analysis focuses on two prominent case studies, specifically the CompStat and PredPol systems, to elucidate the considerable influence that GIS can exert within crime research.

The implementation of the CompStat system by the New York Police Department (NYPD) serves as a notable example of the efficacy of employing GIS-driven crime mapping in reducing crime rates (Smith, 2018). This unique methodology employs GIS to visualize crime incidents, identify clusters of criminal behavior, and strategically allocate resources. Through routine data analysis and feedback mechanisms, law enforcement agencies can adapt their strategies based on evolving crime patterns.

The intricate CompStat mechanism has wielded a marked influence. During the 1990s, there was a noticeable decline in criminal activity within New York City. This shift can be partially attributed to the effective integration of GIS. This technological tool facilitated the rapid monitoring of crime patterns, the distribution of resources, and the ongoing evaluation of progress. By strategically allocating police resources to areas characterized by elevated crime rates, a stronger deterrent effect has been created, significantly contributing to the reduction in illicit activities. The effectiveness of the CompStat framework has served as a driving force for law enforcement agencies worldwide to incorporate GISs as an essential component in their efforts to combat criminal activities.

The use of the PredPol mechanism by various law enforcement agencies stands out as a prominent example of the anticipatory capabilities of GISs within the realm of criminological investigation. By scrutinizing past unlawful incidents, this mechanism harnesses GIS to pinpoint recurring irregularities and predict potential areas with an increased likelihood of criminal activity (Mugari & Obioha, 2021). The integration of this forward-thinking approach enables law enforcement agencies to allocate their resources effectively, thereby enhancing surveillance and community engagement in locales where criminal behaviors are more likely to occur.

Law enforcement's implementation of the PredPol technique in Los Angeles illustrates this phenomenon, as the technique aims to anticipate and deter property-related offenses (Friend, 2013). By utilizing GIS and examining records related to burglary and theft, law enforcement personnel can make informed predictions about future criminal activities. This enables them to concentrate their resources and attention on areas with a heightened likelihood of such incidents occurring. The outcome resulted in a tangible decrease in property crime incidents within the designated areas.

These studies highlight the significant potential of GIS in crime science for bringing about substantial changes and improvements. By integrating spatial data with sophisticated analytics, law enforcement organizations can make informed decisions that lead to measurable decreases in crime rates. GIS technology has evolved from a reactive approach to a proactive strategy in combating criminal activities, becoming an indispensable asset. The ongoing advancement of technology is expected to broaden the impact of GIS in crime science, providing law enforcement agencies with more advanced tools to help create safer communities.

Challenges and Limitations of GIS in Crime Science

While GIS offer significant potential in crime science, their integration presents several challenges. Addressing these challenges necessitates a comprehensive approach that recognizes both the benefits and limitations of GIS technology in crime prevention and investigation.

The effectiveness of GIS-driven crime mapping relies on the quality and accuracy of the underlying data. Inaccurate or incomplete data can result in flawed assessments and misguided decisions regarding resource distribution. Variations in crime reporting, inconsistent data collection methods, and errors in data entry can undermine the reliability of GIS-based insights. Therefore, strict data-gathering procedures and ongoing quality assurance protocols are essential to ensure the integrity of crime mapping.

Combining sensitive demographic and environmental data with crime statistics raises valid privacy concerns. To protect individuals' privacy rights, it is essential to implement strict measures to prevent data breaches, unauthorized access, and inadvertent exposure of personal information. The use of GIS in crime science challenges the balance between informed decision-making and the ethical obligation to safeguard privacy.

The accuracy of GIS analysis depends on the reliability and fairness of the data. Bias in crime data—stemming from factors such as unequal law enforcement practices, socioeconomic disparities, or historical trends—can skew results and perpetuate existing inequities. For example, overpolicing in certain areas may lead to a higher concentration of recorded incidents, distorting the true nature of crime patterns. To address these biases, there must be a continuous commitment to fair and equitable data collection and interpretation.

To fully realize the potential of GIS, a team with specialized knowledge in GIS operation is essential. Training law enforcement officers to effectively use GIS technology and interpret its outputs can be resource-intensive (Chan et al., 2023). Smaller agencies or those with limited training resources may encounter challenges in fully leveraging the capabilities of GIS.

Implementing GIS technology requires a substantial investment in hardware, software, training, and maintenance (Chan et al., 2023). These costs may be prohibitive for some law enforcement agencies, limiting their ability to adopt GIS-based crime mapping strategies. Additionally, technical challenges—such as program compatibility, data integration, and system scalability—can hinder successful implementation.

Understanding these challenges and finding ways to navigate them is crucial for maximizing the benefits of GIS. Transparent data collection, proactive bias prevention, and robust privacy protections are essential for maintaining public trust. By fostering collaboration among law enforcement, researchers, policymakers, and technology vendors, strategies can be developed to leverage GIS' potential while addressing their limitations.

The Future of GIS in Crime Science

The future development of GIS in crime science is expected to undergo significant transformation, providing new opportunities for improving the allocation of police resources. Technological advancements will enhance GIS' ability to analyze crime trends and inform resource allocation through innovative methodologies, diverse data sources, and emerging technologies.

Integrating GISs with advanced analytics, machine learning, and predictive modeling holds significant potential for disruptive impact. By incorporating crime data, environmental factors, and demographic information, law enforcement can generate precise and adaptive forecasts of high-crime areas. This proactive approach enables agencies to strategically allocate resources, thereby reducing the likelihood of crime escalation.

Artificial intelligence (AI) has the potential to revolutionize crime prediction within GIS. AI algorithms can analyze complex relationships within large datasets, revealing patterns that may not be evident to human analysts. AI-powered GIS can process vast amounts of data—including crime incidents, socioeconomic factors, and environmental variables—providing sophisticated insights into the spatial and temporal dynamics of criminal behavior.

Integrating GIS with social media data analysis introduces a new dimension to crime research. Social media provides real-time information and insights into local events, public sentiment, and social trends (Marks et al., 2021). By combining social media data with GISs, law enforcement agencies can detect emerging crime trends and deploy resources more efficiently and flexibly.

The Internet of Things (IoT) presents innovative opportunities for enhancing GIS applications in crime science. Integrating sensor networks—such as surveillance cameras, gunshot detectors, and other IoT devices—with GIS can provide real-time insights into criminal activity (Oladimeji et al., 2023). This integration enables law enforcement to respond more swiftly to incidents and optimize resource distribution.

The future of GIS in crime science will benefit significantly from cross-disciplinary collaboration. Combining expertise from GIS, criminology, urban planning, data science, and social sciences will lead to the development of innovative approaches for analyzing crime and optimizing resource allocation. This interdisciplinary approach enhances our understanding of crime patterns and fosters more effective crime prevention strategies.

The intersection of advanced technologies and innovative methodologies will shape the future of police resource allocation through GIS. As GIS technology evolves, law enforcement will gain deeper insights into crime patterns, risk factors, and prevention strategies. By adopting advanced analytics, AI, social media data integration, sensor networks, and cross-disciplinary collaboration, GIS will remain a vital tool for creating safer and more resilient communities in the face of ever-changing criminal challenges.

Conclusion

GIS are revolutionizing the field of crime science. Research shows that GIS technology has transformed how crime trends are understood and addressed, enabling law enforcement and researchers to visualize, analyze, and evaluate crime data with unprecedented accuracy. GIS-based crime mapping helps in resource allocation that is data-driven and responsive to the specific needs of different communities. Despite challenges such as data quality, privacy concerns, and potential biases, GIS have transformative potential in criminal research.

As technology and methodologies progress, the role of GIS in crime prevention and investigation will continue to expanding. Integrating GIS with advanced analytical techniques, AI, social media platforms, and IoT technology will enhance the precision, proactivity, and responsiveness of crime predictions and resource allocation. With each advancement, GIS solidify their position as a cornerstone of contemporary crime science, contributing to safer and more secure communities both nationally and globally.

References

Bani-Taha, O. I., & Shafiq, M. O. (2020). Combining the richness of GIS techniques with visualization tools to better understand the spatial distribution of data—a case study of Chicago city crime analysis. *International Journal of Big Data Intelligence*, 7(1), 29–46.

Cardone, B., & Di Martino, F. (2022). Fuzzy-based spatiotemporal hot spot intensity and propagation—an application in crime analysis. *Electronics*, 11(3), 370.

Chan, T. N., U, L. H., Choi, B., Xu, J., & Cheng, R. (2023, June). Large-scale geospatial analytics: Problems, challenges, and opportunities. *Companion of the 2023 International Conference on Management of Data*, 21–29.

Flexon, J. L., D'Alessio, S. J., Stolzenberg, L., Cruz, E., & Meldrum, R. C. (2024). Youth access to stolen handguns. *Crime & Delinquency*, 70(3), 672–698.

Friend, Z. (2013). Predictive policing: Using technology to reduce crime. *FBI Law Enforcement Bulletin*.

Hashim, H., Wan Mohd, W. M. N., Sadek, E. S. S. M., & Dimyati, K. M. (2019). Modeling urban crime patterns using spatial space-time and regression analysis. *The International Archives of the Photogrammetry, Remote Sensing and Spatial Information Sciences*, 42, 247–254.

Hossain, S., Abtahee, A., Kashem, I., Hoque, M. M., & Sarker, I. H. (2020). Crime prediction using spatio-temporal data. *Computing science, communication, and security: First international conference, COMS2 2020, Gujarat, India, March 26–27, 2020, Revised selected papers* 1, 277–289. Springer.

Marks, C., Carrasco-Escobar, G., Carrasco-Hernández, R., Johnson, D., Ciccarone, D., Strathdee, S. A. et al. (2021). Methodological approaches for the prediction of opioid use-related epidemics in the United States: A narrative review and cross-disciplinary call to action. *Translational Research*, 234, 88–113.

McDowall, D., Curtis, K., & Loftin, C. (2000). Seasonality of crime: Evidence from the Uniform Crime Reports. *Journal of Quantitative Criminology*, 16(4), 431–452.

Milic, N., Popovic, B., Mijalkovic, S., & Marinkovic, D. (2019). The influence of data classification methods on the predictive accuracy of kernel density estimation hotspot maps. *International Arab Journal of Information Technology*, 16(6), 1053–1062.

Mugari, I., & Obioha, E. E. (2021). Predictive policing and crime control in the United States of America and Europe: Trends in a decade of research and the future of predictive policing. *Social Sciences*, 10(6), 234.

Ogneva-Himmelberger, Y., Ross, L., Caywood, T., Khananayev, M., & Starr, C. (2019). Analyzing the relationship between perception of safety and reported crime in an urban neighborhood using GIS and sketch maps. *ISPRS International Journal of Geo-Information*, 8(12), 531.

Oladimeji, D., Gupta, K., Kose, N. A., Gundogan, K., Ge, L., & Liang, F. (2023). Smart transportation: An overview of technologies and applications. *Sensors*, 23(8), 3880.

Smith, C. (2018). The controversial crime-fighting program that changed big-city policing forever. *New York Magazine*.

Yang, B. (2019). GIS crime mapping to support evidence-based solutions provided by community-based organizations. *Sustainability*, 11(18), 4889.

7 Forensic Technologies

Forensic science serves as a nexus connecting the puzzle of a crime scene with the unwavering pursuit of justice. The multidisciplinary nature of this field involves integrating several academic disciplines, including chemistry, biology, physics, and computer science, to unravel the narratives embedded within the data (Fraser, 2020). By employing empirical analysis and adhering to rigorous scientific methods, forensic scientists play a crucial role in assisting law enforcement agencies in apprehending criminals and establishing the innocence of those wrongly accused.

Unveiling the Three Pillars of Forensic Science

This chapter highlights three significant pillars of forensic technology. Ballistics analysis plays a crucial role in firearm-related investigations. Distinct markings on bullets and cartridge cases create a trail akin to fingerprints, which analysts use to uncover concealed information about firearms. The field of toxicology examines the physiological effects of illicit substances and behaviors. By analyzing biological samples, forensic toxicologists can detect substances such as narcotics, poisons, and alcohol, providing evidence of intoxication, injury, or potential criminal activity. Finally, the field of digital forensics explores the virtual realm, where technological devices reveal concealed information. In an era characterized by constant data flow, professionals in this domain can discover a wealth of evidence from various technological devices, such as computers, smartphones, and digital archives. Rigorous data retrieval and analysis help reveal conversations, linkages, and covert strategies.

This chapter examines the complexities of ballistics analysis, toxicology screening, and digital forensics while emphasizing their combined significance in contemporary investigative practices. As forensic technology advances, its influence affects legal systems and penal institutions, ensuring responsible parties face legal consequences while exonerating the falsely accused. Each of these three domains, characterized by distinct methodologies and technologies, plays a noteworthy role in the integrated narrative of crime prevention, investigation, and resolution. Their amalgamation epitomizes the symbiotic relationship that enables law enforcement agencies to safeguard communities and deliver justice.

Ballistics Analysis: Investigating Firearm Evidence

Within the complex realm of forensic investigation, ballistics analysis is crucial in navigating the interplay between firearms, ammunition, and the enduring traces they leave behind. Its complex nature and significant role characterize this field, serving as a vital tool for meticulously and systematically deciphering crime scenes. By examining firearms, the complexities of ammunition, and interrelated evidence, ballistics analysis constructs a

DOI: 10.4324/9781003558491-7

cohesive narrative by establishing linkages between bullets, cartridge cases, and the specific guns that discharged them. The subsequent sections explore ballistics analysis in depth, examining how each trigger-pull leaves enduring evidence beyond the moment of firing.

The core of ballistics analysis revolves around the complex discipline of firearm identification, which involves a rigorous examination of firearms to reveal the distinct markings they leave on their ammunition. As projectiles travel through the inner chambers of firearms, they accumulate unique characteristics from the manufacturing intricacies of each barrel (Li, 2006). The minute markings manifest as striations and imprints, adorning bullets and cartridge cases with a unique signature. A vast reservoir of valuable data exists within these delineations, eagerly awaiting discovery through the collaborative integration of technological advancements and specialized knowledge.

The process begins with extracting bullets and cartridge cases from the scene, with precision as its fundamental principle. These components serve as the foundation on which the unique characteristics of the firearm are imprinted. By utilizing state-of-the-art imaging equipment, forensic specialists inspect and document these marks, capturing them with utmost precision. The elaborate details and features of firearms are captured and preserved in high-resolution photographs, providing critical visual data about these weapons.

As these photos accumulate in the forensic laboratory, they form a complex mosaic that serves as a storehouse for distinct weapon fingerprints. The National Integrated Ballistic Information Network (NIBIN) is a repository that serves as a central hub for identifying firearms, containing comprehensive data on their make, model, and type (King et al., 2013). The digital platform allows previously unnoticed firearm signatures to be analyzed, turning inert evidence into a powerful witness.

The genuine enchantment, however, arises when these fingerprints are juxtaposed. Like language researchers, forensic professionals engage in thorough and precise comparisons. Researchers meticulously examine the complex patterns engraved on retrieved bullets and cartridge cases, aiming to identify similarities between these patterns and those found on bullets discharged from firearms with known origins. The method seamlessly integrates technological precision and human expertise, wherein patterns are carefully assessed, compared, and conclusions made.

Through these comparisons, a discernible narrative emerges. The striations and impressions, previously enigmatic, now convey a narrative that includes the firearm's historical context, unique characteristics, and role in criminal activity. The trajectory of a bullet discharged from a particular firearm indicates its traversal through an individualized barrel, which exhibits distinct manufacturing characteristics (Fraser, 2020). This expedition, characterized by flaws and unique qualities, establishes a connection between a rifle and its corresponding ammunition. This connection serves as a crucial element in investigative accounts.

Firearm identification seamlessly integrates scientific principles and technical methodologies to provide an exhaustive understanding of key details. With the expansion of the digital archive, the connection between physical evidence and digital data is strengthened, thereby unveiling a novel dimension of forensic discovery (Aggarwal, 2021). At its core, firearm identification involves interpreting implicit information and decoding concealed details embedded within bullet and cartridge case impressions. This process helps investigators pursue factual evidence.

Within the criminal activity, the tools employed act as articulate storytellers, effectively communicating their narratives through the inscriptions they leave behind on diverse surfaces. The field of toolmark analysis serves as a diligent interpreter, methodically decoding these traces that persist as silent witnesses (Guarnera et al., 2023). In ballistics, these marks have consequences beyond their initial lack of visibility, serving as crucial indicators for investigators to unearth new findings.

Toolmark analysis extends beyond the confines of firearm barrels. Its influence encompasses projectiles, casings, and tangible artifacts that can potentially exhibit traces of illicit conduct. When weapons are assembled, disassembled, or fired, tools leave distinctive imprints that serve as unique signatures.

Signatures and toolmarks possess a distinct language that toolmark analysis can decipher. The procedure begins by precisely documenting these impressions, regardless of their location on the exterior of a projectile, a casing, or an item discovered at a forensic site (Fraser, 2020). Within the forensic laboratory, these marks undergo magnification using state-of-the-art imaging equipment, thereby enabling the precise visualization of each contour and groove.

However, these markers' importance becomes apparent when compared with established criteria. Forensic professionals undertake thorough comparisons by gauging the distinct characteristics of each toolmark and examining similarities and correlations with established tools. This procedure entails an amalgamation of accuracy and intuition, thoroughly observing patterns and anomalies to develop a strong association.

Through these comparisons, a richer understanding emerges. A bullet possessing a toolmark can provide insight into the tools used during fabrication, such as a screwdriver for tightening or a pair of pliers for adjustment. These marks indicate manipulation, representing the enduring effects of interaction that reverberate over both temporal and spatial dimensions (Nigrini, 2020). By associating these markings with specific instruments, researchers can extract valuable information about a weapon's history, any potential alterations it may have undergone, and its overall usage.

As a fundamental component, toolmark analysis contributes complex contextual information to the investigative framework. Including this element enriches the storytelling by providing insight into the events before and after pulling a trigger (Gupta & Jain, 2023). Within the field of ballistics, the characteristics exhibited by tools extend beyond their practical function, assuming a narrative role skillfully deciphered by the discipline of toolmark analysis.

In the intricacies of a crime scene, the paths traced by bullets form a narrative that often communicates more effectively than verbal language. Bullet trajectory analysis is a prominent field within crime scene reconstruction, which aims to clarify the trajectory of discharged bullets. This discipline enables investigators to trace bullet paths, facilitating a retrospective examination of events in both temporal and spatial dimensions (Atlam et al., 2020). A narrative that is intertwined with a projectile's trajectory emerges through a detailed analysis of the entry and exit wounds found on victims and the surrounding environment.

Beyond geometry, bullet trajectory analysis also explores a complex interaction of variables. This study encompasses variables such as bullet velocity, angle of impact, and the materials through which the bullet traverses, including air resistance, the yielding texture of clothing, or the unforgiving firmness of bone (Alsop et al., 2021). The confluence of these components establishes a contextual framework within which the narrative of the criminal incident unfolds. As detectives diligently piece together these complexities, a detailed depiction emerges—a tableau that transcends time constraints. The trajectory of each gunshot is akin to a brushstroke on a canvas, offering insight into the dynamics of the event and the emotions permeating the atmosphere. By deciphering the trajectory of a projectile, analysts can unveil the sequence of criminal activities, thereby reconstructing historical events with a high degree of precision. In forensic investigation, bullet trajectory analysis serves as a convergence point between the scientific principles of physics and the nuanced skill of interpretation. The practice involves interpreting the narrative embedded in a bullet's trajectory, elucidating the projectile's path and the complex interconnections among people, objects, and the environment. Was the projectile discharged nearby or from a distance? Was the incident characterized by a deliberate attack or an act of self-defense? The field of bullet trajectory analysis is dedicated to investigating these concerns with a notable level of precision.

Ballistics analysis is an indispensable instrument within the field of crime science, playing a pivotal role in the prevention, investigation, and mitigation of criminal activities. The process of associating bullets and cartridge cases with specific firearms facilitates the identification of weapons and the reconstruction of violent situations, thereby augmenting endeavors in crime prevention. Examining firearms, ammunition, and crime scenes yields significant evidentiary value, thus facilitating the resolution of criminal cases. Moreover, in the context of crime prevention, ballistics analysis bolsters law enforcement agencies' efforts by furnishing valuable perspectives into projectile paths and the locations of perpetrators and victims (Newland et al., 2024). This situation, in turn, aids in the detailed reconstruction of events. In its entirety, it fulfills a crucial role in elucidating the particulars of weapon-related situations.

Toxicology Screening: Detecting Chemical Evidence

Toxicology screening is vital for exploring the chemical composition of biological materials and uncovering concealed information that would otherwise remain undisclosed. This field of forensic science involves a laborious process of analysis, where the examiner carefully examines human fluids and tissues to detect the presence of various chemicals, including narcotics, poisons, alcohol, and others. The depths of this resource hold vital answers about cases involving suspected overdose, poisoning, and impaired driving. These answers can significantly impact the trajectory of investigations and facilitate the administration of justice.

In forensic toxicology, various advanced approaches are used to analyze the intricate routes of biological samples. The pursuit of drug detection is a complex undertaking that systematically uncovers concealed chemical traces within the complicated framework of human physiology. Drug detection utilizes advanced methodologies such as gas chromatography and mass spectrometry, effectively integrating scientific principles with investigative practices and collaborative efforts.

In this orchestration, biological specimens such as blood, urine, and tissue are fundamental elements that harmoniously combine to form the basis of the analysis. These samples undergo analysis, wherein each layer unveils the interplay of chemical components. Gas chromatography and mass spectrometry are widely recognized for their exceptional accuracy and proficiency, demonstrating remarkable performance (Allen & McWhinney, 2019). The process involves separating and identifying discrete chemical fingerprints in the sample, resulting in an all-encompassing dataset that provides insights about the ingested chemicals.

These signatures, resembling musical notes arranged on a scale, enable forensic toxicologists to interpret the specific drugs in an individual's bloodstream. This investigation provides insight into the physiological landscape, exploring the transition from illicit substances to prescribed medications (Alonzo et al., 2022). This phenomenon highlights an individual's engagement with their surroundings and the enduring imprints of their decisions on a molecular level.

Beyond being an essential compilation of chemical elements, the presented knowledge serves as a testimonial to individuals' experiences and existence—a narrative intricately intertwined with the fundamental constituents of our physical beings. The knowledge obtained through drug testing furnishes an extensive understanding of various behaviors and experiences, shedding light on the choices and paths followed. Within forensic investigations, these disclosures manifest as strands that possess the capacity to interlace the tapestry of justice.

The field of toxicology expands its pursuit of knowledge to encompass the captivating domain of alcohol analysis. Toxicologists play a crucial role in this domain by combining rigorous scientific investigation with legal inquiries. They employ techniques such as gas chromatography to accurately assess an individual's level of intoxication, whether in the context of impaired driving events or the examination of alcohol-related crimes (Young & Lurie, 2022). These procedures act as precise tools, providing valuable insights into the subject's state of intoxication.

Amid a multitude of legal inquiries, alcohol analysis emerges as a prominent and illuminating focal point. In suspected impaired driving cases, toxicologists play a pivotal role by utilizing their specialized knowledge to determine if an individual operated a vehicle under the influence of alcohol. This conclusion holds significant legal implications, extending beyond mere technicality (Santhy, 2023). Through blood chemistry analysis, toxicologists provide a reliable tool that assists investigators in reconstructing events and clarifying roles and obligations in administering justice.

The procedure resembles a symphony of analysis, where intricate methods such as gas chromatography coordinate the movement of molecules. Blood samples containing minute amounts of ethanol, the psychoactive compound found in alcoholic beverages, are subjected to rigorous scrutiny. Gas chromatography has emerged as a highly proficient technique, demonstrating an exceptional ability to separate and quantify various components (Girard, 2021). This procedure facilitates the conversion of the biological substrate into a medium that serves as a foundation for toxicologists to depict the state of intoxication.

The findings of this investigation exhibit a dichotomous character, representing scientific discoveries with noteworthy ramifications. The data presented in these findings elucidate how alcohol affects individuals, encompassing the precise numerical representation of physiological reactions. These revelations serve as the foundation for legal cases. Credible evidence substantiates claims and validates or challenges narratives, ultimately contributing to the equitable rendering of judgments.

The domain of alcohol analysis encompasses more than just a simple enumeration of ethanol molecules; it comprises elements of artistic expression. The study goes beyond mere chemical interactions and delves into the intricacies of human behavior, leading to a deeper understanding of the issues involved. By analyzing blood alcohol levels, toxicologists shed light on where decision-making intersects with outcomes (Girard, 2021). The observations provided by individuals help construct a narrative based on the state of intoxication, shedding light on the sequence of events leading up to significant choices, such as operating a motor vehicle or unsteadily navigating a pedestrian pathway.

In forensic investigation, the study of alcohol is not solely a scientific pursuit but rather a critical intersection where the fields of science and law converge. The diverse nature of toxicology is evident in its ability to traverse the complex interplay between human decision-making and societal safety (Bitzer et al., 2019). Like a focused beam of light piercing through a foggy atmosphere, alcohol analysis reveals enlightening insights, providing a lucid perspective on instances of impaired cognitive faculties.

In criminal investigations characterized by concealed truths and unresolved enigmas, poison emerges as a covert and pernicious force capable of devastating consequences for individuals. In this context, toxicologists become key players utilizing their specialized knowledge to expose these hidden threats (Trisnadi, 2021). The scientific approach to justice becomes apparent through the alignment of various poison detection methods, providing a method to expose criminal activities that thrive in clandestine environments.

In instances involving accusations of poisoning, the function of toxicological screening manifests as an unwavering pursuit of truth. Professionals undertake a rigorous exploration, deciphering the complex chemical composition present in biological specimens. In this intricate procedure, the cellular domains are assayed to identify and isolate potentially harmful compounds that could provide crucial insights into the cause of a patient's ailment or fatality. The essence of this undertaking lies in applying laboratory techniques and incorporating the skill of discernment. Through the process of deciphering chemical fingerprints, toxicologists possess the ability to uncover the existence of harmful substances. Equally significant is their ability to determine the extent to which these substances are involved in the incident under investigation. These findings act as beacons, revealing the covert pathways through which toxic substances infiltrate an individual's physiological framework.

The ramifications of poison detection extend beyond the confines of laboratory settings, permeating the realms of legal and medical domains. The correlation between science and reality becomes apparent when toxicologists' discoveries influence medical interventions and the provision of treatment for patients. Toxicologists play a vital role in cases involving poisoning, acting as essential collaborators for medical practitioners by facilitating the connection between analysis and practical therapy. The insights provided by toxicologists into the identification and potency of toxins enable health-care providers to make well-informed decisions that have the potential to save lives.

In essence, poison detection serves a twofold purpose, extending beyond legal considerations to encompass the protection of public health. It is a crucial mechanism for shielding people against poison's insidious harm. Toxicologist's diligent efforts go beyond evidence analysis, encompassing the domain of medical intervention and creating a close collaboration with health-care providers (Trisnadi, 2021). Toxicologists play a crucial role in unraveling the complex web of chemical interactions, significantly contributing to lifesaving medical decisions.

The scientific sector has undergone a significant metamorphosis in the intricate domain of poison detection, adopting a pivotal role as an essential information source for medical practitioners and legal authorities. The far-reaching impact of toxicology is evident as it delves into the most harmful areas to unearth factual information and aid in the recovery and renewal of individuals. The process of poison detection exemplifies the persistent pursuit of scientific investigation, demonstrating the capability to reveal the truth even in the most intricate and formidable situations.

Toxicology screening extends beyond the restricted boundaries of laboratory environments, embarking on a far-reaching exploration of the intricacy's endemic in human biology. This approach explores the intrinsic characteristics of decision-making and behavior, elucidating the enduring impacts of drugs on human psychology (Jung, 2009). This scientific endeavor transforms into a portal that provides momentary insights into the experiences, choices, and journeys humans undertake.

Toxicologists employ various methodologies and tools to analyze the molecular compositions of organisms, revealing hidden chemical interactions. This endeavor encompasses more than just examining chemical substances. It represents a harmonious integration of scientific inquiry and an understanding of human interactions with substances. Examining an individual's choices and connection with the environment contributes to a more complete understanding of intricate behaviors and actions.

Technological progress has resulted in the expansion of toxicology's capacities, thereby uncovering previously inaccessible evidence. These findings have a wide-ranging impact, influencing both personal experiences and large-scale legal proceedings. The revelations unveiled through the field of toxicology possess significant ramifications for the realm of criminal investigations, contributing to the accurate administration of justice.

Toxicology screening is more than a mere scientific compass; it is a fundamental reference point for ensuring accountability and promoting public safety. The insights it provides help protect the integrity of the social structure by revealing hidden realities. As the toxicology field advances, it influences the discourse around criminal science, ensuring that individuals' decisions and behaviors are documented accurately within legal systems.

Notably, toxicology screening is a crucial component of criminal science, as it significantly contributes to crime prevention, investigation, and resolution. Detecting drugs, poisons, and alcohol in biological samples yields crucial insights into suspect's physiological responses, thus contributing to preventing substance-related incidents (Roux et al., 2022). During investigations, there may be evidence indicating the presence of intoxication, drug overdose, or poisoning. Such evidence can be essential in establishing motives and determining responsibility. Furthermore, toxicological screening plays a critical role in assisting law enforcement agencies in fighting substance-related crimes. Providing tangible evidence of substance usage empowers authorities to take effective legal action against those involved in such activities (Bell, 2019). This field of study enhances the capacity to interpret underlying intentions, reconstruct past occurrences, and safeguard community well-being.

Digital Forensics: Investigating Cyber- and Electronic Crimes

Digital forensics has emerged as a distinct domain within modern criminal science. This field of study focuses on recovering, preserving, and analyzing electronic information found within the digital domains of computers, cell phones, and other devices. As the level of global interconnectedness intensifies, the significance of digital evidence transforms from a collection of binary data into a crucial and influential factor (Waltke et al., 2018). This phenomenon plays a key role in preventing, investigating, and combating crime, surpassing its dualistic inception to construct a multifaceted account of veracity within the intricate framework of contemporary criminal terrain.

Within the complex network of digital devices, the data recovery process presents itself as a demanding undertaking combining scientific precision and creative skill. Proficient digital forensics professionals possess a repertoire of specialized tools and methodologies to recover seemingly irretrievable data fragments that have been erased, encrypted, or tampered with (Tully et al., 2020). These small data fragments are valuable, revealing crucial evidence such as transactions, communications, and exchanges that offer insight into the thought processes of suspects.

The pursuit of data recovery is akin to restoring lost digital information. Digital forensic specialists carefully navigate the digital environment during this procedure, following faint traces and concealed pathways. These pathways, resembling digital traces, encompass the digital footprints of various interactions, whether explicit or concealed (Dweikat et al., 2021). Embedded within the complex binary code network, diverse forms of digital content, such as documents, photos, emails, and electronic communication, serve as evidence of the cognitive and affective endeavors of individuals being scrutinized.

The data recovery process might be likened to a digital resurrection, wherein fragmented and lost information is transformed into cohesive narratives. Every component obtained—whether a segment of code or a snippet of text—is an essential element of a larger puzzle, fitting with other pieces to reveal interconnected timelines, actions, and underlying motives (Waltke et al., 2018). The convergence of these digital threads gives rise to a virtual tapestry that intricately weaves together the narrative of the individuals engaged in the complex investigation process.

However, the data recovery process involves more than digital archaeology; it requires a blend of scientific methodologies and intuitive decision-making. Digital forensic professionals navigate through the domains of unprocessed data, utilizing sophisticated technologies to organize and make sense of the chaos (Tully et al., 2020). These fragments are methodically arranged and carefully joined together, akin to bits of a jigsaw puzzle, creating a visual representation of comprehension that serves as evidence of the practitioner's proficiency and the enigmatic nature of the digital realm.

As globalization advances, the digital domain undergoes constant transformation, posing new challenges and opportunities for data recovery. The field of digital forensics is characterized by ongoing adaptation, as tools and procedures are continuously improved to address the evolving nature of the digital landscape. This endeavor is a metaphorical bridge, linking past activities with the current investigative terrain and connecting historical events with contemporary circumstances.

Network analysis serves as a critical tool in the sphere of cybercrime, bringing clarity to the complexities of the digital landscape. Digital forensics professionals act as virtual investigators, combining detectives' skills with technologists' expertise. During their investigation, they delve into the complex structure of interconnections, closely examining network traffic patterns, traces left in logs, and concealed recesses of server data. This expedition represents a harmonious integration of investigative expertise and technological proficiency—a voyage that unravels the digital strands of illicit activities, exposing their origins, vulnerabilities, and strategies.

The network analysis process might be likened to navigating a labyrinth, as one follows a complex path through the sophisticated digital infrastructure. These pathways are formed from the interconnected strands of data packets (Howison et al., 2011). The transient conveyors of data navigate the online environment, bearing the traces of virtual interactions. Network analysts, like contemporary detectives, employ their expertise to decode cryptographic traces left by these data packets, unveiling their sources and carefully tracking their complex routes via virtual channels.

This careful and thorough procedure results in the emergence of intricate patterns, creating a narrative crafted from the encrypted communications of cyber operations. By deciphering these patterns, network analysts acquire valuable knowledge regarding the techniques employed in unauthorized access, the extent of security breaches, and the pathways utilized by cybercriminals to surreptitiously infiltrate computer systems. This wealth of information allows law enforcement to fortify digital strongholds against potential cyberattacks.

Network analysis is a digital tool that closely examines the intricate spaces where illicit activities occur in the virtual realm. Network analysis highlights the ability to shed light on the digital traces left by hackers as they traverse networks, providing insight into their motives and methods. This knowledge acts as a historical account of previous wrongdoings and a strategic plan that law enforcement agencies can use to predict and prevent future attacks.

In criminal science, network analysis plays a crucial role as a safeguard for the digital domain rather than being solely regarded as a tool. It highlights the interdependent nature of science and security, wherein a broad understanding of complex concepts converges with technological expertise to uncover the most obscure aspects of the digital domain.

Within the grasp of many individuals lie vast digital landscapes—microcosms contained within smartphones and mobile devices, teeming with intimate interactions, financial transactions, and immersive involvements. The field of digital forensics encompasses the analysis of handheld devices, wherein skilled specialists conduct thorough investigations to extract and interpret valuable data. The amalgamation of call logs, text messages, Geographic Information System data, and detailed records of application usage intertwine to construct narratives that provide insight into the lives and behaviors of individuals intricately involved in criminal investigations.

From the perspective of analyzing mobile devices, digital forensics professionals assume the role of architects who design timelines resembling a symphony that vividly depict the patterns of communication, movement, and complex connections interwoven within criminal activities (Fukami et al., 2021). Utilizing the proficiency of contemporary cryptographers, intricate details concealed in digital footprints are revealed, wherein every pixel and character plays a role in constructing a depiction of an individual's existence within the digital domain.

The analysis of mobile devices encompasses more than technical aspects; it involves delving into the digital records stored within our portable gadgets. The expanding network of communication channels, including messaging applications, social media platforms, and email services, generates discernible traces that reveal the intricate nature of human interactions (Turvey, 2023). Upon rigorous dissection, these traces unveil intricate threads of intention, interconnections, and actions that hold significant value within the framework of investigative endeavors.

Each instance of a location data marker's ping can be likened to a digital breadcrumb, providing insights into the routes traversed. Similarly, every notification alert can be compared to a melodious note within a symphony of digital interactions. Detectives can transform the abstract and transient characters of virtual lives into concrete narratives through the forensic analysis of mobile devices. This process effectively allows them to navigate the complex circumstances surrounding a crime.

The disclosures encompass more than data points; they offer a contextual understanding that surpasses binary code. Through the analysis of communication patterns and the reconstruction of timelines, experts in digital forensics can reveal people's digital identities, thereby uncovering both the ordinary and the malevolent aspects of their digital presence (Turvey, 2023). This undertaking encompasses more than just data analysis; it involves crafting narratives that unveil the hidden intricacies of human behavior and motivation.

The Role of Forensic Technology in Criminal Justice

The chapter underscores the importance of these forensic technologies in solving crimes, preventing criminal behavior, and shaping legal proceedings. It also addresses their influence on the broader field of criminal justice.

The field of digital forensics extends beyond data analysis, encompassing a complex exploration of the multifaceted landscapes of contemporary society. Within criminal science, it serves as a conduit between the material and immaterial, offering insight into the virtual decisions and behaviors that leave their digital imprints on the digital frontier (Gioe et al., 2020). The field of digital forensics is constantly evolving alongside technological developments. This entity can undergo transformation and adjustment, accompanied by instruments facilitating the revelation of hidden narratives embedded within the digital domain. These narratives can modify investigative processes, bolster judicial proceedings, and strengthen social security.

Digital forensics is a dynamic endeavor that investigates the intricate relationship between human interactions and technology. This field extends beyond electronic and digital boundaries, elucidating the narratives interweaving into the complex choreography of contemporary human existence. It serves as evidence of the interdependent connection among science, technology, and the human condition, exemplifying that the revelation of truth is attainable within the digital realm.

Conclusion

In conclusion, within the complex realm of crime science, forensic technology emerges as a prominent symbol of accuracy and advancement, encompassing ballistics analysis, toxicological screening, and digital forensics. These various aspects provide a framework through which researchers explore the intricate landscape of criminal behavior. Collectively, these tools constitute a formidable arsenal in crime prevention and intervention.

These technologies go beyond basic instruments, guiding law enforcement agencies in navigating intricate mazes and surpassing conventional limitations. To deter criminal activities, individuals in law enforcement employ strategies that involve identifying and disclosing disguised objectives. Additionally, they conduct thorough investigations of incidents, paying attention to detail. Moreover, these professionals oppose unlawful behavior by utilizing the persuasive power of factual evidence. These techniques effectively address emerging difficulties in a constantly changing landscape of criminal activities and technological advancements.

Continuous advancements in various fields of study have resulted in the widespread influence of forensic technology within the realm of justice, significantly shaping courtroom proceedings and policy determinations. Within the overarching framework of criminal science, these technologies serve as protectors of veracity, preserving equity and guaranteeing society's security as it navigates the complexities of human conduct.

References

Aggarwal, A. (2021). Critical analysis of digital forensics in criminal justice. *Supremo Amicus*, 26, 49.

Allen, D. R., & McWhinney, B. C. (2019). Quadrupole time-of-flight mass spectrometry: A paradigm shift in toxicology screening applications. *The Clinical Biochemist Reviews*, 40(3), 135–146.

Alonzo, M., Alder, R., Clancy, L., & Fu, S. (2022). Portable testing techniques for the analysis of drug materials. *Wiley Interdisciplinary Reviews: Forensic Science*, 4(6), e1461.

Alsop, K., Norman, D., Remy, G., Wilson, P., & Williams, M. A. (2021). Quantitative characterization of ballistic cartridge cases from micro-CT. *Forensic Science International*, 326, 110913.

Atlam, H. F., Alenezi, A., Alassafi, M. O., Alshdadi, A. A., & Wills, G. B. (2020). Security, cybercrime, and digital forensics for IoT. *Principles of Internet of Things (IoT) ecosystem: Insight paradigm*, 551–577. Springer.

Bell, S. (2019). *Forensic science: An introduction to scientific and investigative techniques*. CRC Press.

Bitzer, S., Margot, P., & Delémont, O. (2019). Is forensic science worth it? *Policing: A Journal of Policy and Practice*, 13(1), 12–20.

Dweikat, M., Eleyan, D., & Eleyan, A. (2021). Digital forensic tools used in analyzing cybercrime. *Journal of University of Shanghai for Science and Technology*, 23(3), 367–379.

Fraser, J. (2020). *Forensic science: A very short introduction*. Oxford University Press.

Fukami, A., Stoykova, R., & Geradts, Z. (2021). A new model for forensic data extraction from encrypted mobile devices. *Forensic Science International: Digital Investigation*, 38, 1–10.

Gioe, D. V., Goodman, M. S., & Stevens, T. (2020). Intelligence in the cyber era: Evolution or revolution? *Political Science Quarterly*, 135(2), 191–224.

Girard, J. E. (2021). *Criminalistics: Forensic science, crime, and terrorism*. Jones & Bartlett Learning.

Guarnera, L., Giudice, O., Livatino, S., Paratore, A. B., Salici, A., & Battiato, S. (2023). Assessing forensic ballistics three-dimensionally through graphical reconstruction and immersive VR observation. *Multimedia Tools and Applications*, 82(13), 20655–20681.

Gupta, S., & Jain, I. B. (2023). Crime scene investigation and forensic evidence: Forensic analysis and tools. *Journal of Pharmaceutical Negative Results*, 14(2), 3661–3667.

Howison, J., Wiggins, A., & Crowston, K. (2011). Validity issues in the use of social network analysis with digital trace data. *Journal of the Association for Information Systems*, 12(12), 767–797.

Jung, J. R. (2009). *Alcohol, other drugs, and behavior: Psychological research perspectives* (2nd ed.). Sage.

King, W., Wells, W., Katz, C., Maguire, E., & Frank, J. (2013). *Opening the black box of NIBIN: A descriptive process and outcome evaluation of the use of NIBIN and its effects on criminal investigations*. National Institute of Justice.

Li, D. (2006). Ballistics projectile image analysis for firearm identification. *IEEE Transactions on Image Processing*, 15, 2857–2865.

Newland, A., Banks, E., & Halámek, J. (2024). Who shot the bullet? Projectile composition characterization as an evolutionary method for enhancement of ballistics evidence analysis. *ACS Omega*, 9(3), 3342–3348.

Nigrini, M. J. (2020). *Forensic analytics: Methods and techniques for forensic accounting investigations*. Wiley.

Roux, C., Bucht, R., Crispino, F., De Forest, P., Lennard, C., Margot, P., ... & Willis, S. (2022). The Sydney Declaration: Revisiting the essence of forensic science through its fundamental principles. *Forensic Science International*, 332, 111182.

Santhy, D. K. (2023). The role of forensic toxicology in the criminal justice system of India. *International Journal of Law, Policy and Social Review*, 5(1), 42–46.

Trisnadi, S. (2021). The role of forensic medicine in the criminal evidence process. *JPH: Jurnal Pembaharuan Hukum*, 8(3), 455–465.

Tully, G., Cohen, N., Compton, D., Davies, G., Isbell, R., & Watson, T. (2020). Quality standards for digital forensics: Learning from experience in England & Wales. *Forensic Science International: Digital Investigation*, 32, 200905.

Turvey, B. E. (2023). *Forensic victimology: Examining violent crime victims in investigative and legal contexts*. Academic Press.

Young, G. M., & Lurie, I. S. (2022). Recent forensic applications of enhanced chromatographic separation methods. *Journal of Separation Science*, 45(1), 369–381.

Waltke, H., LaPorte, G., Weiss, D., Schwarting, D., Nguyen, M., & Scott, F. (2018). Sexual assault cases: Exploring the importance of non-DNA forensic evidence. *NIJ Journal*, 279, 1–14.

8 Nonlethal Weapons

In the ever-evolving field of criminal science, where the emphasis is on developing novel methodologies, the progression and application of non-lethal weapons represent a crucial advancement in law enforcement tactics. The implementation of non-lethal weapons has instigated a significant transformation, fundamentally reshaping strategies for upholding public safety and managing criminal occurrences. This chapter provides a comprehensive analysis of non-lethal weaponry, focusing specifically on two prominent examples: Tasers and rubber bullets. These technologies have garnered extensive attention for efficiently mitigating fatal outcomes and addressing the intricate challenges law enforcement agencies face.

In contemporary society, there is a pressing need for law enforcement to adopt a comprehensive approach that incorporates effective control methods alongside ethical considerations. Given the prevailing emphasis on safeguarding human life and minimizing unnecessary injury, Tasers and rubber bullets have emerged as viable alternatives, uniquely balancing the use of force with the preservation of human rights. This chapter thoroughly examines these two non-lethal technologies' methodologies, applications, arguments, and breakthroughs, providing valuable insights into their intricate contributions to developing contemporary law enforcement tactics. This inquiry emphasizes the critical importance of non-lethal weapons in criminal science by analyzing their operational challenges and appropriate use in various contexts.

Tasers: Conducted Electrical Weapons in Law Enforcement

Tasers, formally known as conducted electrical weapons (CEWs), have become widely accepted tools in law enforcement, providing officers with a more humane approach to controlling potential offenders. Tasers effectively disrupt the neuromuscular system through a controlled electrical stimulus, resulting in temporary incapacitation. This mechanism triggers increased muscle contractions, effectively immobilizing the individual and enabling authorities to assert control without the severe consequences associated with lethal force. The intricate interplay between electrical technology and knowledge of the human body, which forms the foundation of Tasers, represents a sophisticated solution at the intersection of technology and crime science. This technology underscores the critical role of Tasers in enhancing law enforcement strategies while minimizing the risk of serious harm.

Tasers are widely acknowledged as a notable advancement in non-lethal weaponry due to their combination of technological and physiological components. These devices are skillfully designed to deliver a controlled electric shock, temporarily immobilizing individuals. The core mechanism revolves around the interaction between electrical currents and the human nervous system, resulting in temporary paralysis and muscular incapacitation.

DOI: 10.4324/9781003558491-8

The underlying principle of the Taser focuses on two small electrodes connected to a wiring system. The electrodes are methodically and precisely positioned toward the intended target through the device. When the electrodes contact the target's skin or clothing, they establish a connection that facilitates the electrical current to pass through. This electrical circuit, bolstered by the human body's conductive properties, disrupts the normal function of the nervous system.

The nervous system facilitates the transmission of electrical impulses, enabling communication between the central nervous system, specifically the brain, and various muscle groups. When a Taser's electrical current enters the human body, it induces excessive strain on the body's intrinsic communication system, immediately disrupting the signals necessary for orchestrating muscle coordination. As a result, the targeted individual experiences intense involuntary muscular contractions.

The contractions caused by the Taser have a twofold impact. They cause physical incapacitation, hindering the individual's motor and muscular control. Additionally, the application of an electrical current induces sensory overload, triggering a pain response. This situation acts as an additional deterrent against resistance or aggression (Fridman, 2019). The confluence of these factors provides a brief window for law enforcement to apprehend and control the individual without resorting to lethal measures.

It is salient to acknowledge that while Tasers are designed to reduce lethality, their effectiveness can vary depending on circumstances. Several factors can impact a Taser's efficacy in establishing a reliable electrical connection, including the distance between the Taser and its target, the accuracy of electrode placement, and the individual's clothing (Adams & Jennison, 2007). Additionally, the duration of the electric discharge and the specific physiological reaction exhibited by the individual are essential factors when evaluating the degree of impairment. To promote responsible and efficient use, law enforcement personnel undergo comprehensive training to understand these intricacies and employ Tasers effectively while minimizing potential hazards.

Tasers represent a cutting-edge integration of technology and biology, enabling law enforcement to effectively manage and immobilize suspects without resorting to deadly force. The controlled use of electrical currents interferes with the neural pathways responsible for communication within the neurological system, resulting in a transient state of paralysis and pronounced muscular contractions (Fridman, 2019). Tasers demonstrate the potential of non-lethal weapons in contemporary criminal science by harnessing the complex systems of the human body.

Controversies and Concerns of Tasers

Tasers have sparked significant debate within the realm of non-lethal armaments, encompassing their promising prospects and inherent concerns. The use of Tasers is widely accepted as a strategy to reconcile the tension between employing minimal force and preserving life. However, ongoing debates and concerns underscore the necessity for thorough examination and conscientious implementation.

Tasers are often regarded as safer alternatives to conventional firearms in law enforcement. However, labeling Tasers as "less lethal" rather than "non-lethal" reflects an understanding of their potential dangers. Although most instances involving the deployment of Tasers do not lead to fatalities, a notable number of situations have raised concerns. The occurrence of deaths following the deployment of Tasers has sparked discussions regarding the weapon's potential to elicit lethal consequences, questioning the accuracy of its classification.

A primary focal point revolves around the physiological reactions triggered by a Taser's electrical shock. Applying high voltage and current during an electrical shock can elicit various physiological responses, such as an accelerated heart rate, elevated blood pressure, and in some cases, cardiac arrhythmias (Zipes, 2014). In individuals with pre-existing medical conditions, these effects may be intensified, leading to potentially severe outcomes that could endanger their lives.

One significant area of controversy regarding the use of Tasers is the concept of "excited delirium." This contentious and inadequately understood phenomenon is characterized by heightened restlessness, discomfort, and altered cognitive functioning, frequently accompanied by intense physical activity (Feeney et al., 2010). Although there is a correlation between Taser deployments and increased risk of sudden death, the precise relationship between the two factors remains unclear.

Critics contend that the application of an electrical shock through a Taser can intensify the physiological stress already evident in cases of excited delirium, potentially tipping the equilibrium toward a deadly outcome. This apprehension is amplified by the observation that a significant number of fatalities are probably linked to the use of Tasers involving individuals displaying signs of agitated delirium (Feeney et al., 2010). Understanding the intricate interplay between the use of Tasers and the occurrence of excited delirium poses a significant and urgent challenge for both law enforcement entities and medical scholars.

Another aspect of the contentious discourse surrounding Tasers pertains to the potential for their improper utilization by law enforcement personnel. Instances of inappropriate or excessive use of Tasers have been documented, resulting in unwarranted harm or even death. The potential for overuse of Tasers may be inadvertently heightened due to the ease of their deployment, potentially leading to their application in instances where alternative de-escalation strategies would be more appropriate. This raises questions regarding the accountability of law enforcement personnel and the established procedures governing the use of Tasers. In promoting responsible usage, it is imperative to establish clear protocols and provide thorough training to ensure the limited and appropriate deployment of Tasers, particularly when alternative methods are deemed insufficient.

Considering these concerns, scholars and law enforcement entities are actively engaged in a comprehensive effort to enhance understanding of the physiological and psychological impacts of Tasers. Systematic scientific investigations are currently underway to evaluate the potential hazards related to the deployment of Tasers, its effects on various demographic cohorts, and the potential connections between Taser discharges and subsequent medical issues.

Regulation and policy development are crucial in addressing the controversies surrounding Tasers. Achieving an optimal balance between equipping law enforcement personnel with adequate resources and protecting the civil liberties of individuals necessitates the careful formulation of comprehensive guidelines and regulations. One potential strategy to enhance the responsible use of Tasers is incorporating medical knowledge into law enforcement training, thereby fostering an inclusive understanding and effective management of the associated hazards.

In summary, although Tasers offer a groundbreaking alternative to lethal force within law enforcement, their adoption is not devoid of substantial controversy. The complex interaction between Taser-induced electrical shocks and human physiology, coupled with the challenges presented by excited delirium and improper use, has prompted a collective effort to comprehend their effects and establish suitable protocols for their application. Ongoing research, discussions, and regulatory efforts exemplify a dynamic environment in which criminal science consistently adapts to advancing knowledge, aiming for the prudent and efficient utilization of non-lethal technology to promote public safety.

Training and Guidelines for Using Tasers

Within the complex realm of law enforcement, where maintaining a delicate balance between control and compassion is paramount, the appropriate utilization of Tasers necessitates more than a rudimentary understanding of their operational mechanisms. The responsible employment of Tasers is supported by comprehensive training programs and precisely established guidelines, which are fundamental in ensuring public safety while upholding human rights and well-being.

Law enforcement agencies globally acknowledge the efficacy of Tasers, contingent on the proficiency demonstrated by the officers using these devices. Training programs are salient in guaranteeing the correct utilization of these non-lethal weapons. These programs equip officers with the knowledge, skills, and judgment needed for effective Taser deployment.

The commencement of training involves acquiring a comprehensive understanding of the physiological systems that serve as the foundation for the operation of a Taser. Researchers continue to investigate the intricate relationship between electrical currents and the human nervous system to enhance their understanding of how the weapon effectively generates temporary incapacitation. This knowledge enables law enforcement agents to grasp the probable consequences of deploying a Taser and its impact on individuals' physical well-being.

Although Tasers can be highly effective instruments for de-escalating hazardous situations, their utilization requires a thorough assessment of the prevailing circumstances. It is imperative that police officers thoroughly assess the situation before deploying a Taser. Law enforcement officers need to evaluate various criteria, including the degree of danger presented by the subject, the presence of bystanders and the feasibility of employing less aggressive methods.

The notion of de-escalation is fundamental to this approach, and law enforcement officers are trained to prioritize tactical strategies that minimize confrontations and prevent the unnecessary application of force. De-escalation procedures involve effective communication strategies, establishing a safe physical distance, and implementing vocal commands to gain compliance (Todak & James, 2018). These tactics attenuate the probability of necessitating the use of Tasers and facilitate the cultivation of trust between law enforcement and the community.

Taser training encompasses more than just acquiring technical proficiency; it also delves into the ethical components that underlie the goal of law enforcement. It is strongly recommended that law enforcement officials view Tasers as tools to be employed solely after exhausting all other available techniques of control (Dymond, 2020). This philosophical viewpoint aligns with the principle of proportionality, ensuring that the degree of force used is directly proportional to the level of danger posed.

Furthermore, training programs place substantial emphasis on safeguarding human rights in all interactions. Law enforcement personnel are instructed to uphold dignity and respect for all individuals, irrespective of the prevailing conditions. This commitment to preserving human rights underscores the broader societal responsibility of law enforcement in their engagements with the general population.

Precise and unambiguous directives guide law enforcement personnel as they navigate the many aspects of employing Tasers. The present recommendations aim to clarify the specific circumstances in which Tasers may be utilized, delineating the criteria that justify their deployment. An exhaustive assessment of various factors shapes the multifaceted process through which law enforcement agents make decisions. These include the level of resistance exhibited by individuals, the existence of weapons, and the officer's perception of being endangered.

Moreover, established protocols mandate officers to issue verbal warnings before the deployment of a Taser, allowing the subject to comply with instructions before resorting to the use of force. The significance of precise aiming to ensure appropriate electrode attachment is also underscored, as this factor dramatically influences the effectiveness of the Taser.

Post-deployment measures are crucial for the responsible use of Tasers. Law enforcement officers are trained to ensure that individuals exposed to Taser shocks are promptly provided with necessary medical care. This entails requesting the presence of health-care professionals at the scene to evaluate the individual's condition and administer any required medical attention (Parker, 2021). The correlation between the use of Tasers and potential physiological consequences highlights the need for immediate medical assessment to minimize any unanticipated repercussions. Furthermore, the importance of transparency is emphasized in the documentation process that ensues after the deployment of a Taser. The significance of precise and comprehensive reports cannot be overstated when evaluating the circumstances surrounding an incident, assessing the suitability of Taser deployment, and suggesting potential areas for improvement in subsequent occurrences (Parker, 2021).

Rubber Bullets: Kinetic Impact Projectiles for Crowd Control

Among the options available, rubber bullets—classified as kinetic impact projectiles—have emerged as a prominent choice for managing crowds and dispersing riots due to their ability to minimize the risk of causing fatal injuries (Demir et al., 2022). This section thoroughly analyzes rubber bullets, exploring the underlying mechanics that govern their functioning, the careful balance required between force and safety, and ongoing technological advancements aimed at improving their effectiveness. In the dynamic field of criminal science, the exploration of rubber bullets exemplifies the diligent endeavor to strike a balance between authority involvement and the protection of fundamental human rights.

The complexity of rubber bullets lies in their carefully formulated composition and design, which are precisely manufactured to optimize the utilization of kinetic force while mitigating the potential for severe injury. Rubber bullets derive their name from their composition, which primarily consists of rubber or similar elastic materials. This characteristic sets them apart significantly from traditional weaponry. This section explores the intricate complexities inherent in the composition and design of rubber bullets, elucidating a nuanced interaction between force, impact, and safety that defines their fundamental purpose.

The selection of rubber or elastic materials demonstrates resourcefulness in developing non-lethal weaponry. Unlike conventional weaponry designed to penetrate targets, rubber bullets are specifically designed to incapacitate by inflicting blunt force injuries through targeted deployment (Grocholski et al., 2022). This fundamental difference highlights the commitment to reducing life-threatening harm while efficiently managing circumstances that require prompt attention.

The composition of rubber bullets requires a delicate balance between force and safety, which is essential in this context. The intrinsic property of rubber's elasticity allows it to effectively absorb and distribute energy on contact, minimizing the risk of localized impacts that may lead to serious injury (Mahajna et al., 2002). This design concept aligns with the principles of non-lethal weaponry, as it aims to achieve incapacitation while minimizing loss of life. A critical aspect of the architectural design of rubber bullets is the surface area equation. Distributing force across a wider surface area significantly decreases the likelihood of severe injuries, including fractures or internal trauma. This carefully devised engineering approach aims to achieve an ideal equilibrium, guaranteeing the immobilization of the target while minimizing the potential risks typically associated with conventional armaments.

The trajectory of a rubber bullet commences with its propulsion at carefully calibrated velocities, ensuring the acquisition of optimal kinetic energy. This kinetic energy is the driving force that propels the bullet toward its target. The amalgamation of velocity and kinetic energy confers rubber bullets with the requisite force for efficient immobilization, guaranteeing their efficacy as instruments of regulated confinement.

When a rubber bullet strikes its target, its kinetic energy is dynamically transferred to the recipient's body. This transfer elicits physiological reactions, including blunt force trauma and pain sensations reverberating throughout the recipient's body. This powerful combination disturbs the body's homeostasis, leading to physiological responses that extend beyond simple discomfort and deter subsequent resistance or aggressive conduct.

The interaction between a rubber bullet and the human body triggers a series of physiological responses. The sudden impact of the bullet, accompanied by subsequent physical discomfort, generates a profound sensory experience. This experience elicits a swift reflexive reaction, prompting the individual to reassess their behavior and contemplate further acts of resistance or hostility.

The effectiveness of rubber bullets in a tactical context is contingent on their capacity to elicit a response that discourages the escalation of a situation. The immobilization and pain following an impact provide a critical window for law enforcement personnel to establish control over a situation, thereby avoiding the need to employ fatal force. This calculated strategy aligns with the ethical foundations of non-lethal weaponry, ensuring a deliberate and thoughtful reaction that emphasizes the protection of human rights and the well-being of the general population.

The efficacy of rubber bullets is contingent on a complex interaction of several factors that influence their effects. Several key elements contribute to the outcome of a projectile's trajectory, including firing distance, angle of impact, and precise type of ammunition utilized (Mattijssen & Kerkhoff, 2016). Law enforcement authorities must carefully evaluate these elements to ensure that the impact is powerful enough to achieve its intended objectives while being sufficiently regulated to protect the welfare of all individuals involved.

Overall, the impact dynamics of rubber bullets represent a complex interplay of several physical and physiological variables. The intricate relationship among velocity, energy transfer, and reactive responses highlights the skillful nature of non-lethal crowd management techniques (Mattijssen & Kerkhoff, 2016). The field of impact science embodies the fundamental principles of crime science, grappling with the delicate equilibrium between governmental authority and the protection of human rights. It also navigates the balance between tactical imperatives and ethical considerations.

The Dilemma of Crowd Control

Managing crowds is a significant and complex issue that requires careful navigation between the need for intervention and the preservation of individual rights. Rubber bullets, presented as a non-lethal option, demonstrate law enforcement's dedication to minimizing harm while maintaining societal order. However, using these tools exposes a complex web of ethical challenges and practical issues.

The ethical considerations surrounding the use of rubber bullets are complex and varied. The concept of proportionality, which highlights the relationship between the magnitude of force utilized and the magnitude of the threat presented, holds significant importance. Law enforcement organizations have a vital responsibility to maintain societal order while protecting fundamental human rights. There is a necessity for a balanced approach that effectively deters aggression while minimizing the infliction of unnecessary harm. This need arises from rubber bullets' potential to cause pain and injury.

In the dynamic realm of crowd management, maintaining a delicate balance between prompt intervention and avoiding undue force represents an ongoing challenge. Rubber bullets are intentionally designed to represent a compromise, aiming to disable someone without causing fatal consequences (Baker, 2020). This deliberate compromise reflects the adaptation of ethical norms within contemporary law enforcement, serving as evidence of the recognition that protecting human life is of utmost importance.

Achieving a balanced state in this context depends on carefully formulating procedures that govern the use of rubber bullets. The protocols implemented in this context adopt a hierarchical strategy for using force, emphasizing de-escalation whenever possible (Manhas et al., 2021). Incorporating rubber bullets in the equation necessitates a thorough assessment, considering various factors, such as the threat level, crowd size, and the viability of alternative approaches.

Integrating rubber bullets into a hierarchical force framework establishes a systematic approach for controlled and proportionate responses. Under this paradigm, law enforcement officers are required to utilize non-lethal measures to their fullest extent before resorting to more severe levels of force. Rubber projectiles fit within this conceptual framework, providing a compromise between the use of verbal communication and lethal armaments.

The effectiveness of these protocols relies on the competence of well-trained officers. Training programs help individuals refine their judgment and skills. Law enforcement officers participate in simulated training exercises and scenario-based simulations that resemble real-life events. This immersive training equips individuals with the skills required to assess the dynamics of a situation, determine the appropriate degrees of force, and effectively maintain situational awareness in chaotic circumstances.

Rubber bullets present inherent dangers, necessitating a rigorous approach to risk mitigation. Discharging rubber bullets indiscriminately or intentionally aiming at vulnerable areas can convert a less-lethal alternative into a source of significant harm (Grocholski et al., 2022). Mitigating unforeseen outcomes is crucial for safeguarding lives while maintaining control.

Agencies emphasize the importance of targeting lower body regions to minimize the risk of serious injury. Selective targeting techniques reduce the potential for life-threatening harm while concurrently achieving a high degree of incapacitation for the targeted subject. The primary objective is to immobilize while minimizing the risk to vital organs and avoiding long-term harm by focusing on the lower extremities.

The notion of safety encompasses the fundamental action of firing. Maintaining a safe distance ensures the projectile's impact remains within the prescribed parameters. Moreover, strict adherence to guidelines on impact angle can prevent ricochets or other unexpected consequences.

Evolving Technologies in Non-Lethal Weapons

The evolving field of crowd control is influenced by advancing technology that consistently alters the realm of non-lethal weapons. The pursuit of accuracy, effectiveness, and ethical implementation drives the advancement of rubber bullets, elevating them from basic tools to refined devices of regulated impact. This section explores technological advancements that enhance the effectiveness of rubber bullets while adhering to the principles of responsible law enforcement.

Precision is paramount in crowd management, and current technological advancements aim to enhance it. These advancements are evident in the development of increasingly complex and accurate rubber bullet designs. The primary goal is to optimize precision while minimizing the risk of unforeseen negative consequences.

The utilization of advanced materials and aerodynamic designs is at the forefront of this pursuit. Incorporating advanced materials improves the aerodynamic stability of rubber bullets during their trajectory, minimizing deviations from their intended path. The increased stability ensures the projectiles remain on their planned route, maximizing the likelihood of accurately hitting designated targets.

The enhancement of rubber bullet aerodynamics exemplifies the integration of technology and precision. These advances improve the tool's efficacy in delivering precise immobilization by maintaining impact velocity and minimizing variations. The importance of this accomplishment goes beyond its tactical effectiveness, as it demonstrates a commitment to mitigating any unexpected repercussions that may arise from errant trajectories.

The pursuit of technical advancement also focuses on the effects of rubber bullets upon impact. Emerging technologies are currently investigating the concept of impact force modulation, which holds the potential to enhance control and proportionality in using force.

Consider a hypothetical case in which the magnitude of force applied by a rubber bullet can be adjusted based on the specific demands of the circumstances. Law enforcement agencies can enhance their response control by modifying the impact force to align with the perceived threat level. This nuanced strategy demonstrates a commitment to mitigating negative consequences while optimizing efficacy.

The incorporation of impact force modulation exemplifies the application of proportionality in technology. It is recognized that every circumstance possesses its distinct characteristics, necessitating the calibration of force levels accordingly. This technology surpasses the dichotomous nature of lethal or non-lethal options, offering a range of responses that reflect the complexities of real-world situations.

The development of rubber bullets reflects a broader trend characterized by the seamless incorporation of non-lethal technologies into the arsenal of law enforcement agencies. The advent of diverse and supplementary instruments, encompassing sophisticated tasers and chemical irritants, heralds a period characterized by adaptable and varied approaches. The incorporation of less-lethal technologies recognizes the multifaceted nature of crowd management. The dynamics inherent in each situation exhibit distinct characteristics, necessitating a range of solutions that can be customized to align with the specific conditions. The integration of these technologies facilitates the ability of law enforcement personnel to effectively and accurately address a particular situation by utilizing the most suitable de-escalation strategies.

The incorporation of less-lethal technologies exemplifies the flexibility demonstrated by contemporary law enforcement. This statement reflects an awareness of the rapid evolution of crowd dynamics, which necessitates a similarly adaptable response. By adopting adaptable strategies, organizations can effectively address the dynamic characteristics of collective conduct, reducing the likelihood of escalation. In essence, the transformation of rubber bullets, characterized by enhanced precision, modulation, and integration, mirrors the relentless advancement of technology within law enforcement. These advances go beyond simple technical improvements; they embody a commitment to ethical law enforcement and the protection of human rights (Tumbarska, 2021). Technological advancements in rubber bullets symbolize responsible crowd management, representing a significant aspect of the continuous narrative surrounding the integration of effectiveness, ethical considerations, and the overall welfare of society within the field of crime science.

Conclusion

In conclusion, integrating non-lethal weapons, such as Tasers and rubber bullets, into the inventory of law enforcement agencies reflects an ongoing effort to balance public safety with ethical considerations. These technologies are significant reminders of crime science's dynamic progress in seeking innovative solutions for complex challenges. The intersection of technology and research highlights the crucial importance of law enforcement agencies maintaining vigilance and improving their procedures in tandem with innovations while continually adhering to the principles of prudent and effective use of non-lethal weapons. This symbiotic approach serves as a protective measure against criminal behavior and exemplifies a long-standing commitment to preserving human lives and upholding the fundamental principles of a civilized society.

References

Adams, K., & Jennison, V. (2007). What we do not know about police use of Tasers. *Policing: An International Journal of Police Strategies & Management*, 30(3), 447–465.

Baker, D. (2020). Public order policing approaches to minimize crowd confrontation during disputes and protests in Australia. *Policing: A Journal of Policy and Practice*, 14(4), 995–1014.

Demir, E. E., Tekiner, M. A., & Turan, A. A. I. (2022). The role of non-lethal weapons in public security. *Journal of Criminal Law & Criminology*, 60, 59–75.

Dymond, A. (2020). Towards a socio-technical understanding of discretion: A case study of Taser and police use of force. *Policing and Society*, 30(9), 998–1012.

Feeney, C., Vu, J., & Ani, C. (2010). Acute agitated delirious state associated with Taser exposure. *Journal of the National Medical Association*, 102(12), 1254–1257.

Fridman, O. (2019). *Enemy civilian casualties: Politics, culture, and technology.* Rowman & Littlefield.

Grocholski, K. R., Savitz, S., Wong, J. P., Litterer, S., Khan, R., & Cooper, M. (2022). *How to effectively assess the impact of non-lethal weapons as intermediate force capabilities.* RAND. https://apps.dtic.mil/sti/trecms/pdf/AD1156849.pdf.

Mahajna, A., Aboud, N., Harbaji, I., Agbaria, A., Lankovsky, Z., Michaelson, M., ... & Krausz, M. M. (2002). Blunt and penetrating injuries caused by rubber bullets during the Israeli-Arab conflict in October, 2000: A retrospective study. *The Lancet*, 359(9320), 1795–1800.

Manhas, N. S., Stahl, D., Schellenberg, M., & Gholamrezanezhad, A. (2021). Non-lethal weapon: Injury patterns and imaging correlates for firearm alternatives. *Clinical Imaging*, 79, 165–172.

Mattijssen, E. J., & Kerkhoff, W. (2016). Bullet trajectory reconstruction—Methods, accuracy and precision. *Forensic Science International*, 262, 204–211.

Parker, C. (2021). The safety of medication in patients who have recently received a Taser shock. *Journal of Psychiatric Intensive Care*, 17(2), 75–78.

Todak, N., & James, L. (2018). A systematic social observation study of police de-escalation tactics. *Police Quarterly*, 21(4), 509–543.

Tumbarska, A. (2021). Development and use of less lethal electroshock weapons in law enforcement. *Security & Future*, 5(3), 102–105.

Zipes, D. P. (2014). Taser electronic control devices can cause cardiac arrest in humans. *Circulation*, 129(1), 101–111.

9 Communication Technologies

Given the dynamic and constantly evolving nature of communication technology, it is critical for law enforcement agencies worldwide in crime prevention and investigation. Secure radios and networks have become crucial for facilitating efficient and confidential information exchange, particularly in crime prevention, investigation, and warfare. These technological advancements are pivotal for ensuring streamlined coordination and enhancing overall effectiveness in reducing crime. This chapter thoroughly examines the critical significance of secure communication technology in law enforcement. It emphasizes the substantial impact of these technologies in preventing criminal actions, solving complex investigations, and improving overall public safety by exploring their varied significance. This is accomplished through case studies, specific instances, and analytical perspectives. This in-depth discussion examines these technologies' development, applications, challenges, and future potential, ultimately illustrating their significance as fundamental elements in law enforcement and public safety.

The Role of Secure Radios and Networks in Law Enforcement

Effective communication is essential for efficient operational processes within the complex ecosystem of contemporary law enforcement. As the complexity of crime continues to increase, the need for seamless information exchange among law enforcement organizations becomes increasingly critical. Secure radios and networks are essential components that underpin this demand (Boateng & Kaiser, 2019). These technological advancements go beyond their utilitarian function, as they facilitate the efficient and secure transmission of information and foster collaboration among diverse entities to combat criminal activity.

The concept of effective communication has consistently played a crucial role in the success of law enforcement operations throughout history. The evolution from basic modes of information transmission to the advanced communication technologies of the present era is characterized by significant advancements. Over time, the transmission of information has evolved from simple oral communication to intricate systems of secure radios and networks, resulting in significant transformations in law enforcement.

In the early stages of law enforcement, officers primarily relied on rudimentary verbal communication and visual cues to coordinate their operations effectively. The effectiveness of this form of communication was limited in range and often hindered by various factors such as geographic separation, auditory interference, and the speed of information transmission (Boateng & Kaiser, 2019). As human civilizations advanced and criminal behaviors grew more complex, the imperative for streamlined and efficient communication became increasingly evident.

The emergence of radio technology in the early 20th century marked a pivotal juncture in law enforcement communication. Analog radio technologies facilitated effective

DOI: 10.4324/9781003558491-9

communication among police officers, extending their operational range and significantly enhancing their ability to coordinate responses to emergencies and criminal incidents (Tymoshenko et al., 2022). However, analog radio systems had their drawbacks. Coverage was often limited, especially in areas characterized by natural obstacles, urban canyons, or isolated rural terrains. Additionally, the vulnerability of analog communications to interception raised concerns about safeguarding confidential data.

The advent of digital communication technology marked a significant shift in law enforcement communication, ushering in a new era. Digital systems introduced numerous advancements that effectively addressed the limitations of analog technology. The integration of encryption capabilities into communication equipment played a crucial role in protecting the confidentiality of sensitive law enforcement data. Encryption has significantly increased the difficulty for unauthorized entities to intercept and decode messages, ensuring the protection of investigative methodologies and sensitive information.

The advent of digital communication technologies has also resulted in significant enhancements in both coverage and audio quality. Compared to analog systems, digital radios, and networks exhibit improved resilience against signal degradation, thus facilitating clear communication for police even in situations marked by interference or background noise (Tymoshenko et al., 2022). Enhancing audio clarity is essential in critical situations where accurate communication is vital for effective decision-making and coordination.

The progression of communication technology in law enforcement peaked with the creation of sophisticated, secure networks that effectively integrate diverse communication channels. These networks facilitate the instantaneous sharing of data, the exchange of multimedia content, and collaboration across multiple authorities and jurisdictions. The transition from conventional radio systems to these interconnected networks signifies a fundamental change in law enforcement's communication strategy, emphasizing the importance of efficiency, security, and collaboration among agencies.

Secure Radios: Enhancing Law Enforcement Communication

Within the complex framework of law enforcement communication, encrypted radios are not merely accessories but also essential tools. With integrated encryption algorithms, these meticulously engineered devices help in confidential and secure speech and data transfer, diligently protecting conversations and data and ensuring that only individuals with proper authority can access and interpret the information. A robust encryption mechanism fosters confidence and enables law enforcement organizations to exchange vital information interception by malicious entities.

In addition to ensuring confidentiality, secure radios are designed to address the persistent issue of communication reliability, which has been a long-standing concern in law enforcement operations. Historically, signal interference and dead zones have posed major challenges to achieving uninterrupted communication, particularly during critical moments. In contemporary times, secure radios have overcome these challenges by integrating advanced technology and innovative approaches. By utilizing specific frequencies and employing sophisticated modulation techniques, these radios can navigate the challenges posed by densely populated urban areas and geographically isolated rural regions. This advancement leads to optimal coverage, ensuring officers stationed in any given area can establish unobstructed and coherent communication channels.

The experience of the New York Police Department (NYPD) serves as a quintessential illustration of the revolutionary impact of secure radio communications. New York City, a major metropolis, frequently faces the complexities of communication congestion and interoperability. In response, the NYPD implemented a strategic initiative to transition from traditional communication systems to more reliable and secure digital radio technologies.

This transition sparked a significant change in the prevailing paradigm, leading to enhanced communication clarity among field officers. Implementing secure digital radio systems has improved the clarity and reliability of police communication, alleviating the previous limitations imposed by communication congestion. When patrolling high-traffic areas or responding to major incidents, officers discovered that they possessed a communication infrastructure that surpassed the constraints of previous systems. Consequently, the NYPD's capacity to address multiple incidents promptly and efficiently was greatly enhanced.

Notably, the NYPD's use of secure digital radio systems exemplifies how technology can transform the operational environment of law enforcement organizations. This transition had broader implications beyond communication, empowering officers to carry out their responsibilities more effectively and efficiently, thereby improving public safety in the bustling urban environment of New York City.

Secure Networks: Improving Data and Intelligence Sharing

The communication landscape within law enforcement has expanded beyond the confines of individual officers and agencies, creating a landscape characterized by extensive interconnectivity. Secure networks are pivotal in facilitating communication beyond geographic and jurisdictional limitations. While secure radios enhance direct contact between officers, secure networks expand this communication, enabling real-time collaboration across multiple agencies and jurisdictions.

The foundation of secure networks is built on creating secure channels that allow data to be exchanged without the risk of unauthorized access. These channels are fortified by implementing sophisticated encryption techniques, ensuring that all shared information is securely contained within a specified group of authorized individuals. This capability is particularly crucial in situations that require prompt information dissemination (Aden, 2020). In instances of significant importance, such as ongoing investigations or emergencies, secure networks serve as a means through which various forms of multimedia information, including photographs and videos, can be efficiently exchanged. This situation streamlines decision-making and coordination of responses, thereby accelerating overall response efforts.

The actual effectiveness of secure networks becomes evident in the context of collaborative activities across various agencies. The complexity of contemporary criminal activities often necessitates acquiring resources and knowledge from multiple institutions, including local, state, and federal law enforcement agencies. Secure networks play a crucial role by facilitating seamless, real-time exchange of information across different institutions. Secure networks have enabled law enforcement officers from diverse backgrounds to collaborate electronically in real time by removing communication barriers.

Within the framework of joint task forces, secure networks significantly enhance the overall effectiveness and efficiency of operations. Effective coordination among multiple authorities is crucial for successfully operating task forces that address specific categories of criminal activities, such as drug- or human trafficking. Secure networks enable this cooperation by establishing a digital platform where information can be consolidated, insights can be exchanged, and strategies can be collaboratively developed. The abundance of information in this environment significantly boosts the effectiveness of task forces in identifying and targeting complex criminal networks, apprehending individuals involved in criminal activities, and mitigating the consequences of such offenses.

By integrating a range of communication modalities, secure networks provide law enforcement agents with an extensive array of tools to facilitate collaboration. Video conferencing helps overcome the challenges of geographical distances, enabling real-time visual and auditory communication that simulates face-to-face encounters, thus bridging physical gaps. Instant messaging services serve as efficient tools for facilitating rapid exchanges of information that surpass the speed constraints imposed by conventional modes of communication (Laufs et al., 2020). Shared databases establish repositories containing vital information, which can be promptly accessed by authorized individuals, thereby enhancing situational awareness and informed decision-making.

Joint task forces, which bring together various military branches or agencies, focus on specific criminal activities such as drug- or human trafficking. These task forces involve collaboration among numerous local, state, and federal authorities (Mulcahy, 2023). Implementing secure networks has facilitated the seamless exchange of information across different agencies, augmenting their capacity to consolidate resources, target criminal networks, and apprehend offenders more effectively.

Overcoming Communication Barriers through Interoperability

The lack of compatibility across different communication platforms frequently impedes effective coordination among several agencies. Various entities' use of disparate technology infrastructures can result in communication disruptions and delays, particularly during collaborative processes that require seamless information sharing. Considering this challenge, the emergence of secure communication technologies promotes unity by offering standardized protocols and interfaces that bridge gaps and foster collaboration.

The primary obstacle to achieving interoperability lies in communication systems' segmented and isolated characteristics. Law enforcement agencies, characterized by their distinct instruments and technologies, operate within their respective domains. Adopting an insular strategy can engender fragmentation, restricting crucial information within the system of a particular organization. In critical situations where prompt reaction and synchronized efforts are of utmost importance, fragmentation can cause inefficiencies, thus jeopardizing the efficacy of law enforcement operations.

Secure communication systems facilitate effective collaboration across agencies by establishing shared communication standards that transcend organizational boundaries. These standards act as a universal communication tool, enabling the seamless exchange of information between various systems. This situation effectively eliminates obstacles that hinder collaborative efforts. Law enforcement agencies can overcome previous barriers to real-time information exchange by adopting standard protocols and interfaces (Laufs et al., 2020). The endeavor to build interoperable communication channels has driven the development of integrated communication networks. These networks are collaborative platforms facilitating information sharing among multiple agencies, regardless of technological differences. The integration of secure radios and networks in these environments facilitates seamless collaboration, enabling officers from several agencies to communicate as though they were operating within a cohesive system.

The National Capital Region Wireless Network (NCRWIN) initiative exemplifies the significant influence of interoperability in enabling transformative processes. The primary objective of this project was to surmount jurisdictional boundaries by creating a unified communication network linking various law enforcement agencies across the metropolitan area of Washington, D.C. The NCRWIN program was to address the widespread issue of agencies using fragmented communication systems. Implementing a collective communication infrastructure enables organizations to establish direct communication channels during emergencies and critical events. The effective dissemination of information allows seamless coordination, enabling law enforcement officials from multiple jurisdictions to collaborate in real time, thereby enhancing the region's ability to navigate complex scenarios efficiently. The NCRWIN project underscores the significance of interoperability in improving law enforcement capabilities. The initiative aims to create a cohesive environment by eliminating agency boundaries. This unified front fosters collaboration, supports informed decision-making, and ensures synchronized responses. Consequently, the challenges of divergent communication systems are successfully surmounted, thus facilitating a cohesive and determined approach to public safety and crime prevention.

Situational Awareness and Real-Time Decision-Making

Situational awareness transcends ordinary communication and encompasses the utilization of real-time, up-to-date information. Conditions can change rapidly, threats may evolve, and new opportunities might emerge. Facilitating the exchange of information is paramount when navigating this dynamic landscape, necessitating the emergence of communication technology that guarantees confidentiality. These technologies empower law enforcement officers by providing them with real-time situational awareness, which is invaluable in their work.

The empowerment stems from integrating secure communication technologies with tools beyond conventional communication paradigms. Integrating mapping interfaces with Global Positioning System (GPS) tracking generates real-time geographic data, forming a complex interconnected network (Milić & Milidragović, 2021). Utilizing this mosaic enhances location identification accuracy and facilitates the evolving visualization of the environment. Through extensive spatial comprehension, law enforcement personnel can discern crucial locations, monitor movement patterns, and develop tactical approaches that effectively leverage geographic knowledge.

Live video feeds offer direct insight into ongoing operations within this dynamic information ecosystem. Video feeds serve as a medium for law enforcement agents to obtain a firsthand visual perspective beyond the limitations of textual or auditory information (Milić & Milidragović, 2021). By utilizing video feeds transmitted over secure communication channels, law enforcement officials can analyze scenarios effectively, assess potential risks, and arrive at well-informed judgments.

The collective effect of these techniques designed to enhance situational awareness is significant. Law enforcement officers acquire a comprehensive perspective of developing circumstances, encompassing accurate, real-time information. This knowledge enables law enforcement personnel to make well-informed decisions, adapt real-time tactics, and respond effectively to incidents (Joyce & Laverick, 2022). Situational awareness surpasses conventional communication concepts, providing law enforcement officers with cognitive resources to navigate intricate situations, anticipate potential challenges, and capitalize on favorable circumstances.

Challenges and Considerations in Secure Communication Technologies

In the realm of secure communication technologies, characterized by a proliferation of innovation and efficiency, addressing the challenges and considerations that arise is imperative. While these technologies offer significant potential, they also face complexities associated with adoption, operation, and maintenance. As organizations endeavor to leverage their capabilities, numerous obstacles arise, each possessing the capacity to influence the future of secure communication technology.

One of the primary concerns that warrants particular attention is the pervasive threat of cybersecurity risks. Although secure communication technologies are intended to enhance the confidentiality and integrity of information, they remain susceptible to the strategic actions of cyber adversaries. The fundamental challenge lies in ensuring the robustness of communication networks against these attacks. Encryption algorithms, which serve as the foundation for secure communication, must be fortified to withstand ongoing and advanced threats aimed at compromising security measures (Nguyen et al., 2021). Protecting sensitive information from unauthorized access depends on the efficacy of these algorithms, necessitating an ongoing pursuit of innovation to stay ahead of emerging dangers.

In addition to the domain of digital fortifications, a significant obstacle is the financial burden that secure communication technologies can impose on agency budgets. The field of law enforcement is not exempt from fiscal realities. Thorough financial planning is essential for acquiring specialized equipment, implementing system updates to match the evolving technological landscape, and training staff to utilize these technologies. As governmental organizations emphasize the establishment of secure communication technology, they face the challenge of striking a careful balance between technological advancement and financial responsibility.

The susceptibility of law enforcement organizations to cyber threats was underscored by a significant incident, serving as a clear reminder of the potential consequences at hand. In 2019, the Baltimore Police Department experienced a distressing ransomware attack that severely impacted its communication systems (Skertic, 2021). This incident significantly disrupted the department's communication capabilities, degrading its effectiveness at a critical moment. This occurrence highlighted the pressing need for cybersecurity to help ensure a secure communication infrastructure.

The Baltimore incident had far-reaching consequences that extend beyond the scope of a single organization, drawing attention to the broader repercussions of insufficient cybersecurity protocols. This situation underscores that law enforcement organizations are vulnerable to cyber threats. The incident serves as a sobering reminder that the effectiveness of secure communication systems extends beyond encryption; it encompasses the entirety of cyber resilience. Implementing robust cybersecurity protocols is the primary means of safeguarding secure communication channels from potential digital threats.

Organizations adopting secure communication technologies must consider the valuable insights derived from this case study. The Baltimore incident underscores the critical importance of cybersecurity, prompting agencies to strengthen their digital defenses, increase their vigilance, and allocate resources toward a comprehensive strategy that not only harnesses the potential of these technologies but also protects them from digital vulnerabilities.

The Future of Law Enforcement Communication Technologies

In the ever-evolving landscape of secure communication technology, the future holds promising possibilities for groundbreaking innovations that could significantly impact the field of crime science. Continuous technological progress is anticipated to improve secure communication technologies, boost efficiency, introduce preventative measures, and enhance security in law enforcement operations.

Incorporating artificial intelligence (AI) is a crucial aspect of ongoing technological advancement and can profoundly influence communication technologies within law enforcement. Predictive analysis is considered one of the most significant applications of AI. By employing machine learning and data analytics techniques, law enforcement agencies can forecast and detect patterns and trends in criminal behavior (Leese, 2023). This empowers them to take proactive measures to prevent potential threats from materializing. The ability to anticipate future events provides government agencies with a valuable strategic edge, allowing them to transition from reactive measures to proactive initiatives aimed at protecting communities.

Blockchain technology is an emerging innovation that can profoundly transform the existing paradigm of law enforcement. Renowned for generating immutable and tamper-proof records, blockchain technology promises to reshape the dynamics of information transmission and interaction within law enforcement institutions (Dolliver, 2019). Through blockchain technology, authorities can guarantee the integrity and validity of data, thereby mitigating any apprehensions regarding tampering or unauthorized modifications. This technology revolutionizes secure communication by extending its scope beyond confidentiality to include data integrity, a crucial aspect that holds significant relevance in law enforcement.

Advanced biometric authentication systems are emerging as a key component of future secure communication technologies. As these systems develop, ensuring the security of communication channels is of paramount importance. A range of authentication technologies, including facial recognition and fingerprint scanning, help ensure that only authorized users are granted access to secure communication channels (Leese, 2023). Integrating biometrics with secure communication technologies creates a connection between identification and access control, creating an unprecedented level of security.

As technology advances into unexplored domains, law enforcement organizations must act as stewards of accountability. The ethical adoption of these advancements reflects their dedication to upholding societal well-being while embracing technological progress (Ben Farah et al., 2022). In formulating this trajectory, agencies must carefully manage the intricate balance between fostering innovation and upholding the fundamental principles of justice, fairness, and the inviolability of individual rights.

Within secure communication technologies, the future trajectory unfolds as a gradual and escalating musical progression—an ever-increasing harmony of inventive advancements, untapped possibilities, and ethical obligations. As governmental agencies increasingly utilize artificial intelligence, blockchain technology, and advanced biometrics, they are dramatically reshaping criminal science (Bozdag, 2023). In doing so, they configure a future in which technology serves as a tool and a guiding force that shepherds society toward enhanced safety and security.

The complex interaction between secure communication technology and law enforcement gives rise to real-world situations that illuminate the significant influence of these tools in the pursuit of justice. The presented case studies exemplify practical applications, highlighting specific instances where integrating technology and strategic approaches has led to significant outcomes in crime prevention, investigation, and warfare.

The historical records of law enforcement provide evidence of a significant event highlighting the crucial importance of secure communication technologies—the investigation into the devastating 2013 Boston Marathon bombing (LaLone et al., 2020). Following this tragic incident, law enforcement authorities launched a thorough investigation to bring those responsible to justice. At the core of this endeavor was the application of secure communication technologies, which emerged as the digital conduits that interconnected real-time information, photos, and videos.

Establishing secure networks aided the exchange of crucial information and evidence across law enforcement organizations, surpassing geographical and temporal constraints. The rapid identification and subsequent apprehension of the culprits were facilitated by the collaborative nature promoted by these technologies (LaLone et al., 2020). Encrypted communication tools in this high-stakes inquiry had broader implications beyond the investigation, demonstrating the power of technology in challenging circumstances.

The Project Greenlight program in Detroit acts as a platform where innovation and security intersect. This initiative utilized sophisticated video monitoring and secure communication technology to address criminal activities. The project witnessed the active adoption of a forward-thinking strategy by participating businesses, which installed high-definition cameras seamlessly integrated into a secure network. The effort has had a significant impact. Law enforcement agencies have gained the capability to monitor and respond to situations in real-time, transcending the constraints associated with conventional surveillance techniques. The outcome yielded a measurable decrease in criminal activity within the geographical regions encompassed by the project (Circo et al., 2020). The convergence of technology, collaboration, and proactive intervention exemplifies the transformative capabilities of secure communication technologies in reconfiguring urban environments, reinstating security measures, and improving the overall welfare of communities.

The presented case studies provide evidence of the practical and measurable effects of secure communication technology in real-world scenarios. The efficacy of these techniques is evident across a range of domains, including counterterrorism operations and cybercrime investigations. Law enforcement agencies continue to integrate secure communication technologies into their strategies, contributing to the establishment of a safer and more secure society. These technologies, which have emerged from innovative thinking and are utilized with specific objectives, highlight the interconnectedness between human creativity and technological capabilities, ultimately crafting a future in which the effectiveness of secure communication plays a key role in achieving justice.

Ethical and Legal Considerations in Secure Communication

Adopting secure communication technology in law enforcement, encompassing secure radios and networks, presents a multifaceted array of ethical and legal challenges. The key to reconciling the goals of public safety and individual rights lies in carefully considering privacy, transparency, and accountability.

The ethical dilemma agencies face becomes apparent when considering the intricate balance between ensuring public safety and respecting individuals' privacy rights. The effectiveness of secure communication technologies resides in their ability to promote efficient information transmission, thereby enhancing law enforcement authorities' capabilities in preventing and combating criminal activities. Nevertheless, it is crucial to ensure that pursuing these aspirations does not overshadow the ethical obligation to uphold individuals' rights to privacy. Achieving this balance requires establishing clear rules and processes that guarantee the legal interception of communication, reinforced by the principles of due process and judicial oversight.

Establishing unambiguous and well-defined limits on secure communication technology is essential for maintaining ethical standards. Secure communication technology must be underpinned by the unwavering principles of transparency, accountability, and justice (Soroka & Kurkova, 2019). Law enforcement organizations should prioritize the development of protocols that effectively address the legal aspects of intercepting communications, ensuring that these technologies are employed responsibly and according to constitutional protections.

Amid ethical deliberations, establishing public trust is a fundamental element that comes to the forefront. Transparent data management is crucial in fostering and upholding public confidence in law enforcement institutions. The successful deployment of secure communication technologies necessitates a commitment to safeguarding data privacy. This includes establishing protocols that guarantee the proper management, retention, and elimination of confidential data (Karale, 2021). The ethical obligation of effectively managing and safeguarding data is fundamental in a contemporary context characterized by the potential erosion of public confidence due to data breaches.

Exploring secure communication technology goes beyond technological aspects, becoming a moral and legal obligation. Ethical issues are central to responsible deployment that upholds individual privacy rights while fulfilling the obligation to safeguard public safety. The legal aspects of this process underscore the necessity for flexible legislative frameworks that can adapt to the rapidly evolving technological landscape. As law enforcement agencies navigate these challenges, they exemplify the core principles of responsible innovation, strategically mapping out a trajectory that upholds the principles of justice, integrity, and the fundamental rights that form the foundation of a democratic society.

Conclusion

In conclusion, the field of criminal science encompasses a dynamic environment where the narrative surrounding communication technologies serves as evidence of the profound impact of innovation. The utilization of secure radios and networks, which serve as the fundamental components of this discourse, has significantly transformed how information is shared, utilized, and capitalized on by law enforcement entities. Integrating various secure communication technologies facilitates effective coordination, upholds confidentiality principles, and unprecedentedly enhances real-time cooperation.

The continuous advancement of technology has opened new possibilities for the future development of communication in crime science. Law enforcement organizations will incorporate higher levels of creativity, interconnectedness, and efficiency into their communication frameworks and initiatives. In the immediate future, secure communication technologies will take on a prominent position, significantly influencing the trajectory of law enforcement and its ability to prevent, investigate, and mitigate criminal activities. Moreover, secure communication technologies will continue to play a lasting role across temporal and spatial dimensions, aligning human innovation with the pursuit of justice.

References

Aden, H. (2020). Information sharing, secrecy, and trust among law enforcement and secret service institutions in the European Union. *Secrecy in European politics*, 157–178). Routledge.

Ben Farah, M. A., Ukwandu, E., Hindy, H., Brosset, D., Bures, M., Andonovic, I., & Bellekens, X. (2022). Cyber security in the maritime industry: A systematic survey of recent advances and future trends. *Information*, 13(1), 22.

Boateng, F. D., & Kaiser, K. (2019). Trust and confidence in media and criminal justice institutions. *International Journal of Offender Therapy and Comparative Criminology*, 63(12), 2213–2233.

Bozdag, A. A. (2023). AIsmosis and the pas de deux of human-AI interaction: Exploring the communicative dance between society and artificial intelligence. *Online Journal of Communication and Media Technologies*, 13(4), e202340.

Circo, G., Rogers, J. W., McGarrell, E. F., Julie M.Krupa, J. M., De Biasi, A., Liebler, J., Cartwright, S., & Carter, T. (2020). *Project Greenlight Detroit: Evaluation report*. Michigan State University Justice Center.

Dolliver, D. S. (2019). Emerging technologies, law enforcement responses, and national security. *ISJLP: Journal of Law and Policy for the Information Society*, 15(1–2), 123–150.

Joyce, P., & Laverick, W. (2022). *Criminal justice: An introduction*. Routledge.

Karale, A. (2021). The challenges of IoT addressing security, ethics, privacy, and laws. *Internet of Things*, 15, 100420.

LaLone, N., Toups, Z., & Tapia, A. (2020). The structure of citizen bystander offering behaviors immediately after the Boston Marathon bombing. *Proceedings of the 53rd Hawaii International Conference on System Sciences*, 2177–2186. HICSS.

Laufs, J., Borrion, H., & Bradford, B. (2020). Security and the smart city: A systematic review. *Sustainable Cities and Society*, 55, 102023.

Leese, M. (2023). Enacting criminal futures: Data practices and crime prevention. *Policing and Society*, 33(3), 333–347.

Milić, N., & Milidragović, D. (2021). The use of technologies in achieving real-time situational awareness during police intervention. *Archibald Reiss Days* (11).

Mulcahy, D. T. (2023). The use of task forces internationally: Mitigating socio-political risks for law enforcement agencies. *Socio-political risk management: Assessing and managing global insecurity*, 207–222. De Gruyter.

Nguyen, V. L., Lin, P. C., Cheng, B. C., Hwang, R. H., & Lin, Y. D. (2021). Security and privacy for 6G: A survey on prospective technologies and challenges. *IEEE Communications Surveys & Tutorials*, 23(4), 2384–2428.

Skertic, J. (2021). Cybersecurity legislation and ransomware attacks in the United States, 2015–2019 [Doctoral dissertation, Old Dominion University].

Soroka, L., & Kurkova, K. (2019). Artificial intelligence and space technologies: Legal, ethical and technological issues. *Advanced Space Law*, 3(1), 131–139.

Tymoshenko, Y. P., Kozachenko, O. I., Kyslenko, D. P., Horodetska, M. S., Chubata, M. V., & Barhan, S. S. (2022). Latest technologies in criminal investigation (testing of foreign practices in Ukraine). *Amazonia Investiga*, 11(51), 149–160.

10 Vehicle Technologies

Crime science is a dynamic and multidisciplinary field that effectively integrates various strategies, procedures, and technologies to address, analyze, and combat illegal activity. Vehicle technologies have become essential in contemporary law enforcement efforts within the complex realm of crime prevention and investigation. This chapter explores two significant vehicle technologies that have dramatically changed law enforcement: Automatic License Plate Recognition (ALPR) and Global Positioning System (GPS) tracking. By seamlessly integrating diverse strategies and technologies, law enforcement agencies can proficiently trace stolen vehicles, monitor suspicious behaviors, execute pursuit operations, and enhance overall crime prevention and investigation efforts. This chapter highlights the essential roles of ALPR and GPS tracking within the field of crime science by examining their mechanisms, applications, advantages, concerns, and ethical considerations.

Automatic License Plate Recognition: A Breakthrough in Law Enforcement

ALPR represents a significant advancement in visual character interpretation and image processing. The fundamental purpose of ALPR is its inherent ability to extract relevant license plate information from a collection of vehicles. The operational methodology of ALPR systems involves several key components, prominently including high-resolution cameras that accurately capture images of license plates. These images undergo a series of operations in image processing software, during which the alphanumeric characters displayed on the license plates are carefully extracted and analyzed.

The operational process relies on a sophisticated network of technology that integrates various components for efficient functioning. The ALPR ecosystem is strengthened by essential elements, including complex image processing algorithms, data repositories that store extensive license plate information, and a collection of high-quality cameras. The convergence of these factors results in enhanced operational efficiency, positioning ALPR prominently in modern law enforcement implementations. The dominance of this technology arises from its diverse range of applications, including rapid vehicle identification, real-time monitoring, and efficient detection of stolen vehicles and those linked to criminal activities (Hodge, 2020). The following sections elucidate the various intricate aspects of ALPR, including its wide-ranging capabilities, practical applications, inherent benefits, and associated concerns. These discussions will underscore its status as an innovative technology leading to advancement in crime science.

ALPR technology is characterized by the seamless integration of complex components, carefully coordinated to provide law enforcement agencies with a significant advantage in their operations. ALPR systems play a crucial role in automotive surveillance and follow a systematic process involving multiple stages.

DOI: 10.4324/9781003558491-10

The orchestration begins with specialized cameras strategically positioned to capture license plate images from various vehicles. The high-resolution cameras diligently capture and record the intricate details of license plates, preserving a visual representation of the alphanumeric data inscribed. These captured images contain essential vehicle information and are processed within the ALPR technology system.

The ALPR system incorporates advanced software intricately integrated into its architecture, serving as the central processing unit. This software is designed to analyze the collected photos and extract the embedded alphanumeric characters that make up the license plate number through a complex and challenging process. Converting an image into data involves the remarkable abilities of pattern recognition and visual interpretation, performed by software with exceptional proficiency.

The collection of extracted data represents a comprehensive digital representation of vehicle identifications, ready to be compared against databases containing vehicular information. The ALPR system conducts a comparison, demonstrating its ability to accurately detect stolen vehicles, vehicles involved in illegal activities, or vehicles associated with outstanding warrants. The rapid and thorough execution of this iterative process serves as evidence of the complex operational nature that forms the foundation of ALPR capabilities. This empowers law enforcement agencies with a digital toolkit that significantly enhances the landscape of crime prevention and investigation.

One of the critical aspects of ALPR's application is its ability to detect stolen vehicles and those involved in criminal activities quickly. The symbiotic relationship between ALPR technology and law enforcement organizations is particularly evident when a stolen car or a vehicle involved in criminal activities passes by a camera equipped with ALPR capabilities. At this juncture, the ALPR system instigates a series of processes that ultimately lead to prompt and decisive action.

When the ALPR system processes a license plate image, the software employs several algorithms to extract the alphanumeric characters displayed on the plate. The digitized license plate data is then compared against law enforcement databases. In this context, the extracted data are compared against meticulously cataloged documents maintained by law enforcement authorities. The outcome is a rapid comparison, as the ALPR system aims to determine whether the vehicle in question is flagged as stolen or linked to criminal activity.

The consequences of this rapid identification profoundly impact various levels of the law enforcement hierarchy. A real-time alert is sent when a vehicle of interest or concern is detected. Law enforcement personnel are quickly alerted, prompting them to take immediate action, which often results in the successful apprehension of stolen vehicles, the prevention of potential criminal activities, and the limitation of criminals' mobility. The ability to rapidly and automatically detect vehicles significantly strengthens the effectiveness of law enforcement operations, thereby enhancing public safety and providing law enforcement with a tactical advantage.

The significance of ALPR extends beyond conventional identification, encompassing the realm of vehicle tracking. ALPR systems, equipped with advanced high-resolution cameras and intricate algorithms, can effectively integrate various vehicular movement patterns. ALPR technology has become a vital tool in criminal investigations, offering significant advantages for law enforcement. Law enforcement agencies can monitor the paths of vehicles suspected of engaging in criminal behavior, revealing the routes they traverse and the locations they frequently visit. Digital traces are crucial in delineating connections, establishing temporal order, and furnishing substantiation to corroborate or contest alibis. The ALPR system efficiently transforms vehicle movement patterns into a beneficial and instructive asset, thereby assisting in resolving complex criminal cases.

Furthermore, ALPR technology demonstrates proficiency in accurately detecting and monitoring vehicles of concern. Integrating ALPR technology into traffic monitoring and law enforcement has enhanced its role in law enforcement activities. ALPR adopts a proactive stance in this capacity, broadening its purview to monitor vehicle compliance with traffic laws. ALPR systems employ precise optical observation techniques to scan the movement of vehicles, thereby expanding their digital capabilities to acquire license plate data. This network can effectively capture alphanumeric sequences, operating as a digital instrument specifically designed to detect and address vehicle infractions that jeopardize road safety and traffic compliance.

The ALPR system diligently monitors and detects expired registrations, unpaid fines, and other vehicular infractions. The system identifies these violations with a discerning perspective, directing them toward examination and investigation by law enforcement agencies. Implementing automated detection in this context enables the effective administration of road safety, offering law enforcement agencies a streamlined tool for enforcing traffic regulations (Etomi & Onyishi, 2021). ALPR systems play a crucial role in deterrence and enforcement, with strategically positioned ALPR equipment acting as a significant deterrent to potential violators. The recognition that vehicle violations will not escape detection contributes to the development of a compliance-oriented culture, ultimately leading to a safer and more orderly traffic environment.

Advantages and Concerns of ALPR Technology

The incorporation of ALPR technology into the field of law enforcement demonstrates its versatility and potential. Although the use of ALPR provides law enforcement agencies with numerous benefits, it is essential to analyze the associated concerns that arise from its deployment.

One notable attribute of ALPR technology lies in its remarkable efficiency. ALPR systems serve as vigilant and efficient monitors, capable of processing many license plates in real time. This proficiency allows for the rapid identification of suspicious vehicles, such as stolen vehicles, those linked to criminal activity, and those connected to outstanding warrants. It thus helps law enforcement authorities initiate swift, focused, and rapid responses. This efficiency is especially beneficial in situations involving car pursuits, where the real-time capabilities of ALPR are crucial.

The operational mechanics of ALPR systems highlight its non-intrusive characteristics. The system does not require direct interaction with vehicles or their occupants. The process of capturing license plate images occurs smoothly and without the need for interruption or engagement with moving vehicles. This non-intrusive methodology optimizes the data-gathering process and demonstrates consideration for the smooth flow of vehicular traffic, thus minimizing traffic disruptions and augmenting the general public's acceptance of the technology.

Data integration involves combining and consolidating data from multiple sources into a unified and coherent system. ALPR technology exemplifies this concept due to its effective integration with other law enforcement systems, facilitating seamless information sharing and collaboration. The data collected through ALPR systems can be effectively incorporated into broader investigative efforts, resulting in a comprehensive compilation of information that strengthens the overall landscape of crime prevention and investigation (Sánchez-Cambronero et al., 2021). This integration enhances the capabilities of law enforcement organizations by offering them a comprehensive perspective on vehicular movements and patterns. This, in turn, strengthens their ability to make connections, create timelines, and confirm or challenge hypotheses.

While ALPR serves as a crucial tool for law enforcement, its ability to collect extensive license plate data also raises significant privacy concerns related to surveillance. Continuous monitoring of vehicle activities, essential for deterring criminal activities, raises concerns regarding the potential infringement on personal privacy. The challenge lies in striking a balance between using ALPR's functionalities in law enforcement and safeguarding individuals' rights to privacy. This necessitates ensuring that the implementation of this technology complies with ethical and legal standards.

The field of ALPR is susceptible to the unpredictable effects of external variables. Various factors, such as unfavorable weather conditions or challenging lighting circumstances, can obstruct the accurate deciphering of license plate information (Shashirangana et al., 2020). Environmental conditions, such as dust, rain, or glare, can hinder the correct acquisition and subsequent processing of license plate images. Consequently, these factors may result in misinterpretation and errors throughout the identification process. The efficacy of ALPR systems depends on their capacity to overcome these obstacles and deliver reliable information. It is crucial to prioritize this concern through maintenance and calibration of ALPR equipment, ensuring the continued effectiveness of the technology, even when confronted with unfavorable circumstances.

Legal and Ethical Considerations of ALPR

Integrating ALPR technology into the domain of crime science entails a complex interplay of legal and ethical considerations. Due to its notable capacity to augment law enforcement capabilities, a thorough evaluation of the impact of this technology on individual rights and societal norms is essential.

Utilizing ALPR technology requires strict compliance with a complex network of regulatory frameworks, particularly the fundamental principle of Fourth Amendment protections, which secure individuals against unjustifiable searches and seizures (Dattani, 2022). The process frequently involves acquiring appropriate legal authority, such as search warrants or court orders, to conduct surveillance using ALPR technology. Establishing a clear and understandable legal framework acts as a protective measure against the excessive exercise of authority, ensuring that actions remain within the boundaries set by existing legislation.

Ethical considerations surrounding ALPR technology reflect the intricate interplay between crime prevention objectives and individual privacy protection. The technology's capacity to effectively collect and retain substantial amounts of license plate data raises concerns about widespread surveillance and the possible infringement on individual privacy (Dattani, 2022). The ethical discussion revolves around inquiries regarding the scope of data retention, the sharing of data among different entities, and the risk of data misuse. Achieving a balance between leveraging the potential of ALPR technology for law enforcement objectives and safeguarding individual rights necessitates thoughtful, ethical consideration.

Data usage and transparency are fundamental principles in the domain of data-driven technologies. The successful deployment of ALPR technology necessitates the establishment of clear and open policies that outline the specific purposes for how the collected data will be utilized. The level of openness exhibited by authorities includes disseminating information to the public regarding the presence and extent of ALPR systems. This practice alleviates apprehensions and promotes a perception of responsibility and accountability.

Accountability and oversight are critical ethical concerns. Agencies that use ALPR systems must have comprehensive processes for monitoring data access, usage, and storage. Periodic audits and assessments play a crucial role in safeguarding against potential misuse, ensuring that the technology maintains its intended purpose of promoting justice rather than becoming a means of violating rights.

GPS Tracking: Revolutionizing Vehicle Surveillance and Investigation

GPS tracking is a technology that utilizes the GPS to determine the precise location of an object or individual. This technology has gained significant popularity and has been adopted widely in various fields, including crime science. GPS technology has emerged as a powerful force within law enforcement, fundamentally altering the dynamics of tracking vehicles and suspects. The significant importance of this technology in crime science is attributed to its ability to offer real-time tracking and precise location data. This section delves into the complex network that GPS technology has created, revealing its numerous capabilities, wide-ranging applications, benefits, and key considerations. GPS technology is pivotal in law enforcement, as it facilitates vehicle retrieval and augments investigative procedures. This situation underscores the notable correlation between technological advancement and the dedication of law enforcement agencies to upholding justice and safeguarding the well-being of the general population.

The core of GPS technology consists of a complex network of satellites orbiting the Earth, forming a worldwide network essential for precise location tracking. Within this satellite network, strategically positioned GPS receivers embedded in a wide array of devices, including cell phones, vehicles, and specialized tracking units, play a key role in decoding signals (Lawal et al., 2019). The primary function of these devices is to intercept and decipher the signals transmitted by the satellites in orbit, thereby facilitating the complex process of triangulation.

Triangulation serves as the fundamental basis for GPS's operational mechanics. A GPS receiver utilizes the convergence of signals emitted by multiple satellites to perform complex computations, thereby determining the exact coordinates of its location. These computations encompass more than just latitude and longitude; they incorporate altitude values and horizontal and vertical placement dimensions.

However, identifying and specifying a location is only beneficial when the data are placed to practical use. The result of this process is the utilization of location data. The presented data, resembling digital mapping, transforms geographic coordinates into a cohesive depiction of tangible spatial elements (Lawal et al., 2019). These data consist of three fundamental components—latitude, longitude, and altitude—each associated with a temporal reference point in the form of a time stamp, recording the precise moment of data capture.

The subsequent transmission of these data navigates through several communication networks to centralized monitoring systems. These systems provide advanced real-time tracking capabilities, allowing them to process and share location data with relevant entities. This enables a seamless connection between devices in different areas and central command centers. The result is converting location data into practical insights, forming the foundation of law enforcement's monitoring and tracking operations.

The integration of position data from many devices exemplifies the primary goal of GPS, which is to decipher the intricate patterns of movement. The integration and organization of data are essential for implementing GPS in crime science applications. The integration of advanced technology in law enforcement has ushered in a new era characterized by enhanced safety in vehicle pursuits and improved surveillance capabilities to monitor suspects' activities. This comprehensive approach to tracking represents a significant development, as it combines technology with the quest for justice and public safety.

Applications of GPS in Law Enforcement

The consequences of GPS monitoring in the context of vehicle pursuit are significant and far-reaching. This technology has become increasingly essential for law enforcement, as it can fundamentally alter their approach to high-speed pursuits and the retrieval of stolen vehicles. GPS technology facilitates various benefits through its strategic implementation, such as heightened safety during pursuits, improved operational productivity, and preventive measures against criminal activities. Combining GPS technology and law enforcement expertise in the context of vehicle pursuit leads to a significant transformation in tactics and operational strategies. GPS tracking mitigates the risks associated with high-speed pursuits, which can harm law enforcement personnel, individuals being pursued, and innocent bystanders (Verma et al., 2024). Law enforcement agencies can discreetly affix GPS trackers to cars of interest, creating a connection for indirect monitoring.

The implementation of remote monitoring represents a transformative aspect of law enforcement efforts. Law enforcement agencies, equipped with real-time data on the movements of suspect vehicles, acquire an advantageous position surpassing the constraints imposed by geographical boundaries. The necessity for life-threatening high-speed pursuits is attenuated, as law enforcement officials can now monitor and pursue suspects from a safe distance. This prevents potential injuries and enables agencies to develop tactical apprehension methods, reducing the likelihood of escape and enhancing the success rate of pursuits.

The various applications of GPS technology in crime science are particularly evident in suspect surveillance and investigation. Law enforcement agencies utilize this technology to effectively transform vehicles into valuable sources of information, providing unprecedented visibility into the actions and whereabouts of criminals. The operational method employed in this deployment is characterized by its subtle nature, which entails the covert installation of GPS trackers on vehicles owned or operated by individuals under suspicion. This nuanced integration transforms the vehicles of suspicious individuals into channels of information, making them essential for assembling the complex puzzle of illicit actions.

The data obtained via GPS tracking provides an unbiased account of the activities of individuals under investigation. It reveals a comprehensive depiction of the locations visited, routes taken, and interactions, offering a wide-ranging perspective into the lives of suspects that often elude the usual scrutiny of law enforcement. The data obtained are the pivotal point around which law enforcement constructs its legal arguments. Within the field of investigations, the utilization of GPS technology enhances the array of tools available for acquiring evidence. The data produced through GPS tracking technology function as definitive digital evidence, either confirming or refuting the alibis of individuals under investigation (Koops et al., 2018). Accurate chronological and spatial coordinates are vital for challenging suspect narratives and enhancing law enforcement's ability to prove their truthfulness and reliability.

Moreover, the abundance of data plays a crucial role in intricate investigations. It facilitates the formation of linkages, timelines, and relationships. GPS tracking provides valuable information that aids law enforcement in navigating the complex landscape of criminal behavior and uncovering enigmas. Integrating GPS technology into crime science provides law enforcement with essential information for their investigations. This technology enhances efforts to achieve justice and maintain public safety by offering an unparalleled perspective on the intricate interactions between vehicles, suspects, and criminal activities. The close relationship between technology and investigative ingenuity revolutionizes the practice of tracking, monitoring, and analyzing the intricacies of criminal activities.

Advantages and Concerns of GPS Tracking

GPS tracking technology serves as a vigilant tool for providing real-time awareness. The ability of this technology to rapidly transmit location data enables law enforcement to respond promptly and effectively. In a rapidly evolving world marked by criminal incidents, overcoming geographic limitations and promptly reacting becomes paramount. The real-time capabilities of GPS tracking technology can significantly enhance law enforcement organizations' operational efficiency, enabling them to protect the public by responding to emerging threats.

Evidence collection is a crucial aspect of the legal process, and GPS tracking technology has emerged as a valuable tool. The data obtained through this technology hold significant evidentiary value in legal contexts. GPS data are a neutral and supportive instrument in court procedures marked by conflicting narratives. These data are reliable evidence, reinforcing or challenging a defendant's defense (Koops et al., 2018). The comprehensive record formed by the digital imprints of movements captured through GPS tracking enhances the credibility of law enforcement narratives. Using data-driven objectivity in investigations provides a solid basis for establishing the truth, strengthening the reliability of findings.

Using GPS tracking technology significantly mitigates risks in pursuit scenarios and improves the safety of law enforcement officers. The involvement of GPS tracking recalibrates the inherent hazards associated with high-speed pursuits, which pose risks to law enforcement agents, suspects, and innocent bystanders. Law enforcement agencies strategically work toward limiting the need for dangerous activities, orchestrating a decrease in the likelihood of harm. The significant risk reduction can be attributed to the crucial role of technology in promoting public safety, as it effectively mitigates situations that could potentially escalate into fatal outcomes.

The implementation of GPS tracking technology occurs within the parameters of legal frameworks. Adherence to legal principles is not discretionary but rather a necessary obligation. The Fourth Amendment is a significant safeguard against unjustified searches and seizures, emphasizing the importance of obtaining appropriate authority. The deployment of GPS tracking typically requires warrants or legal approvals. This measure guarantees that the GPS technology's powerful capabilities are responsibly utilized while adhering to recognized regulatory frameworks.

The effectiveness of GPS tracking technology is linked closely to its level of precision, which several circumstances can impact. Tall buildings and high activity levels in urban areas can hinder signal reception and affect location accuracy. An urban environment and varied topography also pose challenges in achieving precise tracking (Merry & Bettinger, 2019). These issues are further compounded by intentional signal interference. The endurance of the technology is contingent on its capacity to navigate intricate terrains, making it essential to ensure that precise data form the foundation of its usefulness.

Legal and Ethical Considerations of GPS Tracking

Incorporating GPS tracking technology into crime science creates a domain where technological expertise intersects with personal liberties and societal norms. This convergence creates a complex interplay of legal and ethical factors, necessitating a careful balance to maintain justice, privacy, and transparency.

The cornerstone of GPS tracking in the legal domain is based on the fundamental principle of obtaining appropriate authorization. Law enforcement agencies frequently encounter a complex network of legal procedures, which typically culminate in acquiring warrants or official authorizations for deploying GPS devices. This rigorous procedure ensures that the powerful functionalities of GPS tracking are utilized per legal regulations. The Fourth Amendment serves as a protective measure against unjustifiable searches and seizures, guiding the course of tracking efforts. These legal precautions are not merely bureaucratic obstacles but rather protective measures that firmly establish technology within the framework of individual rights.

Legal considerations regarding technology become increasingly complex as they transcend jurisdictional boundaries. In a globalized society characterized by interconnected information networks, the legality of cross-border tracking presents intricate challenges (Shi, 2020). This situation underscores the importance of international collaboration and adherence to foreign legal systems. The pursuit of justice extends beyond geographic boundaries, requiring the alignment of technology's capabilities with the legal framework that supports its implementation.

GPS tracking falls within the ethical domain, particularly concerning privacy, data utilization, and transparency. Even when conducted for valid law enforcement reasons, the ongoing surveillance of individuals' movements encroaches on the fundamental right to personal privacy. The possibility of excessive governmental authority is a significant concern, raising fears of omnipresent surveillance reminiscent of George Orwell's dystopian vision.

The ethical discourse necessitates the establishment of clear policies and methods that serve as the foundation for obtaining informed consent. Individuals must be provided with comprehensive information regarding the implementation of GPS tracking technology, including its intended objectives and the extent of data acquisition. Transparent policies are crucial in ensuring that individuals fully understand the technology's function, empowering them to make well-informed decisions about their movements and privacy.

The ethical discussion also concerns the duration of data retention. Data collection via GPS monitoring, especially in cases with legitimate law enforcement objectives, must conform to the criteria of necessity and proportionality. Prolonged data storage beyond the necessary scope of an inquiry may infringe on individuals' rights and raise concerns over potential misuse. Additionally, ethical considerations pertain to the responsible management of collected data. Law enforcement authorities are responsible for protecting these valuable data from unlawful access or breaches. Implementing strong cybersecurity measures is paramount, as the data repository may be susceptible to exploitation without rigorous protection.

Conclusion

In conclusion, the amalgamating of ALPR with GPS tracking technologies represents a significant and transformative paradigm shift within the contemporary law enforcement landscape. These advancements in vehicle technology serve as foundational elements within the field of crime science, fundamentally transforming methods of tracking, prevention, and investigation. The combination of ALPR technology's rapid identification of stolen vehicles and those linked to criminal activity enhances law enforcement effectiveness. Additionally, the precise surveillance of suspect movements enabled by GPS tracking contributes to a novel understanding of operational efficiency.

Combining optical character recognition and image processing in ALPR facilitates the expeditious retrieval of license plate data. These advanced technological capabilities not only promote the detection of stolen vehicles but also provide law enforcement with a crucial means of monitoring suspicious activity in real time. Similarly, using satellite constellations in GPS tracking offers unparalleled capabilities for real-time monitoring and precise location determination. GPS tracking has emerged as a crucial tool in crime science, serving many purposes, such as assisting with vehicle recovery and closely monitoring suspects' actions. Its ability to provide precise and agile surveillance has positioned it as critical to ensuring effective law enforcement.

However, ethical and legal considerations arise when incorporating these technologies into law enforcement protocols. While ALPR and GPS tracking systems offer numerous benefits, adopting a cautious approach to safeguard individuals' privacy and rights is crucial. The responsible use of technology necessitates the inclusion of legal frameworks that mandate appropriate authorization for deployment and address ethical issues related to transparency and data utilization.

Consequently, the combined use of ALPR and GPS tracking technology constitutes a powerful alliance in the field of crime science. It equips law enforcement agencies with the means to proactively deter criminal activities, conduct thorough investigations, and protect the general public. The efficacy of these tools extends well beyond the surveillance domain, paving the way for a new era of law enforcement characterized by the harmonious integration of technology and ethics. These tools act as guiding lights by effectively balancing technological advancement and societal norms, illuminating a trajectory where justice and security intersect.

References

Dattani, Y. (2022). Big brother is scanning: The widespread implementation of ALPR technology in America's police forces. *Vanderbilt Journal of Entertainment and Technology Law*, 24(4), 749–785.

Etomi, E. E., & Onyishi, D. U. (2021). Automated number plate recognition system. *Tropical Journal of Science and Technology*, 2(1), 38–48.

Hodge, S. D., Jr. (2020). Big brother is watching: Law enforcement's use of digital technology in the twenty-first century. *University of Cincinnati Law Review*, 89(1), 30–54.

Koops, B. J., Newell, B. C., & Skorvanek, I. (2018). Location tracking by police: The regulation of tireless and absolute surveillance. *UC Irvine Law Review*, 9(3), 635–698.

Lawal, L. S., Chatwin, C. R., & Chatwin, C. R. (2019). A review of global navigation satellite and augmentation systems. *IJRDO—Journal of Electrical and Electronics Engineering*, 5(3), 1–21.

Merry, K., & Bettinger, P. (2019). Smartphone GPS accuracy study in an urban environment. *PLoS ONE*, 14(7), e0219890.

Sánchez-Cambronero, S., Álvarez-Bazo, F., Rivas, A., & Gallego, I. (2021). Dynamic route flow estimation in road networks using data from automatic number of plate recognition sensors. *Sustainability*, 13(8), 4430.

Shashirangana, J., Padmasiri, H., Meedeniya, D., & Perera, C. (2020). Automated license plate recognition: A survey on methods and techniques. *IEEE Access*, 9, 11203–11225.

Shi, K. (2020). GPS Tracking at the border: A mistaken expectation or a chilling reality. *Washington and Lee Journal of Civil Rights and Social Justice*, 27(1), 161–229.

Verma, R., Singh, B. K., & Zahidi, F. (2024). Management of GPS tracking systems in transportation. *Intelligent transportation system and advanced technology*, 251–263. Springer.

11 Wearable Technology

The integration of wearable technology in crime science has significantly altered law enforcement practices, reconfiguring operational approaches and enhancing effectiveness and accountability. This chapter investigates this evolving landscape, focusing on the convergence of wearable technology and crime science. A key topic of discussion is the use of body-worn cameras by law enforcement personnel. These discreet devices have substantial potential for documenting and contextualizing encounters between law enforcement agents and the public, capturing pivotal moments with unprecedented objectivity. Their role as instruments of transparency and documentation underscores their importance as catalysts in contemporary law enforcement practices.

Body Cameras: A Game Changer in Law Enforcement

Body cameras are a prominent and enduring choice within wearable technology applications. This popularity is attributed to their ability to genuinely document occurrences, thus reinforcing accountability and filling gaps in evidence during investigative and legal proceedings. The implementation of body-worn cameras in law enforcement has initiated a paradigm shift toward increased transparency and accountability, altering the interactions between police officers and the communities they serve. These inconspicuous devices have transformed from discretionary tools to integral components of contemporary policing, offering unparalleled insights into law enforcement engagements. This section explores the various benefits of body cameras, highlighting their significant impact on reducing instances of force, enhancing the professionalism of law enforcement officers, and providing an impartial record of incidents.

One of the most noteworthy contributions of body cameras is their ability to decrease incidents of force. The existence of a camera serves as a deterrent, prompting both law enforcement personnel and individuals to modify their conduct and engagements. Simultaneously, individuals in the public may also adjust their behavior, recognizing the presence of an impartial observer who can validate their claims or behaviors. This shift fosters an environment where de-escalation tactics are prioritized, reducing confrontations that could escalate to employing force. The use of body cameras among law enforcement officials promotes a higher level of professionalism. The awareness that their actions are recorded encourages officers to consistently adhere to their departments' established standards and best practices. By analyzing their interactions, law enforcement agents can reflect on their decision-making processes and identify areas for improvement (Koen & Mathna, 2019). This continuous feedback loop fosters a culture of personal growth and ensures that officers maintain the highest standards of conduct during their operations. The camera acts as a passive observer. It cultivates an environment conducive to high performance by ensuring police officers comply with their training and responsibilities.

DOI: 10.4324/9781003558491-11

One of the primary advantages of implementing body cameras is their ability to provide an impartial and transparent record of incidents. Recorded audio and video evidence offer a neutral account of events, reducing discrepancies and potential biases potentially arising from eyewitness statements (Adams et al., 2020). This thorough and objective documentation is crucial in investigations and legal proceedings. Body camera footage is considered credible and reliable evidence that can either substantiate or challenge the reliability of witness testimony, thereby enhancing the overall integrity of the judicial system and the credibility of law enforcement agencies.

Building trust between law enforcement organizations and the communities they serve requires the implementation of body-worn cameras. These cameras demonstrate a commitment to transparency, indicating that interactions are subject to scrutiny and accountability. Consequently, community members are more likely to perceive law enforcement as acting reasonably, responsibly, and with a genuine concern for public welfare (Crow et al., 2017). Maintaining detailed records of interactions helps reduce confrontations, clarify misunderstandings, and foster improved communication between law enforcement and the public. This transparency may strengthen community bonds and encourage collaboration between law enforcement and citizens.

Evidentiary Value in Investigations and Prosecutions

In contemporary criminal justice, body camera footage has emerged as a powerful evidentiary tool, fundamentally reshaping methodologies in investigations and the dynamics of legal proceedings. The inherent objectivity of recorded audio and video provides a vivid and unfiltered perspective of events, enabling law enforcement agencies and legal professionals to construct accurate narratives (Petersen et al., 2021).

The primary benefit of body camera footage lies in its ability to reconstruct occurrences accurately. The cameras capture real-time visual and audio data as law enforcement officials respond to various situations, capturing the chronological progression of actions, responses, and conversations. The comprehensive documentation allows investigators to reconstruct the sequence of events in a manner consistent with how they occurred, serving as a reliable and sequential record. The nuanced information recorded by body cameras, including facial expressions, body language, and background sounds, can further enhance the reconstruction of events. These subtle cues provide additional context that might be missed through verbal accounts alone.

Body camera footage can either confirm or refute the accuracy of witness statements, significantly impacting the credibility of reports provided by involved parties. By reviewing the footage, investigators can identify patterns of agreement and divergence between eyewitness accounts and the visual evidence (Petersen et al., 2021). This process aims to enhance the credibility of testimony and provide a more accurate account of events. Body cameras offer crucial visual evidence that is invaluable for substantiating or disproving claims, ultimately influencing investigations and legal proceedings.

In addition to documenting the chronological order of events, body camera footage offers an unmatched perspective on the complexities and interactions within crime scenes. The body camera footage from officers' viewpoints provides valuable perspectives on spatial relationships, personnel positioning, and contextual nuances that can significantly influence the understanding and analysis of incidents (Robertson et al., 2024). This detailed visual documentation aids investigators in comprehending the context in which incidents occurred, thereby highlighting various factors that potentially impacted the decision-making processes of law enforcement officers and civilians involved. The ability to examine these subtle intricacies enhances the profundity of investigative analyses and the accuracy of legal proceedings.

Numerous empirical examples underscore the critical importance of body camera footage in securing convictions and upholding justice. In cases where law enforcement actions have been scrutinized, body-worn cameras have proven instrumental in clarifying the situational factors that played a role in their rapid decision-making processes. This is especially relevant in police use-of-force incidents (Zamoff, 2019). The recorded video is salient in providing visual evidence of a suspect's hostile behavior, which in turn can justify the officer's conduct. Similarly, body camera recordings can corroborate an officer's testimony in criminal prosecutions. The documented interactions between the law enforcement officer and the accused individual can yield crucial evidence, ultimately leading to the safeguarding of the officer and the defendant's conviction.

Challenges and Considerations in Implementing Body Cameras

While the implementation of body cameras in law enforcement offers numerous advantages, it also presents a series of complex challenges that require careful management. This section explores the intricate obstacles associated with body camera use, including privacy, data management, selective recording, and potential biases arising from different camera angles and perspectives. Additionally, this section addresses the complexities of storing, redacting, and efficiently handling the large volume of video data generated by these cameras.

The deployment of body-worn cameras raises significant concerns regarding personal privacy and public surveillance. While body cameras enhance transparency and accountability, it is essential to recognize that they can inadvertently capture footage of individuals not directly involved in the intended purpose, thereby infringing on their privacy (White & Malm, 2020). Achieving a balance between overseeing law enforcement operations and protecting individuals' rights and privacy presents a nuanced challenge. Establishing explicit policies that dictate when body cameras should be activated, as well as the circumstances and locations in which they should be used, is crucial to prevent unwarranted intrusions into individuals' privacy.

The extensive production of body camera footage generates significant amounts of data that require effective administration and storage solutions. Law enforcement agencies face logistical challenges related to data storage, including security, accessibility, and long-term preservation (Police Executive Research Forum, 2018). The substantial volume of recorded material necessitates the establishment of advanced storage systems capable of managing the influx of data, which is essential for protecting crucial evidence and complying with data retention policies.

Moreover, body cameras allow law enforcement officers to exercise discretion in starting and concluding recordings, which creates the potential for selective recording that may impact the interpretation of an incident. The timing of initiating the recording process can unintentionally influence the portrayal of an event, highlighting the importance of implementing established procedures to guarantee thorough documentation and avoid omitting essential contextual details. The primary challenge lies in formulating precise criteria for determining the appropriate moments to activate and deactivate cameras, which would minimize the risk of introducing subjective perspectives or intentional bias (White & Malm, 2020).

The placement of body-worn cameras on law enforcement uniforms can also inadvertently introduce biases into the recorded footage. Limitations in camera angles may obscure specific aspects of an incident, potentially affecting the accuracy and comprehensiveness of the recorded events (Boivin et al., 2020). It is imperative to mitigate these biases by providing training on optimal camera placement and promoting situational awareness among law enforcement agents.

Law enforcement agencies face the formidable task of effectively handling and processing substantial video data generated by body cameras. Efficient mechanisms for reviewing, evaluating, and redacting sensitive content are crucial for extracting relevant information while maintaining privacy. Incorporating redaction techniques into data management processes adds a layer of intricacy, particularly when obscuring sensitive information such as the identities and personal details of uninvolved individuals.

Ethical and Legal Implications of Body Cameras

The ethical and legal implications of a particular issue or action are essential and warrant careful consideration. These implications pertain to the moral and legal consequences of engaging in certain behaviors or making specific decisions. Integrating body cameras into contemporary police practices raises diverse ethical and legal concerns that demand thorough scrutiny and analysis. This section explores the complex ethical considerations associated with using body cameras, addressing public surveillance, consent, and privacy invasion. It also addresses the potential for unauthorized use of recorded footage and the delicate balance between transparency and the fundamental right to privacy.

The primary challenge presented by body cameras is the intricate task of striking a balance between the principles of transparency and the protection of personal privacy. The prevalence of body camera footage raises concerns about encroaching on individual privacy (Lin, 2016). Individuals engaged in their daily activities may unintentionally have their actions documented, leading to a sense of constant surveillance. This ethical dilemma necessitates comprehensive regulations that clearly define the circumstances of body camera activation to protect privacy in private settings and sensitive situations. Furthermore, data security is critical, necessitating measures to prevent unauthorized access to confidential recordings that could jeopardize personal data.

The issue of consent becomes particularly relevant when considering the use of body cameras. While law enforcement agents possess the legal authority to document contacts as part of their official duties, it is not always clear that individuals involved will be aware of or understand the consequences of such recordings (Lawrence et al., 2018). Effective communication regarding the utilization of body-worn cameras can facilitate informed decision-making, enabling citizens to modify their conduct or make conscious choices about engaging with law enforcement personnel while being aware of the recording.

The accumulation of comprehensive body camera recordings raises the risk of misuse, including inadvertent disclosures and intentional alterations. The primary ethical consideration revolves around ensuring that recorded material is used solely for its intended purposes: enhancing transparency, fostering accountability, and facilitating investigative processes. Robust regulations regarding data processing, the implementation of access controls, and the establishment of accountability systems are crucial to preventing the illegal utilization of recorded material and minimizing the potential for malicious exploitation against individuals.

Body cameras can significantly impact community relations, yielding both advantages and disadvantages. On the one hand, body cameras can reduce citizens' complaints against the police by fostering trust through transparency (Stolzenberg et al., 2018). On the other hand, concerns about surveillance and the potential for misuse can undermine community confidence in law enforcement (Poirier et al., 2024). Ensuring open and transparent communication regarding body camera policies and their anticipated benefits is imperative to cultivating positive community relationships and alleviating concerns.

The notion of consent for utilizing body cameras is characterized by its multi-dimensional nature. Although officers have the authority to document their interactions while performing official tasks, obtaining agreement from individuals captured in the recorded footage may not always be practical. Complex situations, such as interactions involving vulnerable individuals, require careful and nuanced examination of ethical principles. Achieving a balance between the pressing operational needs of law enforcement and the imperative to uphold the rights of individuals being recorded necessitates meticulous deliberation and the establishment of clearly defined protocols.

Implementation Strategies and Best Practices

To successfully integrate body cameras into law enforcement procedures, a well-thought-out plan is required to ensure compliance with legal requirements and promote honesty, accountability, and ethical conduct. This section examines the crucial best practices essential for successfully implementing body cameras, emphasizing the importance of clearly defined policies, strategic directives, data management, officer education, community engagement, accountability mechanisms, and ongoing policy adaptation to account for changing circumstances.

A key component of successful integration is the establishment of explicit norms and procedures that provide a framework for body camera use. Law enforcement organizations need to develop comprehensive guidelines that encompass all facets of body camera operation. These policies should clearly define the conditions that warrant recording information and include procedures for activation and deactivation. Additionally, to protect the privacy and security of recorded footage, regulations must establish strict guidelines for the duration of data retention, outline standards and methods for redacting sensitive material, and implement stringent access controls for recorded footage.

Establishing clear policies is vital to mitigate any potential uncertainty among law enforcement officers and ensure their comprehensive understanding of their responsibilities regarding body-worn cameras. Transparent and accessible policies provide a reference point for officers facing ethical or procedural dilemmas.

Defining strategic rules for activating and deactivating body cameras is necessary for maximizing their effectiveness while upholding privacy rights. Law enforcement officers must receive comprehensive training on the appropriate circumstances for initiating recordings, particularly in situations that may escalate or during service calls (Police Executive Research Forum, 2014). Implementing situational triggers, such as activating cameras during traffic stops or in response to domestic incidents, establishes standardized protocols for determining when to begin recording. Simultaneously, it is essential to define deactivation protocols to minimize the risk of unauthorized recording in contexts requiring heightened sensitivity or within private domains. Practical training for officers on the appropriate exercise of discretion following these guidelines ensures the production of relevant, defensible recordings that respect individuals' privacy rights.

The substantial volume of data generated by body cameras requires a resilient data storage and management method. Law enforcement agencies should allocate resources to establish secure storage solutions based on cloud technology while complying with data protection standards. This infrastructure facilitates the effective retrieval, examination, and redaction of video recordings as needed for investigative or legal purposes.

Additionally, implementing a structured data management system that categorizes video recordings by event type, date, and location streamlines the retrieval and examination processes. Organizations can ensure the authenticity and confidentiality of recorded material by prioritizing data security measures, such as encryption protocols and access control mechanisms, thereby maintaining public confidence in protecting sensitive data.

Equipping law enforcement officers with the necessary skills to effectively utilize body cameras is crucial for optimizing the advantages while mitigating potential drawbacks. Comprehensive training programs should encompass various technological components, including camera operation, data management, and redaction procedures (Police Executive Research Forum, 2014). Training courses should also address ethical considerations related to privacy invasion, consent, and the appropriate use of body cameras.

Scenario-based training can enhance law enforcement officers' ability to navigate complex situations that require prompt decision-making regarding the activation or deactivation of body-worn cameras. Furthermore, ongoing training programs ensure officers stay informed about policy changes, legal advancements, and emerging best practices. This approach ensures their continued competence in effectively utilizing body cameras as an integral part of their standard operating procedures.

The implementation of body-worn cameras has the potential to influence community perceptions and foster trust in law enforcement organizations. Proactive community engagement is crucial to ensure that community members fully understand these devices' objectives, benefits, and constraints. Collaboration with community leaders, advocacy groups, and stakeholders is vital for agencies to gather feedback and address privacy, surveillance, and accountability concerns. Transparent communication initiatives that disseminate information about body camera policies, usage guidelines, and privacy protection measures can enhance understanding and promote collaboration. This dialogue fosters a shared recognition of the role of body cameras in improving transparency and accountability, ultimately strengthening the relationship between the community and law enforcement.

Implementing effective accountability measures is crucial to ensure that the use of body cameras aligns with established policies and guidelines. It is advisable for designated personnel or supervisors to regularly review recorded footage to assess compliance and identify areas for improvement. Regular audits provide valuable opportunities to rectify deviations and offer constructive feedback to officers. Promptly addressing instances of policy violations or inappropriate use of footage is imperative. Establishing transparent systems for reporting issues related to body camera deployments, such as dedicated hotlines or internal reporting channels, empowers law enforcement officers and citizens to hold each other accountable and address potential ethical violations swiftly.

Regulations governing the use of body cameras should be considered flexible documents that adapt to technological advancements, legislative modifications, and societal perspectives. Law enforcement agencies should be open to seeking input from officers, community members, and legal experts. Periodic policy assessments facilitate the proactive identification and resolution of emerging challenges, refinement of guidelines, and incorporation of insights gained from real-world experiences. Ongoing consultation with legal counsel ensures policies comply with applicable laws, mitigating potential legal complexities. Maintaining the relevance and effectiveness of policies in a dynamic environment requires flexibility and adaptability.

The effective incorporation of body cameras into law enforcement necessitates a comprehensive approach that covers well-defined regulations, strategic directives, efficient data management, officer education, community engagement, accountability mechanisms, and a commitment to policy refinement. By following these recommended guidelines, law enforcement agencies can effectively navigate the intricate process of implementing body cameras. This approach promotes transparency, accountability, and public trust while enhancing interactions with the communities they serve.

Future Directions and Technological Advancements

Body camera technology is an evolving field, continually adding new features to enhance these devices' efficiency, transparency, and use. Ongoing technological advancements enable body cameras to offer a variety of unique capabilities and integration opportunities beyond simple documentation. This section examines prospective technological developments anticipated in the immediate future, including real-time analytics, automatic event detection, integration with law enforcement systems, and incorporating AI and machine learning for in-depth analysis.

The integration of real-time analytics represents a paradigm shift in body camera technology. By leveraging onboard processing capabilities and connectivity, body cameras can provide law enforcement officers with real-time situational analysis. Real-time analytics can assist in detecting potential threats, providing relevant information about the surrounding environment, and alerting law enforcement personnel to unusual patterns or behaviors (Crow & Smykla, 2019). For example, facial recognition algorithms can help identify individuals with outstanding warrants or known criminal histories. This technological application can equip law enforcement officials with valuable information, enabling them to make informed decisions while performing their duties.

Integrating automatic event detection capabilities in body cameras holds great potential for transforming law enforcement practices. These cameras can detect motions, sounds, or gestures that indicate potentially hazardous situations. One potential application of automatic event detection involves recognizing acoustic signals, such as gunshots, which can trigger the recording process (Crow & Smykla, 2019). This technology plays a vital role in capturing essential evidence in time-sensitive situations, thereby enhancing the safety of law enforcement officers and providing a more accurate record of high-pressure incidents.

Incorporating technology systems within law enforcement organizations has become an increasingly significant aspect of criminal justice. This integration facilitates the seamless exchange of information and data across multiple platforms, augmenting the effectiveness and efficiency of law enforcement operations.

Incorporating body cameras into existing law enforcement systems presents significant potential for facilitating information exchange and enhancing situational awareness. The integration of body camera footage with computer-aided dispatch, Geographic Information Systems, and records management systems creates a comprehensive data network (Strom, 2017). This integration improves decision-making processes by enabling law enforcement agents to access contextual information about specific locations, prior occurrences, or individuals associated with a particular situation.

The incorporation of AI and machine learning algorithms signifies a paradigm shift in the application of body cameras. AI enables the automated detection of patterns, anomalies, and trends within recorded material, providing valuable insights that might be overlooked in manual reviews (Watts et al., 2024). AI algorithms can identify objects, gestures, and emotions, facilitating a deeper understanding of human interactions and potentially aiding investigative efforts. Furthermore, this technology can assist in the automated categorization of video footage, streamlining retrieval and redaction processes.

The application of technological advancements in body cameras can also extend to training and performance evaluation. Integrating body camera footage into virtual reality simulations allows law enforcement personnel to engage in immersive experiences that closely resemble real-life situations. This technology provides a controlled environment where officers can refine their decision-making skills. Additionally, AI-driven algorithms can analyze officers' interactions recorded on body cameras, offering personalized feedback and identifying areas for improvement in communication, de-escalation techniques, and adherence to established protocols.

Conclusion

The incorporation of wearable technology, particularly body cameras, has initiated a significant transformation within the realm of crime science, fundamentally altering how law enforcement interacts with the public and manages criminal incidents. The exploration of various sections of this work highlights the substantial impact of body cameras on enhancing transparency, promoting accountability, and strengthening the evidentiary foundation of investigations and legal proceedings. Despite the challenges and ethical considerations presented, the benefits of body cameras are unequivocally evident. These devices enhance law enforcement organizations' capabilities in effectively managing complex situations, offering a thorough and unbiased record of events, and ensuring that principles of fairness and equity are upheld. Body cameras have become crucial in fostering trust, deterring misconduct, and safeguarding due process by documenting interactions between law enforcement and the public.

The rapid evolution of technology has positioned the field of crime science at the intersection of innovation and responsibility. The advancement of body camera technology offers a glimpse into a future where real-time analytics, automatic event recognition, and AI-driven insights will redefine law enforcement operations. Law enforcement agencies must remain vigilant in modern society, ensuring their ability to adapt to technological advancements while upholding ethical standards, protecting privacy rights, and encouraging meaningful community involvement. Wearable technology exemplifies how innovative solutions and time-tested principles can coexist harmoniously in crime science. The integration and evolution of wearable technologies in law enforcement must prioritize justice, transparency, and public trust. This approach ensures that law enforcement's use of wearable technology is characterized by fairness, integrity, and progress.

References

Adams, D., Paterson, H. M., & MacDougall, H. G. (2020). Law and (rec) order: Updating memory for criminal events with body-worn cameras. *PLoS ONE*, 15(12), e0243226.

Boivin, R., Faubert, C., Gendron, A., & Poulin, B. (2020). Explaining the body-worn camera perspective bias. *Journal of Qualitative Criminal Justice & Criminology*, 9(1), 1–28.

Crow, M. S., & Smykla, J. O. (2019). Police body-worn cameras: Research developments on an emerging technology. *Criminal Justice Review*, 44(3), 257–262.

Crow, M. S., Snyder, J. A., Crichlow, V. J., & Smykla, J. O. (2017). Community perceptions of police body-worn cameras: The impact of views on fairness, fear, performance, and privacy. *Criminal Justice and Behavior*, 44(4), 589–610.

Koen, M. C., & Mathna, B. (2019). Body-worn cameras and internal accountability at a police agency. *American Journal of Qualitative Research*, 3(2), 1–22.

Lawrence, D. S., Peterson, B. E., & Thompson, P. S. (2018). *Community views of Milwaukee's police body-worn camera program: Results from three waves of community surveys*. Urban Institute.

Lin, R. (2016). Police body-worn cameras and privacy: Retaining benefits while reducing public concerns. *Duke Law & Technology Review*, 14(1), 346–365.

Petersen, K., Mouro, A., Papy, D., Castillo, N., & Ariel, B. (2021). Seeing is believing: The impact of body-worn cameras on court outcomes, a cluster-randomized controlled trial in Miami Beach. *Journal of Experimental Criminology*, 19, 191–211.

Poirier, B., Charbonneau, É., & Boivin, R. (2024). Police body-worn cameras and privacy: Views and concerns of officers and citizens. *International Journal of Police Science & Management*, 26 (2), 170–181.

Police Executive Research Forum. (2014). *Implementing a body-worn camera program: Recommendations and lessons learned*. Police Executive Research Forum.

Police Executive Research Forum. (2018). *Cost and benefits of body-worn camera deployments*. Police Executive Research Forum.

Robertson, O. N., McCluskey, J. D., Smith, S. S., & Uchida, C. D. (2024). Body cameras and adjudication: Views of prosecutors and public defenders. *Criminal Justice Review*, 49(1), 15–29.

Stolzenberg, L., D'Alessio, S. J., & Flexon, J. L. (2018). *Eyes on the street: Police use of body-worn cameras in Miami-Dade County*. Weston Publishing.

Strom, K. (2017). *Research on the impact of technology on policing strategy in the 21st century, final report*. U.S. Department of Justice.

Watts, S., White, M. D., & Malm, A. (2024). Automating body-worn camera footage review through AI: Preliminary findings from a multi-site randomized control trial. *Policing: A Journal of Policy and Practice*, 18. https://doi.org/10.1093/police/paae107.

White, M. D., & Malm, A. (2020). *Cops, cameras, and crisis: The potential and the perils of police body-worn cameras*. New York University Press.

Zamoff, M. (2019). Assessing the impact of police body camera evidence on the litigation of excessive force cases. *Georgia Law Review*, 54(1), 1–61.

12 Financial Investigation Tools

The significance of financial investigation techniques in the dynamic realm of crime science cannot be overstated. Given the evolving digital landscape, law enforcement agencies and financial institutions must continually adapt their strategies and practices to combat the activities of technologically savvy criminals. In contemporary times, criminal activities have transcended geographical boundaries, necessitating the usage of advanced technology and innovative approaches to counteract them. Two significant tools have emerged as transformative elements in the battle against financial crimes: blockchain analysis and anti-money laundering (AML) software.

Utilizing blockchain analysis has significantly transformed how law enforcement and regulatory authorities conduct financial investigations. Blockchain technology's transparency and immutability allow for meticulous tracking and analysis of complex transactions, thereby unraveling the intricate networks established by those engaged in illicit financial activities (Wu et al., 2024). Recently, AML software has assumed a crucial role in safeguarding the financial industry by employing sophisticated algorithms and machine learning techniques to identify potentially illicit financial activities, such as money laundering and other fraudulent schemes. As these technologies evolve in response to emerging risks, they serve as essential foundations of protection against the increasingly complex nature of financial crimes in the digital era.

Blockchain Analysis: A Key Tool in Financial Investigations

Blockchain technology, frequently lauded as a transformative force, is the foundation of cryptocurrencies and plays a crucial role in financial investigations. It is imperative to elucidate the fundamental aspects of blockchain technology to comprehend its importance. Fundamentally, a blockchain is a digitally implemented, immutable ledger that is shared across interconnected computers. Each page within this ledger is conceptualized as a distinct unit, referred to as a block, dedicated to recording a series of transactions (Yli-Huumo et al., 2016). The blocks within a blockchain are sequentially interconnected, forming a chronological chain, hence the term "blockchain."

In contrast to conventional centralized databases, which are governed by a single entity, blockchains are decentralized and dispersed across a network of nodes (computers). Thus, blockchain security relies on this fundamental principle of decentralization (Yli-Huumo et al., 2016). The decentralization process effectively mitigates the risk associated with a single point of failure. Thus, it helps ensure resistance to tampering or illegal modifications. In contrast, another mechanism, proof of stake, relies on the possession of cryptocurrency tokens, wherein validators are selected to generate new blocks in proportion to the number of tokens they hold.

DOI: 10.4324/9781003558491-12

Once a transaction is appended to the blockchain, modifying it becomes exceedingly challenging due to cryptographic hashing, which ensures the blockchain's immutability. Consequently, altering any element within a block necessitates modifying all subsequent blocks, which is nearly impossible.

Each block in the chain is characterized by a distinct cryptographic hash of the preceding block, establishing a robust and tamper-proof link between them. If a hacker were to manipulate a transaction within a block, the resulting action would modify the hash of that block (AlShamsi et al., 2022). Utilizing each block's hash in the subsequent block results in the propagation of modifications throughout the entire chain, thereby alerting the network of tampering attempts.

Blockchain's immutability guarantees the preservation of data integrity, thereby establishing it as a reliable and trustworthy source of information. The potential applications of blockchain technology extend beyond cryptocurrencies, encompassing various domains such as supply chain management, voting systems, and legal contracts.

Cryptocurrencies are digital assets created and maintained using blockchain technology. Blockchain technology records transactions and manages ownership rights (Trozze et al., 2022). Bitcoin, the pioneering digital currency, was the first to adopt blockchain technology, leading to the development of other cryptocurrencies such as Ethereum, Ripple, and Litecoin.

Bitcoin, developed by Satoshi Nakamoto, demonstrated the viability of blockchain technology. This technology enables individuals to transmit monetary value directly to one another, bypassing intermediaries such as financial institutions. Bitcoin transactions are recorded on the publicly accessible Bitcoin blockchain.

Ethereum, another prominent cryptocurrency, introduces the innovative concept of smart contracts. Self-executing contracts, commonly called smart contracts, are contractual arrangements wherein the terms and conditions of the agreement are explicitly embedded into computer code (Trozze et al., 2022). The Ethereum blockchain enables programmers to develop decentralized applications (DApps), expanding the capabilities of blockchain technology beyond traditional peer-to-peer transactions.

In contrast, Ripple primarily emphasizes facilitating rapid and economically efficient cross-border payment transactions. The swift settlement of transactions has garnered attention from financial institutions. Additionally, Litecoin, often referred to as Bitcoin's silver counterpart, is a digital currency that exhibits numerous parallels with Bitcoin while providing expedited transaction processing times.

Blockchain technology serves as the fundamental infrastructure on which cryptocurrencies are built. Its decentralized, immutable, and transparent nature has the potential to revolutionize industries like supply chain management, health care, and government services beyond just banking. A comprehensive understanding of the fundamental principles behind blockchain technology is essential to fully grasp its significance in financial investigations and its potential to address complex criminal activities associated with digital currency.

Role of Blockchain in Criminal Activities

The disruptive potential of blockchain extends beyond authorized use cases. Criminals have utilized this technology to engage in a range of illicit operations, leveraging its inherent features to maintain anonymity, streamline transactions, and facilitate money laundering practices (AlShamsi et al., 2022). Criminals exploit the pseudonymous nature of blockchain transactions to partake in various illicit activities, such as drug trafficking, ransomware attacks, tax evasion, and other unlawful pursuits (Kethineni & Cao, 2020).

One of the critical advantages for individuals engaged in illicit activities is their capacity to operate within a relatively anonymous and decentralized environment.

Silk Road, an infamous online marketplace for facilitating illicit drug transactions, exemplifies how blockchain technology enables criminal activity. Silk Road operated behind the confines of the dark web, facilitating anonymous and illegal narcotics trade (Ahmad et al., 2023). This situation was made possible by the use of cryptocurrencies, with Bitcoin being the predominant digital currency employed. The platform offered a convenient and ostensibly secure means for individuals involved in the illicit drug trade to establish connections. Ross Ulbricht, the individual responsible for orchestrating the Silk Road enterprise, was ultimately apprehended and subsequently convicted, receiving a life sentence in prison. The investigation into Silk Road involved the utilization of advanced blockchain analysis methodologies, which enabled law enforcement authorities to track Bitcoin transactions on the blockchain, ultimately leading to Ulbricht's apprehension. Ulbricht was pardoned by President Donald Trump in 2025.

Ransomware attacks have emerged as a notable threat in the contemporary era of digital technology, wherein hackers routinely coerce their targets into paying ransoms using cryptocurrencies, particularly Bitcoin. During a conventional ransomware attack, the perpetrator employs malicious software to encrypt the target's files, rendering them inaccessible (Connolly & Wall, 2019). Subsequently, the assailant demands a monetary sum in cryptocurrency in exchange for the decryption key. This strategy offers numerous benefits to individuals engaged in cybercriminal activities. Cryptocurrencies allow individuals to receive payments while concealing their identities. Utilizing blockchain technology presents challenges for authorities in their efforts to track the movement of financial resources. The global nature of cryptocurrency transactions enables attackers to target victims across international borders. Cryptocurrency transactions are executed quickly, allowing criminals to receive funds swiftly and intensifying the coercive influence on victims to comply with their demands. These incidents have garnered considerable media attention and have brought attention to the involvement of cryptocurrencies in acts of extortion and criminal financial acquisition. Law enforcement authorities have diligently formulated measures to monitor and apprehend ransomware operators, frequently employing blockchain analysis techniques and fostering international cooperation.

Blockchain Analysis Techniques for Law Enforcement

Combating criminal activities facilitated by blockchain technology requires the utilization of advanced analysis methodologies and technologies to conduct a comprehensive examination of transactions within a blockchain system. This effort aims to discern repeating trends, track fund movements, and ultimately reveal the identities of individuals engaged in unlawful endeavors (Pelker et al., 2021). The following section examines the procedures and tools utilized in blockchain analysis.

One of the core techniques within blockchain investigation is the scrutiny of transaction flow. This approach entails observing fund movements within the blockchain by inspecting transaction input and output components (Wang et al., 2019). This analytical method assists investigators in monitoring the progression of monetary resources and establishing connections among diverse cryptocurrency addresses.

Transaction flow analysis is similar to tracking the trajectory of money as it navigates through a series of financial transactions. By dissecting data within the blockchain, investigators can discern the origin of financial resources, their distribution, and their ultimate destinations. This methodology plays a pivotal role in comprehending the transfer of assets within illicit endeavors and revealing concealed associations.

Address clustering, or address linkage analysis, is a strategic technique employed in blockchain examination. Its primary purpose is to associate multiple cryptocurrency addresses with a single entity or user. In blockchain analysis, this methodology is indispensable for tracking fund flow amid diverse wallets tied to illicit activities (Pelker et al., 2021). Perpetrators often attempt to obscure their financial transactions by deploying multiple addresses, thereby introducing a formidable challenge in monitoring the currency's trajectory. Address clustering relies on an amalgamation of various data indicators, including the concept of shared input ownership and transaction behaviors. These disparate data points reveal concealed address connections. Once these linkages are successfully identified, investigators gain the capacity to formulate a more comprehensive understanding of the intricate web of fund transfers and money laundering activities operating within the criminal network.

Heuristic analysis is a methodology that employs algorithms and heuristics to detect potentially suspicious patterns within blockchain transactions. Detecting potential criminal actions is crucial to blockchain forensics. One common heuristic involves examining transaction quantities. For example, dividing substantial transactions into smaller, difficult-to-trace sums could suggest illicit money laundering efforts. This behavior is frequently linked to individuals involved in illegal activities who attempt to obfuscate the origin of their finances through "mixing" or "tumbling." Another heuristic involves identifying unusual transaction patterns, such as an abrupt increase in activity or the use of particular mixing services recognized for their association with illicit undertakings (Collins, 2022). These anomalies can trigger further investigation.

The utilization of data visualization is of utmost importance in the examination of blockchain technology. Visual depictions such as transaction flows, address linkages, and network interactions enhance the comprehensibility of intricate data for investigators. Data visualization techniques such as heat maps, network graphs, and interactive dashboards assist in analyzing blockchain data (Song et al., 2022). Heat maps, for instance, can reveal concentrated patterns of activity within the blockchain, providing insights into the movement of funds. Network graphs are valuable tools for visualizing the relationships between addresses, thereby facilitating the tracking of asset movements within a criminal network (Collins, 2022). Data visualizations in blockchain data analysis allow investigators to gain a holistic perspective, facilitating the identification of patterns that may not be readily discernible in unprocessed data.

Machine learning and artificial intelligence (AI) have achieved notable advancements in blockchain analysis. These technologies facilitate the automation of pattern recognition and anomaly detection, thus expediting the investigative process and enhancing precision. Machine learning algorithms can be trained to identify patterns associated with various categories of blockchain-enabled criminal activities, including but not limited to ransomware attacks, darknet marketplaces, and fraudulent initial coin offerings. Through ongoing analysis of blockchain data, machine learning models can detect potentially illicit transactions and raise alerts for further scrutiny.

AI-powered solutions can also assist in natural language processing, aiding investigators in analyzing extensive textual data about blockchain transactions, forum discussions, and online conversations. The examination of this text can reveal significant insights into criminal activity and the individuals implicated therein. Moreover, the utilization of machine learning and AI has the potential to facilitate risk assessment and predictive analysis. By analyzing historical data and detecting recurring trends, these technologies can predict potential future hazards and vulnerabilities within the blockchain ecosystem.

Legal and Ethical Considerations in Blockchain Investigations

The examination of blockchain technology presents intricate legal and ethical dilemmas. Although it possesses considerable efficacy in deterring criminal activities, utilizing this tool raises substantial concerns about privacy, civil liberties, and the delicate balance between monitoring and investigative measures.

Blockchain transactions are commonly characterized as pseudonymous rather than anonymous. This situation implies that although the identities of individuals or companies engaged in transactions are not explicitly disclosed, they are linked to cryptographic addresses. The degree of pseudonymity exhibited by cryptocurrency users depends on their address and transaction management methods.

The traceability aspect of blockchain technology gives rise to privacy concerns, as individuals may express reservations about the ease with which their financial activities can be tracked. Preserving privacy is an inherent and essential entitlement of every individual, constituting a fundamental human right. Consequently, individuals possess valid and justified concerns for safeguarding the confidentiality of their financial matters. The dual nature of blockchain transactions, characterized by their pseudonymous attributes, has both advantageous and disadvantageous qualities. On the one hand, it affords users a certain level of privacy. On the other hand, it presents avenues for potential surveillance.

Nations across the globe are developing legislative frameworks to regulate the utilization of blockchain analysis within the context of criminal investigations. Implementing these frameworks is crucial for establishing the rights and obligations of law enforcement agencies and individuals involved in cryptocurrency activities (Teichmann & Falker, 2021). The primary objective is to actualize a balance between the imperative to address unlawful behaviors and the safeguarding of individual liberties, including the entitlement to financial confidentiality. Balancing these ethical considerations is challenging. Deploying blockchain analytical techniques necessitates compliance with legal norms and a dedication to preserving ethical principles and values. Implementing ethical norms and oversight systems guarantees the responsible and ethical use of blockchain analysis in criminal investigations.

AML Software: Enhancing Financial Crime Detection

Money laundering facilitates illicit operations by enabling criminals to legitimize their unlawfully acquired profits and seamlessly integrate them into the legitimate financial framework. It is a complex process that entails disguising the origin of finances to create an appearance of legitimacy.

Money laundering involves three main processes: placement, layering, and integration. The placement phase involves entering unlawfully obtained funds into the financial system through various methods, such as cash deposits, asset acquisitions, or cross-border transfers (Han et al., 2020). In the subsequent stage, complexity is introduced due to layering by reallocating funds between various accounts, diversifying investments, and executing transactions across multiple financial institutions. The integration phase involves reintegrating the "cleaned" money back into the legitimate economy, making it appear legitimate.

AML software plays a crucial role in combating the illicit practice of money laundering. Singh and Best (2019) assert that the process involves examining transaction data by utilizing predefined rules, algorithms, and more recently, machine learning methodologies to identify potentially suspicious trends. AML software fulfills various essential duties in this context. First, the system monitors transactions to detect anomalies or deviations from established norms. Transactions displaying atypical attributes, such as substantial cash deposits, frequent international transfers, or rapid fund transfers between accounts, are flagged for further examination.

Second, AML software supports the implementation of customer due diligence procedures. This software assists in verifying client identities and evaluating their risk profiles. It is crucial to exercise caution when engaging with clients who constitute a high level of risk, such as politically exposed persons or individuals from regions classified as high risk.

Moreover, AML software provides alerts when potentially suspicious activity is identified. These alerts serve as cues for compliance officers to conduct thorough examinations and make informed decisions about reporting such activities to the relevant authorities (Han et al., 2020). This approach aids financial institutions in meeting their regulatory reporting responsibilities.

Many legal measures and international standards have been implemented globally to enhance the efficacy of AML efforts (Gaviyau & Sibindi, 2023). These regulations delineate the criteria that financial institutions must follow to build and sustain robust AML programs and reporting protocols. Prominent instances include the USA PATRIOT Act, Bank Secrecy Act, Financial Action Task Force (FATF) Recommendations, European Union Anti-Money Laundering Directive, and the Proceeds of Crime Act in the United Kingdom.

The performance of AML software depends on sophisticated algorithms and, increasingly, machine learning methods to effectively execute its operations. The fundamental role of transaction monitoring entails observing client transactions using predetermined rules and algorithms to detect potentially suspicious conduct by analyzing various transaction data. Additionally, the customer due diligence process benefits from AML software and is crucial for onboarding customers and monitoring their activities. These components encompass verifying identities, evaluating risk profiles, and implementing more rigorous due diligence measures for higher risk level clients.

Alert generation is another crucial aspect in which AML software is devised to initiate alerts upon identifying potentially illicit or suspicious activities. The risk ratings assigned to these alerts are determined by the degree of abnormalities detected, and it is the responsibility of compliance officers to assess them to ascertain the necessity of additional measures or reporting to regulatory bodies (Gerbrands et al., 2022). Additionally, sanctions screening is a crucial functionality of AML systems, ensuring that customer identities, entities, and transactions are validated against government sanctions lists, politically exposed persons lists, and other relevant watch lists. Furthermore, specific AML systems incorporate transaction filtering, which involves real-time monitoring to detect and prevent transactions that meet predefined criteria indicative of potential money laundering or terrorist financing activities.

The effectiveness of AML software hinges on the sophisticated algorithms and machine learning methodologies it employs. These technologies enhance the precision and efficiency of identifying potentially illicit behaviors by examining intricate patterns and deviations within extensive databases. Anomaly detection, for instance, involves machine learning techniques to discern patterns and anomalies in transactional data, making the technology particularly adept at identifying new or evolving money laundering methods (Chen et al., 2018). The machine learning system learns from historical transaction data and adapts to changing tactics. Additionally, risk scoring utilizes machine learning algorithms to assign risk scores to transactions and clients based on their historical behavior and associations. High-risk ratings trigger alerts for further investigation.

Machine learning models are leveraged by behavioral analytics to establish client baseline behavior profiles and detect deviations from these established patterns. This approach is invaluable for identifying atypical account behavior. Predictive modeling, another technique used in AML software, employs historical patterns to anticipate potential instances of suspicious behavior. This adaptive approach is essential in staying ahead of evolving risks.

Challenges in Implementing AML Software

Financial institutions face various challenges and considerations when implementing AML software. Initial expenditures, encompassing software procurement, customization efforts, and ongoing maintenance, can be substantial, necessitating effective resource allocation (Geiger & Wuensch, 2007). Furthermore, institutions must address compatibility issues, facilitate data migration, and implement necessary system changes to optimize operational efficiency.

Since the effectiveness of AML software relies on the quality and quantity of the data it receives, data quality management and handling of the substantial volume of daily transaction data are paramount. The utilization of AML software can lead to the generation of false positive alerts, requiring unnecessary investigations and incurring compliance expenses. Striking the right balance between minimizing false positives and accurately detecting suspicious activity requires careful software calibration.

Despite significant advancements, criminal organizations involved in money laundering consistently adapt their methods. Thus, evaluating the effectiveness of AML measures remains an ongoing area of investigation. Effectiveness is assessed based on the software's ability to identify new or evolving money laundering strategies, reduce false positives, streamline regulatory reporting, and support due diligence and risk assessment processes.

Regulatory compliance is critical for financial institutions to avoid legal sanctions and actively participate in global efforts to combat money laundering and terrorist financing. Oversight entities, such as the Organization for Financial Compliance Oversight, the Financial Crimes Enforcement Network (FinCEN), and the European Banking Authority, establish regulatory frameworks and reporting requirements for financial organizations. Non-compliance can result in substantial fines, damage to the institution's reputation, operational disruptions, and regulatory interventions.

AML software facilitates compliance by automating transaction monitoring and customer due diligence workflows, generating accurate reports for regulatory authorities, detecting and mitigating AML risks, and maintaining comprehensive audit trails. Citations of relevant financial regulatory documents, such as FATF Recommendations or FinCEN directives, provide precise guidance on AML compliance requirements.

Case Studies and Real-World Examples

The application of blockchain analysis has proven valuable in crime resolution and the apprehension of offenders. In 2017, a notable achievement in blockchain research occurred with the successful dismantling of AlphaBay, a widely recognized illicit online marketplace operating on the dark web that facilitated the illegal trade of prohibited commodities and services, including narcotics, firearms, and stolen information. Law enforcement organizations, including the Federal Bureau of Investigation and Europol, collaborated to dismantle AlphaBay. Blockchain analysis played a crucial role in identifying and apprehending Alexandre Cazes, the individual responsible for operating the network. Cazes was found deceased within his confinement shortly after his arrest. The confiscation of a substantial amount of cryptocurrencies by authorities exemplifies the efficacy of blockchain analysis in dismantling criminal networks.

Blockchain analysis tools have also proven crucial in tracking misappropriated funds in instances where cryptocurrency exchanges fall victim to hacking incidents. Cryptocurrency exchanges are highly appealing to malicious actors due to the significant cash rewards that may be obtained. Nevertheless, employing blockchain analysis can facilitate tracing illicitly acquired cryptocurrencies as they traverse multiple addresses, thereby enabling the identification of the individuals responsible for such activities. Although complete restitution of stolen money is not always achieved in such instances, they offer significant insights and enhance the overall security of the Bitcoin ecosystem.

Criminals consistently adapt their strategies to evade detection. Individuals utilize sophisticated mixing services, decentralized exchanges, and privacy-centric coins to disguise their transactions and identities. Consequently, it is imperative for blockchain analysis tools to continuously advance and augment their functionalities to remain aligned with the ever-evolving strategies. The ongoing advancement and exploration of blockchain forensics are vital to maintaining a proactive stance against illegal activities.

Privacy coins like Monero and Zcash pose significant challenges to blockchain research by prioritizing user privacy. The design of these coins provide users with increased privacy and anonymity. Sophisticated cryptographic techniques, such as zero-knowledge proofs, ensure the secrecy of transactional data. Consequently, investigators encounter significant challenges in tracing transactions and identifying individuals. The use of privacy currencies is becoming more prevalent among criminals for illegitimate purposes, necessitating the blockchain analysis community to develop novel approaches to tackle this issue while upholding the principles of privacy rights.

AML software has played a crucial role in detecting and preventing financial crimes in major cases worldwide:

In 2012, the Hong Kong and Shanghai Banking Corporation (HSBC), a major global financial institution, faced accusations of financial misconduct and sanctions violations. Utilizing AML software played a notable role in spotting and flagging potentially illicit activities, resulting in official examinations and substantial fines of approximately $1.9 billion (Bearpark, 2022).

AML software also played a crucial role in uncovering a significant money laundering scheme within the Estonian branch of Danske Bank. The bank faced significant legal repercussions due to investigations prompted by the software's identification of questionable transactions amounting to billions of euros.

In 2012, Standard Chartered Bank encountered allegations of engaging in transactions with Iranian companies, contravening U.S. sanctions (Xian, 2014). Implementing AML software facilitated identifying these unlawful activities, ultimately leading to a substantial settlement of $667 million with U.S. authorities.

These case studies emphasize the crucial importance of AML software in detecting and preventing illegal financial activities. AML technology serves the dual purpose of detecting potentially illicit actions and facilitating regulatory reporting and collaboration with authorities. The implementation of AML legislation aids in ensuring the accountability of financial institutions and acts as a deterrent to those engaging in money laundering activities.

Conclusion

In summary, blockchain analysis with AML software integration is imperative in the current realm of crime science. The detection and prevention of financial crimes, such as money laundering and terrorist financing, are efficiently managed and minimized by the substantial efforts of individuals who fulfill vital roles in these endeavors. The need for continuous advancements in blockchain analysis and AML software remains critical due to the dynamic characteristics of financial offenders. Adopting new strategies, maintaining constant vigilance, and adhering to evolving regulatory standards are crucial to combating financial crimes effectively.

Utilizing blockchain analysis and AML software emerges as crucial allies in combating financial crimes. Technology and data analysis usage have become essential in monitoring and deterring illicit financial activity. Blockchain analysis has enabled law enforcement agencies to meticulously trace the financial transactions of individuals involved in illegal activities, disrupting and dismantling major crime syndicates. Concurrently, AML software has strengthened the protective measures of financial institutions, serving as a solid initial barrier against money laundering and other unlawful financial practices.

The necessity for ongoing technological innovations becomes increasingly apparent as financial crimes grow more complex and sophisticated. The field of blockchain technology undergoes continuous development, resulting in the emergence of new challenges and opportunities. Similarly, it is crucial for AML software to adeptly adapt and counteract the constantly evolving tactics deployed by individuals engaged in illicit money laundering endeavors. Maintaining a proactive stance against financial criminals necessitates the continued prioritization of collaboration among law enforcement agencies, financial institutions, and regulatory entities. Despite the dynamic nature of the landscape, a steadfast commitment to addressing financial crimes guarantees the resilience and security of financial institutions, even in the presence of constantly evolving threats.

References

Ahmad, A. A., Jusoh, A. F., Zain, M. N. M., & Ahmad, S. (2023). Conspiracy of Silk Road: Dread Pirate Roberts to cybercrime and money laundering. *Malaysian Journal of Social Sciences and Humanities (MJSSH)*, 8(6), e002354.

AlShamsi, M., Al-Emran, M., & Shaalan, K. (2022). A systematic review on blockchain adoption. *Applied Sciences*, 12(9), 4245.

Bearpark, N. T. (2022). *Deconstructing money laundering risk*. Springer.

Chen, Z., Van Khoa, L. D., Teoh, E. N., et al. (2018). Machine learning techniques for anti-money laundering (AML) solutions in suspicious transaction detection: A review. *Knowledge and Information System*, 57, 245–285.

Collins, J. (2022). *Crypto, crime and control: Cryptocurrencies as an enabler of organized crime*. Global Initiative Against Transnational Organized Crime.

Connolly, L. Y., & Wall, D. S. (2019). The rise of crypto-ransomware in a changing cybercrime landscape: Taxonomising countermeasures. *Computers & Security*, 87, 101568.

Gaviyau, W., & Sibindi, A. B. (2023). Global anti-money laundering and combating terrorism financing regulatory framework: A critique. *Journal of Risk and Financial Management*, 16(7), 313.

Geiger, H., & Wuensch, O. (2007). The fight against money laundering: An economic analysis of a cost-benefit paradoxon. *Journal of Money Laundering Control*, 10(1), 91–105.

Gerbrands, P., Unger, B., Getzner, M., & Ferwerda, J. (2022). The effect of anti-money laundering policies: An empirical network analysis. *EPJ Data Science*, 11(1), 1–33.

Han, J., Huang, Y., Liu, S., & Towey, K. (2020). Artificial intelligence for anti-money laundering: A review and extension. *Digital Finance*, 2(3), 211–239.

Kethineni, S., & Cao, Y. (2020). The rise in popularity of cryptocurrency and associated criminal activity. *International Criminal Justice Review*, 30(3), 325–344.

Pelker, C. A., Brown, C. B., & Tucker, R. M. (2021). Using blockchain analysis from investigation to trial. *Department of Justice Journal of Federal Law and Practice*, 69, 59–100.

Singh, K., & Best, P. (2019). Anti-money laundering: Using data visualization to identify suspicious activity. *International Journal of Accounting Information Systems*, 34, 1–18.

Song, W., Zhang, W., Wang, J., Zhai, L., Jiang, P., Huang, S., & Li, B. (2022). Blockchain data analysis from the perspective of complex networks: Overview. *Tsinghua Science and Technology*, 28(1), 176–206.

Teichmann, F. M. J., & Falker, M. C. (2021). Cryptocurrencies and financial crime: Solutions from Liechtenstein. *Journal of Money Laundering Control*, 24(4), 775–788.

Trozze, A., Kamps, J., Akartuna, E. A., Hetzel, F. J., Kleinberg, B., Davies, T., & Johnson, S. D. (2022). Cryptocurrencies and future financial crime. *Crime Science*, 11, 1–35.

Wang, Y., Singgih, M., Wang, J., & Rit, M. (2019). Making sense of blockchain technology: How will it transform supply chains? *International Journal of Production Economics*, 211, 221–236.

Wu, H., Yao, Q., Liu, Z., Huang, B., Zhuang, Y., Tang, H., & Liu, E. (2024). Blockchain for finance: a survey. *IET Blockchain*, 4, 101–123.

Xian, K. (2014). The price of justice: Deferred prosecution agreements in the context of Iranian sanctions. *Notre Dame Journal of Law, Ethics & Public Policy*, 28(8), 631–664.

Yli-Huumo, J., Ko, D., Choi, S., Park, S., and Smolander, K. (2016). Where is current research on blockchain technology? A systematic review. *PLoS ONE*, 11(10), e0163477.

13 Inmate Monitoring and Management

The monitoring and managing of inmates is an essential component of the criminal justice system, playing a crucial role in ensuring public safety and promoting effective reintegration of offenders into society. Given the complexity of these responsibilities, supervision, repair, and rehabilitation must be carefully balanced. Furthermore, the field of inmate administration has undergone significant changes due to ongoing technological advancements. This evolution has ushered in an era where precision, data-driven analysis, and real-time surveillance are essential tools.

Electronic Monitoring: A Key Tool in Inmate Management

One critical aspect of inmate management is electronic monitoring, which encompasses a variety of tools designed primarily to supervise offenders at different stages in the criminal justice system. Ankle monitors have become a recognizable and versatile component of electronic surveillance in this complex environment (Scott-Hayward & Eife, 2021). These devices are known for using advanced technology, which has evolved significantly over time.

Ankle bracelets, also known as ankle monitors or electronic monitoring devices, are wearable electronics typically fastened to the user's ankle. These devices are frequently employed in the criminal justice system for oversight. Ankle monitors are essential to modern inmate monitoring systems, designed to track movements and activities accurately. They have gained attention as a potential alternative to traditional incarceration, offering a unique balance between maintaining public safety and granting offenders the freedom necessary for rehabilitation.

Ankle monitors integrate numerous sensors and communication technologies that allow the continuous tracking of an individual's movements and activities. These devices use Global Positioning System (GPS), cellular connectivity, and tamper detection mechanisms to create a virtual boundary around the individual (Williams & Weatherburn, 2022). GPS technology is crucial for location tracking, relying on satellite systems to accurately determine an individual's geographic coordinates. Cellular communication technologies transmit location data to a centralized monitoring center, ensuring a constant flow of information to authorities regarding the wearer's whereabouts. This virtual perimeter functions as an active surveillance system, enabling real-time tracking of individuals under law enforcement and correctional facilities' supervision, 24/7.

Ankle monitors were first implemented in the criminal justice system during the 1980s, primarily to monitor individuals awaiting trial or under parole. Early versions relied on basic radio frequency technology. Over time, ankle monitors have undergone significant advancements. Miniaturization, battery durability, and communication technology improvements have transformed these devices into sophisticated tracking tools. The

DOI: 10.4324/9781003558491-13

introduction of GPS technology marked a substantial shift in electronic surveillance, enabling precise tracking of geographical positions. This development has significantly improved the effectiveness of ankle monitors, allowing law enforcement agencies to monitor an individual's movements with exceptional accuracy.

Moreover, ankle monitors are equipped with tamper detection features, designed to identify any efforts to dislodge or interfere with the apparatus. If tampering is detected, an alert is activated that immediately notifies authorities of a potential violation. The integration of GPS technology in ankle monitors can be augmented with additional functionalities, such as geofencing. Geofencing allows authorities to set designated areas that individuals are permitted or prohibited from accessing. If an individual wearing the device crosses these boundaries, the system instantly triggers an alert, enabling law enforcement to take immediate action.

Ankle monitors have been widely adopted for monitoring and controlling criminal offenders due to their many advantages. One compelling benefit is the significant cost reduction compared to traditional incarceration (Yeh, 2010). Electronic monitoring systems enable offenders to serve their sentences within their communities rather than in costly correctional institutions, alleviating the financial burden on the criminal justice system.

They also facilitate the rehabilitation and reintegration of offenders into society. While under supervision, these individuals can maintain family relationships, pursue employment opportunities, and actively engage in rehabilitative programs (Scott-Hayward & Eife, 2021). This community integration is often more effective in addressing the root causes of criminal behavior and reducing recidivism rates.

Despite these benefits, ankle monitors have limitations that require careful consideration. Privacy concerns have emerged as a significant issue, as the pervasive nature of electronic surveillance raises questions about protecting individual privacy rights (Casey, 2007). Critics argue that electronic monitoring may infringe on fundamental civil liberties, leading to discussions about the delicate balance between ensuring public safety and preserving personal autonomy. Additionally, ankle monitors are not infallible; offenders may attempt to manipulate or remove the devices, introducing vulnerabilities in the surveillance process. Continuous technological advancement and vigilant oversight by monitoring authorities are essential to address these difficulties effectively.

Other Electronic Monitoring Tools

In addition to ankle monitors, various electronic monitoring methods are employed to verify adherence to court orders and parole requirements. These tools encompass a range of features and capabilities, all designed to enhance the supervision and rehabilitation of individuals within the criminal justice system.

Biometric monitoring systems are electronic surveillance tools that rely on individuals' unique physical or behavioral characteristics—such as fingerprints, retinal patterns, or voice recognition—to verify identity and monitor whereabouts (Milone, 2001). One application of voice recognition technology is to confirm a parolee's identity during scheduled telephone check-ins. Voice recognition systems utilize algorithms for speech analysis to verify an individual's identity by analyzing vocal characteristics such as pitch, rhythm, and intonation (Rashid et al., 2008). Although facial recognition systems have also been utilized in electronic surveillance, their use is limited due to ethical and privacy concerns. These systems compare an individual's facial features with a pre-existing database of approved individuals to verify their presence at designated locations.

GPS tracking devices are used to monitor individuals under supervision, extending beyond the conventional use of ankle monitors. These portable devices can be discreetly carried, providing monitoring authorities with location data. Biometric ankle monitors combine electronic monitoring devices with biometric sensors, enabling simultaneous tracking of an individual's location and collecting physiological data, such as heart rate and skin conductance. For example, remote breathalyzer tests are employed when individuals must abstain from alcohol as a condition of their supervision. These tests allow authorities to monitor the blood alcohol levels of these individuals by analyzing breath samples remotely (Sweeney et al., 2022). They provide instantaneous data and can trigger notifications in the event of any breaches.

The effectiveness of electronic monitoring tools relies on their design, implementation, and alignment with the unique requirements of the criminal justice system. Evaluating these technologies requires examining several critical factors. Numerous scholarly investigations have assessed the effects of electronic monitoring on reducing recidivism rates. These studies provide valuable insights into the techniques and strategies that are most effective in achieving this pivotal objective. Electronic monitoring systems are vital in ensuring that individuals adhere to court-imposed conditions, including curfews, movement restrictions, and sobriety requirements. Assessing compliance rates yields significant data regarding the effectiveness of these instruments. Community safety is a fundamental goal of electronic monitoring, as it protects the public by supervising individuals who may pose potential threats. Evaluating these tools' capacity to enhance community safety requires examining their accuracy and promptness. The cost-effectiveness assessment is crucial when comparing the financial implications of electronic monitoring services with those of traditional incarceration or supervision methods.

House Arrest Programs: An Alternative to Incarceration

House arrest programs are a vital component of contemporary penal methodologies. They offer an alternative to conventional imprisonment by allowing offenders to remain connected to their local communities under vigilant supervision. This section thoroughly examines house arrest, highlighting its objectives, advantages, and the crucial role of electronic surveillance in ensuring effectiveness.

House arrest, also known as community detention or home confinement, represents a corrective approach that diverges from the traditional method of incarcerating offenders in penitentiary facilities. Instead, it permits eligible persons to serve their sentences within the confines of their homes while remaining under strict supervision (Hurwitz, 1986). The primary objective of house arrest is to safeguard public welfare by limiting offenders' capacity to engage in unlawful activities while allowing them to maintain essential connections with their families and communities.

House arrest operates on the premise that separating offenders from their social circles can exacerbate their criminal tendencies and obstruct their rehabilitation prospects. By allowing offenders to remain within their familiar environments, house arrest seeks to address the root causes contributing to criminal behavior, such as substance abuse or familial discord. Moreover, it alleviates the burden on correctional institutions, mitigating concerns about prison overcrowding.

House arrest programs have several goals that enhance their effectiveness and appeal within the criminal justice system. A primary advantage of these programs is their ability to generate significant financial efficiencies compared to conventional incarceration methods (Yeh, 2010). By circumventing costs associated with housing, feeding, and caring for individuals within correctional institutions, these programs present an economically prudent approach to managing correctional matters.

Offender rehabilitation is essential to house arrest programs. Offenders can engage in educational programs, vocational training, and therapeutic interventions that are believed to be more effective in a community-based setting (Lipsey & Cullen, 2007). The main goal of this rehabilitative approach is to effectively address the underlying issues contributing to criminal behavior and promote lasting transformation. Overcrowding is a significant challenge faced by correctional institutions globally. In response to this issue, house arrest programs have emerged as a potentially viable solution (Padgett et al., 2006). By providing community-based supervision for non-violent offenders, these programs effectively alleviate strain on correctional institutions, allowing them to reallocate resources to those involved in more serious crimes.

Electronic monitoring plays a salient role in house arrest programs, providing authorities with the necessary tools to enforce compliance and closely monitor participants' actions. The primary goal of electronic monitoring in house arrest programs is to track and document the whereabouts of individuals under supervision. Using technology such as GPS, participants' movements can be tracked in real time, ensuring they remain within the parameters outlined in their court orders.

Court-imposed limitations, such as curfews, restricted locations, and prohibitions on specific activities, can be monitored electronically to ensure compliance. Alerts are triggered instantly by deviations from these conditions, enabling authorities to respond promptly. Implementing tamper detection systems in electronic monitoring equipment is crucial to safeguarding the program's integrity. These systems notify authorities if a participant attempts to remove or tamper with the monitoring device, helping to deter potential violations.

Data collection and reporting involve gathering information on participants' movements and activities through electronic monitoring devices. This information is conveyed to a centralized monitoring facility, where it is analyzed to ensure adherence to regulations and subsequently used to generate reports for law enforcement and judicial evaluation.

Parole Compliance and Supervision

Parole is a vital component of the criminal justice framework, allowing individuals who have served part of their incarceration sentences to reintegrate into society while under state supervision. Its significance extends beyond mere early release, symbolizing the system's commitment to rehabilitation and reintegration, aiming to disrupt the cycle of criminal behavior.

Parole serves several critical purposes. It allows individuals to gradually reintegrate into society, fostering the growth of essential life skills, including employment, education, and social connections. A well-designed parole program supported by effective monitoring can significantly attenuate recidivism rates (Henneguelle et al., 2016). By providing support and supervision, parole aims to prevent individuals from returning to criminal activity. It enables non-violent offenders to serve their sentences under community supervision, freeing up correctional resources for more serious cases and helping to alleviate prison overcrowding.

While parole facilitates rehabilitation and reintegration, it also presents unique challenges for monitoring offenders' return to society. Ensuring that parolees adhere to their release conditions can be difficult. Parolees must maintain employment, attend counseling, follow curfews, and avoid specific individuals or locations (Travis & Stacey, 2010). Effective monitoring of these conditions is essential. Assessing a parolee's risk level involves multiple steps and requires a nuanced approach to determine the necessary level of supervision and the likelihood of reoffending. Successful reintegration relies on access to support services, including housing, employment opportunities, and substance abuse treatment. Coordinating these services can be challenging. Balancing public safety and achieving reintegration remains an ongoing challenge, as parolees must not pose a danger to their communities.

Electronic monitoring technologies are essential for addressing these challenges and enhancing parolee supervision. They provide a comprehensive strategy for monitoring parolees. Authorities can track parolees' whereabouts in real time using GPS-enabled ankle bracelets and other monitoring tools. This capability ensures they remain within designated geographic limits and comply with curfews. Some electronic monitoring systems can detect alcohol or drug use by analyzing physiological measures such as sweat alcohol content or breath alcohol concentration. This approach addresses substance abuse, a common factor in recidivism. By alerting authorities of rule violations, electronic monitoring devices help enhance neighborhood safety by enforcing curfews and location restrictions. Violations are discouraged when individuals know their movements and activities are being monitored.

Data indicate that electronic monitoring may play a crucial role in reducing recidivism rates among parolees by increasing supervision, providing access to support services, and enabling prompt intervention in cases of violations. Numerous examples demonstrate how electronic monitoring has facilitated effective reintegration into society, highlighting individuals who have complied with their parole terms and made noteworthy efforts to begin anew (Hawkes et al., 2024). Despite its benefits, electronic monitoring has drawbacks, including device tampering, false alerts, and privacy concerns, highlighting the need for continuous advancements and modifications in technology and procedures.

In summary, electronic monitoring is a vital tool for supervising parolees, offering a sophisticated approach that enhances compliance, supports rehabilitation, and helps achieve the primary objectives of parole—reintegration and recidivism reduction.

Legal and Ethical Considerations in Inmate Monitoring

Navigating electronic surveillance in correctional facility oversight involves a multifaceted matrix of legal and ethical dilemmas, necessitating thorough examination and resolution. Striking a harmonious balance between public safety demands and personal liberties preservation is a primary concern in this evolving landscape.

Electronic monitoring raises various legal and ethical questions, requiring a comprehensive investigation of relevant issues. Because electronic monitoring involves continuous surveillance, privacy rights are substantially challenged. Reconciling the imperative of safeguarding public safety with the fundamental right to privacy creates a complex ethical dilemma. Implementing electronic surveillance can encroach on an individual's civil liberties, including their right to freedom of association and mobility (Casey, 2007). Achieving a fair balance between individual rights and law enforcement demands is paramount. There is also a risk of power abuse within the electronic monitoring framework, necessitating robust safeguards and supervision systems to prevent overreach by law enforcement or monitoring authorities.

A major concern is the intersection of technological monitoring and privacy rights. Individuals subjected to electronic surveillance may feel like their private lives are intruded on by constant monitoring. Electronic monitoring systems, particularly those utilizing GPS technology, enable continuous tracking of individuals. The scope and depth of this surveillance raise concerns regarding an individual's ability to lead a private life free from unwarranted interference. Location tracking, a fundamental component of electronic monitoring, can be particularly intrusive, as it reveals a person's precise location at all times, raising questions about the limits of surveillance. It is also essential to consider how long data collected through electronic monitoring will be retained and who will have access to it. These data may be misused or accessed without authorization, posing serious privacy risks.

Challenges and Future Trends in Inmate Monitoring

As technology continues to evolve, electronic monitoring faces persistent challenges and exciting new trends in the supervision of offenders. Understanding these dynamics is essential for shaping the future of this critical area. The expense of technology remains a recurring issue when using electronic monitoring programs. The acquisition, maintenance, and modernization of monitoring equipment and systems require substantial financial investment (Yeh, 2010). Striking a balance between program effectiveness and cost-effectiveness is an ongoing challenge. Various stakeholders, including the public, lawmakers, and criminal justice professionals, often oppose implementing electronic monitoring systems. Overcoming this opposition and promoting acceptance of electronic monitoring as a practical and valuable tool remains challenging. Additionally, skilled personnel must effectively utilize electronic monitoring technologies. The program's success depends on ensuring that staff in monitoring centers and parole offices are trained to operate and interpret data from these devices.

Integrating artificial intelligence (AI) with predictive analytics is an emerging trend in inmate monitoring. AI algorithms can analyze vast datasets to identify trends and predict violations or risks, enabling authorities to take preventive action. Facial recognition and fingerprint scanning are increasingly being incorporated into electronic monitoring. These technologies not only enhance identity verification but also deter parolees from attempting to evade supervision. Blockchain technology is a novel concept for tracking offender records. Blockchain technology's immutability and inherent security can ensure the integrity of parolee data, reducing the possibility of fraud or manipulation.

The criminal justice system's use of electronic surveillance is poised for significant transformation. Technological developments and the adoption of creative methods will shape this future. By leveraging data analytics, electronic monitoring programs can gain insights into criminal behavior and facilitate individualized interventions and risk assessments. The seamless integration of electronic surveillance with support services, such as mental health counseling and substance abuse treatment, will likely become standard practice (Nellis, 2023). Electronic monitoring programs can also be developed to support international cooperation, allowing the tracking of parolees across borders, particularly in cases involving transnational crimes.

Case Studies and Real-World Applications

Real-world examples of successful implementation underscore the practical effectiveness of house arrest programs. By analyzing select instances where these programs have yielded favorable results, we can gain insights into their impact on participants' lives and the pivotal role electronic monitoring plays in their success.

The Stockholm model is a well-regarded example of a successful house arrest program. Implemented in Sweden, it emphasizes rehabilitation and reintegration. Offenders are provided with electronic supervision tools, primarily ankle monitors, and are permitted to continue their employment, educational pursuits, or therapeutic endeavors. This program has notably reduced recidivism rates and garnered substantial employment effects among those involved (Al Weswasi & Bäckman, 2024). These programs also result in significant cost savings and help alleviate inmate overcrowding in confinement facilities (Hurwitz, 1986).

Minnesota's Electronic Monitoring Program (EMP) serves as a prime illustration of the success of electronic monitoring. The EMP is designed for low-risk, non-violent offenders who qualify for early release or community monitoring. The program employs GPS ankle bracelets to track participants' whereabouts and ensure compliance with curfews and location restrictions. The Minnesota EMP has demonstrated encouraging results, with participants exhibiting high compliance rates with their parole requirements. Furthermore, unlike traditional parole programs, the EMP has significantly reduced recidivism (Duwe, 2012). This success underscores the role of electronic surveillance in enhancing public safety and supporting rehabilitation.

The innovative electronic monitoring approach utilized by the Thames Valley Integrated Offender Management (IOM) program in the United Kingdom has garnered international notice. The IOM employs advanced monitoring tools, such as biometric ankle monitors, to oversee high-risk offenders with a history of violent or sexual offenses (Annison et al., 2015). The program prioritizes risk assessment and intervention. By leveraging biometric data and real-time tracking, authorities can respond swiftly to deviations from prescribed conditions or potential risk factors. Participants' reoffending rates have significantly decreased due to this proactive strategy, further demonstrating the potential of electronic monitoring to enhance public safety.

These case studies highlight the diverse strategies employed in house arrest programs, showcasing their capacity to adapt to legal jurisdictions and offender characteristics. Furthermore, they illustrate the mutually beneficial relationship between house arrest and electronic monitoring, demonstrating how technology enhances the effectiveness of these programs in upholding public safety, minimizing costs, and fostering rehabilitation.

Conclusion

Thanks to technological advancements, inmate monitoring and management have become essential components of the modern criminal justice system. This chapter has highlighted the critical importance of these practices, as they collectively enhance community safety, promote rehabilitation, and reduce recidivism. Technological advancements increase the potential for developing increasingly effective inmate management strategies.

Electronic monitoring can transform lives, as demonstrated by the success stories of recovery and the real-world impacts presented in case studies. However, a fair and balanced relationship between individual rights and public safety must exist. Looking ahead, we envision a future where electronic monitoring seamlessly integrates with support services, employs advanced data analytics, and fosters global collaboration to ensure community safety as we navigate ongoing challenges and embrace emerging trends in this field.

References

Al Weswasi, E., & Bäckman, O. (2024). The effects of replacing incarceration with electronic monitoring on crime, mortality, and labor market exclusion. *Journal of Quantitative Criminology*, 1–38.

Annison, H., Bradford, B., & Grant, E. (2015). Theorizing the role of "the brand" in criminal justice: The case of integrated offender management. *Criminology & Criminal Justice*, 15(4), 387–406.

Casey, T. (2007). Electronic surveillance and the right to be secure. *University of California Davis Law Review*, 41, 977–1033.

Duwe, G. (2012). Evaluating the Minnesota Comprehensive Offender Reentry Plan (MCORP): Results from a randomized experiment. *Justice Quarterly*, 29(3), 347–383.

Hawkes, A. L., Sellbom, M., & Gilmour, F. E. (2024). Under surveillance: Does global positioning system monitoring of offenders reduce recidivism? *Criminology & Criminal Justice*, 24(4), 862–881.

Henneguelle, A., Monnery, B., & Kensey, A. (2016). Better at home than in prison? The effects of electronic monitoring on recidivism in France. *Journal of Law and Economics*, 59(3), 629–667.

Hurwitz, J. N. (1986). House arrest: A critical analysis of an intermediate-level penal sanction. *University of Pennsylvania Law Review*, 135, 771–811.

Lipsey, M. W., & Cullen, F. T. (2007). The effectiveness of correctional rehabilitation: A review of systematic reviews. *Annual Review of Law and Social Science*, 3, 297–320.

Milone, M. G. (2001). Biometric surveillance: Searching for identity. *Business Lawyer*, 57(1), 497–512.

Nellis, M. (2023). Smartphone electronic monitoring (EM), artificial intelligence and the mass supervision question in the USA. *Tracking People*, 137–160. Routledge.

Padgett, K. G., Bales, W. D., & Blomberg, T. G. (2006). Under surveillance: An empirical test of the effectiveness and consequences of electronic monitoring. *Criminology & Public Policy*, 5(1), 61–92.

Rashid, R. A., Mahalin, N. H., Sarijari, M. A., & Aziz, A. A. A. (2008). Security system using biometric technology: Design and implementation of Voice Recognition System (VRS). *May 2008 international conference on computer and communication engineering*, 898–902. IEEE.

Scott-Hayward, C. S., & Eife, E. (2021). Correctional and sentencing law commentary: Electronic monitoring. *Criminal Law Bulletin*, 57(3), 407–422.

Sweeney, M. M., Holtyn, A. F., Stitzer, M. L., & Gastfriend, D. R. (2022). Practical technology for expanding and improving substance use disorder treatment: Telehealth, remote monitoring, and digital health interventions. *Psychiatric Clinics*, 45(3), 515–528.

Travis, L. F., III, & Stacey, J. (2010). A half-century of parole rules: Conditions of parole in the United States, 2008. *Journal of Criminal Justice*, 38(4), 604–608.

Williams, J., & Weatherburn, D. (2022). Can electronic monitoring reduce reoffending? *Review of Economics and Statistics*, 104(2), 232–245.

Yeh, S. S. (2010). Cost-benefit analysis of reducing crime through electronic monitoring of parolees and probationers. *Journal of Criminal Justice*, 38(5), 1090–1096.

Index

FSC
www.fsc.org
MIX
Papier | Fördert gute Waldnutzung
FSC® C083411

Kolibri 360 GmbH
Ferdinand-Jühlke-Straße 7
99095 Erfurt, Deutschland
produktsicherheit@kolibri360.de